JAVA/J2EE Interview Questions

(Including Core Java , Servlets, JSP, Architecture, Project Management, EJB, STRUTS and General Interview Questions)

By

Shivprasad Koirala

BPB PUBLICATIONS

B-14 Connaught Place, New Delhi-110 001

FIRST EDITION 2007

Distributors:

MICRO BOOK CENTRE
2, City Centre, CG Road,
Near Swastic Char Rasta,
AHMEDABAD-380009 Phone: 26421611

COMPUTER BOOK CENTRE
12, Shrungar Shopping Centre, M.G. Road,
BANGALORE-560001 Phone: 25587923, 25584641

MICRO BOOKS
Shanti Niketan Building, 8, Camac Street,
KOLKATTA-700017 Phone: 22826518, 22826519

BUSINESS PROMOTION BUREAU
8/1, Ritchie Street, Mount Road,
CHENNAI-600002 Phone: 28410796, 28550491

DECCAN AGENCIES
4-3-329, Bank Street,
HYDERABAD-500195 Phone: 24756400, 24756967

MICRO MEDIA
Shop No. 5, Mahendra Chambers, 150 D.N. Road,
Next to Capital Cinema V.T. (C.S.T.) Station,
MUMBAI-400001 Ph.: 22078296, 22078297

BPB PUBLICATIONS
B-14, Connaught Place, **NEW DELHI-110001**
Phone: 23325760, 23723393, 23737742

INFO TECH
G-2, Sidhartha Building, 96 Nehru Place,
NEW DELHI-110019
Phone: 26438245, 26415092, 26234208

INFO TECH
Shop No. 2, F-38, South Extension Part-1
NEW DELHI-110049
Phone: 24691288

BPB BOOK CENTRE
376, Old Lajpat Rai Market,
DELHI-110006 PHONE: 23861747

> **NOTE: THE CD-ROMS INCLUDED WITH THE BOOK HAS NO COMMERCIAL VALUE AND CANNOT BE SOLD SEPARATELY.**

Price : Rs. 198/-

ISBN 81-8333-173-4

Published by Manish Jain for BPB Publications, B-14, Connaught Place, New Delhi-110 001 and Printed by him at Akash Press, New Delhi.

"Cheers to the true fighting spirit of IT professionals"

Introduction

Dedication

This book is dedicated to my kids Sanjana and Simran, whose dad's play time has been stolen and given to this book. I am thankful to my wife for constantly encouraging me.I am also thankful to BPB Publication to give new comer a platform to perform. Finally on top of all thanks to the two old eyes my mom and dad for always blessing me. I am blessed to have Raju as my brother who always keeps my momentum moving on.

Thanks to Mr Soumen Deb for clearing my technical doubts. He is almost like a co-author for this book.

I am grateful to Bhavnesh Asar who initially conceptualized the idea of the interview question series.I believe concept thinking is more important than execution.

Tons of thanks to my reviewers whose feedback provided an essential tool to improve my writing capabilities.

About the author

Author works in a big multinational company and has over 8 years of experience in software industry. He is working presently as project lead and in past has led projects in banking, travel and financial sectors.

But on top of all, I am a simple developer like you all guys there doing an 8 hour job. Writing is something I do extra and I love doing it. No one is perfect and same holds true for me .So anything you want to comment, suggest, and point typo / grammar mistakes or technical mistakes regarding the book you can mail me at shiv_koirala@yahoo.com. Believe me guys your harsh words would be received with love and treated to the top most priority. Without all you guys I am not an author.

Writing an interview question book is really a great deal of responsibility. I have tried to cover maximum questions for the topic because I always think probably leaving one silly question will cost someone's job there. But huge natural variations in an interview are something difficult to cover in this small book. So if you have come across such questions during interview which is not addressed in this book do mail at shiv_koirala@yahoo.com .Who knows probably that question can save some other guys job.

Features of the book

√   Around 400 plus interview questions from live JAVA interviews.

√   Section wise JAVA interview question coverage according to multinational companies.

√   Short and to the point answers (no hitting around the bush).

√   Every question is classified in to Basic,Intermediate and advanced category, thus providing more focus to readers on specific category.

√ During interviews other than main technology companies expect other areas to be strong for example UML, Project management, Architecture, Database etc. Other sections is the most strong point of the book, which makes reader prepared for theunexpected questions.

√ Full range of interview questions right from junior JAVA developers to senior architects or project manager.

√ CD has all the software you need to start for practice, sample resume and sample code to understand fundamentals.

√ Book covers important points like salary negotiations, resume making and general points to be remembered during interview.

√ Recommended for JAVA interviewers who are looking for what questions to be asked to get better and decent JAVA professionals

√ Recommended for Fresher and students who want to have a feel of what JAVA questions are asked in multinational companies.

√ Developers who are looking for Quick reference and FAQ.

I am sure after reading this book readers will have extra confidence and a better approach for JAVA interviews.

What's in the CD?

Well the CD has everything you need to really startup your career as a Java professional or to prepare practically for an interview.

√ Interview rating Sheet with 1000 Interview questions to measure yourself.

√ Java sample source code which this books explains.

√ Estimation free ebook.

√ JDK setup (1.4 and 1.5)

√ Eclipse setup which is copyright of The Eclipse Foundation. For more detail you can refer to http://www.eclipse.org/

√ PostgresSql setup. PostgreSQL is Copyright © 1996-2005 by the PostgreSQL Global Development Group and is distributed under the terms of the license of the University of California below. Postgres95 is Copyright © 1994-5 by the Regents of the University of California.

√ JBOSS 4.0.4 setup.

√ ANT tool apache-ant-1.6.5-bin.

√ Struts 1.2.9 zip file.

√ JBOSS Eclipse IDE.

√ Jakarta tag libs jakarta-taglibs-standard-1.1.2.zip

√ jwsdp-2_0-windows-i586 Java web services developer pack

√ Tomcat50-jwsdp has the tomcat container for deploying application made using JWSDP.

√ aspectj-1.5.2

√ WTP

Introduction

"Changes trigger opportunity" and if you have bought this book you are looking for change. But these opportunities knock at your doorsteps giving you very little time for preparation. How many times has it happened you are working on a tight dead line project and you get a call that there is an interview tomorrow morning. Then comes the reaction hey man lot to prepare I will not be able to make it up tomorrow morning.

Working in projects is practical based, but interviews are more of how you present yourself theoretically. It's very much possible you can do anything practically in JAVA but when you are approached with simple questions you stumble very badly. Let's say you are working on a project which deals with struts. You know struts in and out but when you go for an interview you flunk in simple JDBC and OOPS questions. That does not mean you are bad, just that you have not revised the basic stuffs.

Ok now the so called basic stuff is very much from interviewer perspective and it varies from individual to individual. Multinational companies try really hard to standardize the interview procedure. But I am sure if you give an interview twice in the same company you can easily see huge variations because of individual perspective.

Other than basic stuff an interviewer will ask you some creamy questions like "What's passivation in EJB?". "Explain EJB Architecture?" is a fundamental basic question but "What's passivation in EJB?" is a creamy question. Creamy questions have no pattern and are extremely difficult to predict. But basic question have a regular pattern and if you are ok with the basic question you are in a good position. This book attempt's to cover those basic questions and make you ready for an interview.

From freshers point of view this book gives a complete picture of what's expected during JAVA / J2EE interviews. From experienced professional point of view it attempts to give you a quick revision.

In this book we have tried to cover interview questions from Core Java, OOP's, JDBC, EJB, STRUTS, Servlets, JSP , Web services , Design patterns and project management point of view. We hope this book will be your true friend during your job search struggle phase.

Do not get panic by couple of failures. If there are no failures how do we measure success.Keep similing and Happy job hunting.

How to read this book

If you can read English, you can read this book....kidding. There are some legends which will make your reading more effective. Every question has simple tags which mark the rating of the questions.

These rating are given by Author and can vary according to companies and individuals.

(B) Basic Questions

Basic Grade means according to the interviewer it's a fundamental question and should be answered. Example What's the difference between an Abstract and a Interface ? Guy's stumbling on this question will rarely pass interviews.

(I) Intermediate Questions

These are Mid-level questions and will be expected to be answered if you are looking for a decent position in the company.

(A) Advanced Questions

These are advanced level question which are expected when they are looking for specialist in the field.

(P) Psyche Questions

These level of questions do not judge anything for a candidate but I see it as a attitude problem of the interviewer.

Note

While reading you can come across section marked as "Note", which highlight special points of that section.

One advice do not read this book from top to last. Read the index and see which sections you are targeting and revise those.

Software Company hierarchy

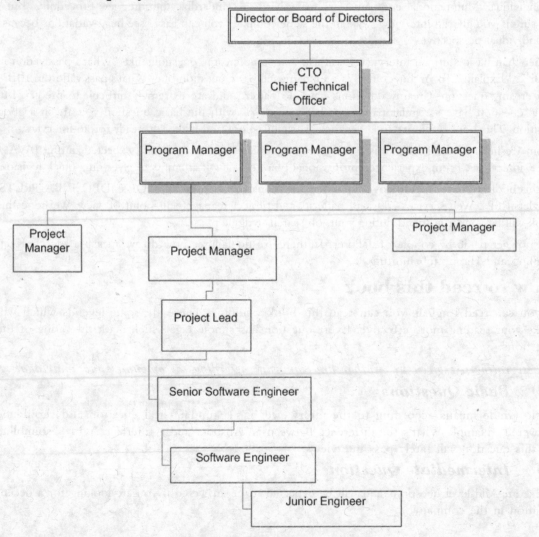

Figure: 0.1 IT Company hierarchy

Its very important during interview to be clear about what position you are targeting. Depending on what positions you are targeting the interviewer shoots you questions. Example if you are looking for a project manager position you will be asked around 20% technical questions and 80% management.

> *Note:* *In small scale software house and mid scale software companies there are chances where they expect a PM to be very much technical. But in big software houses the situations are very much different, interview are conducted according to positions.... Unless the interviewer changes the rule.*

Above is a figure of a general hierarchy across most IT companies.

> *Note:* *There are many small and medium software companies which do not follow this hierarchy and they have there own adhoc way of defining positions in the company.*

So why is the need of hierarchy in a interview.

> *"Interview is a contract between the employer and candidate to achieve specific goals."*

So employer is looking for a suitable candidate and candidate looks for a better career. Normally in interviews the employer is very clear about what type of candidate he is looking for.But 90% times the candidate is not clear about the positions he is looking for.

How many times it has happened with you that you have given a whole interview and when you mentioned the position you are looking for...pat comes the answer, " we do not have any requirements for this position". So be clarified about the position right from when you start the interview.

Following are the number of years of experience according to position.

√   Junior engineers are specially fresher and work under software engineers.

√   Software engineers have around 1 to 2 years of experience. Interviewer expects software engineers to be technically at a medium level.

√   Senior Software Engineers have around 2 to 4 years of experience. Interviewer expects them to technically be very strong.

√   Project leads should handle majority technical aspect of project and should have around 4 to 8 years of experience. They are also indirect architect of the project. Interviewer expects them to be technically strong and in terms of architecture to be decent. Interviewer also expects them to have people management skills.

√   Project Manager are expected to be around 40% technically strong and should have experience above 10 years plus. But they are more interviewed from aspect of project management, client interaction, people management, proposal preparation etc.

So now judge where you stand, and where you want to go...........

Resume Preparation Guidelines

> *First impression is the last impression*

> Note: *A sample resume is provided in "SampleResume" folder.*

Before even the interviewer meets you he will first meet your resume. Interviewer looking at your resume is almost a 20% interview happening with out you knowing it. I was always a bad guy when it comes to resume preparation. But when I looked at my friends resume they where gorgeous. Now that I am writing series of book on interviews I thought this will be a good point to put in. You can happily skip it if you are confident about your resume. There is no hard and fast rule that you have to follow the same pattern but just see if these all check list are attended.

√   Use plain text when you are sending resumes through email. For instance you sent your resume using Microsoft word and what if the interviewer is using Linux he will never be able to read your resume. You can not be sure both wise, you sent your resume in Word 2000 and the guy has Word 97…uuhhh.

√   Attach a covering letter it really impresses and makes you look traditionally formal. Yes, even if you are sending your CV through email send a covering letter.

Check list of content you should have in your resume:

√   Start with an objective or summary, for instance, "Working as a Senior Database administrator for more than 4 years. Implemented quality web based application. Follow the industry's best practices and adhered and implemented processes, which enhanced the quality of technical delivery. Pledge to deliver the best technical solutions to the industry."

√   Specify your Core strengths at the start of the resume by which the interviewer can make a quick decision are you eligible for the position. For example :-

❑   Looked after data mining and data warehousing department independently. Played a major role in query optimization.

❑   Worked extensively in database design and ER diagram implementation.

❑   Well versed with CMMI process and followed it extensively in projects.

❑   Looking forward to work on project manager or senior manager position.

This is also a good position to specify your objective or position which makes it clear to the interviewer that should he call you for an interview. For instance, if you are looking for senior position specify it explicitly 'looking for this job profile'. Any kind of certification like JCP, MCSD etc you can make it visible in this section.

√   Once you have specified briefly your goals and what you have done its time to specify what type of technology you have worked with. For instance RDBMS, TOOLS, Languages, Web servers, process (Six sigma, CMMI).

√   After that you can make a run through of your experience company wise that is what company you have worked with, year / month joining and year / month left. This will give an overview to the interviewer what type of companies you have associated your self.

Now its time to mention all your projects you have worked till now. Best is to start in descending order that is from your current project and go backwards. For every project try to put these things:

√   Project Name / Client name (It's sometimes unethical to mention clients name; I leave it to the readers).

√   Number of team members.

√   Time span of the project.

√   Tools, language, RDBMS and technology used to complete the project.

√   Brief summary of the project.

Senior people who have huge experience will tend to increase there CV with putting in summary for all project. Best for them is to just put description of the first three projects in descending manner and rest they can say verbally during interview. I have seen CV above 15 pages... I doubt who can read it.

√   Finally comes your education and personal details.

√   Trying for onsite, do not forget to mention your passport number.

√   Some guys tend to make there CV large and huge. I think an optimal size should be not more than 4 to 5 pages.

√   Do not mention your salary in CV. You can talk about it during interview with HR or the interviewer.

√   When you are writing your summary for project make it effective by using verbs like managed a team of 5 members, architected the project from start to finish etc. It brings huge weight.

√   This is essential very essential take 4 to 5 Xerox copies of your resume you will need it now and then.

√   Just in case take at least 2 passport photos with you. You can escape it but many times you will need it.

√   Carry all your current office documents specially your salary slips and joining letter.

Salary Negotiation

Ok that's what we all do it for: MONEY. This is probably the weakest area for techno savvy guys. They are not good negotiators. I have seen so many guys at the first instance they will smile and say "NEGOTIABLE SIR". So here are some points:-

√   Do a study of what is the salary trend? For instance have some kind of baseline. For example what is the salary trend on number of year of experience? Discuss this with your friends out.

√   Do not mention your expected salary on the resume?

√   Let the employer first make the salary offer. Try to delay the salary discussion till the end.

√   If they say what you expect ?, come out with a figure which is little at higher end and say negotiable. Remember never say negotiable on something which you have aimed, HR guys will always bring it down. So negotiate on AIMED SALARY + some thing extra.

√   The normal trend is that they look at your current salary and add a little to it so that they can pull you in. Do your home work my salary is this much and I expect this much so whatever it is now I will not come below this.

√   Do not be harsh during salary negotiations.

√   It's good to aim high. For instance I want 1 billion dollars / month but at the same time be realistic.

√   Some companies have those hidden cost attached in salary clarify that rather to be surprised at the first salary package.

√   Many of the companies add extra performance compensation in your basic which can be surprising at times. So have a detail break down. Best is to discuss on hand salary rather than net salary.

√   Talk with the employer in what frequency does the hike happen.

√   Take everything in writing, go back to your house and have a look once with a cool head is the offer worth it of what your current employer is giving.

√   Do not forget once you have job in hand you can come back to your current employer for negotiation so keep that thing in mind.

√   Remember the worst part is cribbing after joining the company that your colleague is getting more. So be careful while interview negotiations or be sportive be a good negotiator in the next interview.

√   One very important thing is that the best negotiation ground is not the new company where you are going but the old company which you are leaving. So once you have offer on hand get back to your old employee and show them the offer and then mak your next move. It's my experience that negotiating with the old employer is easy than with the new one….Frankly if approached properly rarely any one will say no. Just do not be aggressive or egoistic that you have an offer on hand.

Top of all some time some things are worth above money: JOB SATISFACTION. So whatever you negotiate if you think you can get JOB SATISFACTION aspect on higher grounds go for it. I think its worth more than money.

Applicable to only India	
Years of Experience	**Amount in Rupees CTC (Cost to Company)**
Fresher's	5000 to 8000
1 to 2 yrs	10000 to 20000
3 to 4 yrs	25000 to 30000
4 to 6 yrs	30000 to 40000
6 to 8 yrs	40000 to 60000
12 to 15 yrs	70000 to 100000
15 yrs and above	Depends upon negotiations

Figure: 0.2 Salary Card for India

Applicable to US Only	
Years of Exp	**Amount in Dollars (Per Annum)**
Freshers	40000 to 50000 Dollars
2 to 4 yrs	50000 to 55000 Dollars
4 to 6 yrs	55000 to 60000 Dollars
6 to 8 yrs	60000 to 70000 Dollars
8 to 12 yrs	70000 to 80000 Dollars
12 yrs and above	Depends on negotiations
Note: - If you are a Non-US resident like Indian, Philippine etc who is going on H1 then you start from a fresher level or the 2 to 4 yrs of salary slab. Also one note if you come back from US and then want to try again how much ever experience you have you will need to start from the either of first three slabs.	

Figure: 0.3 US Salary Card

> Note: The above US Salary card is based on my experience and some talk which I had with my friends who are staying on longer term basis outside. In case you are finding discrepancies please do mail me at shiv_koirala@yahoo.com probably we can standardize it better for the community.

The score card shown above is completely derived from author's experience and interaction he had in his circle. It is not an approved score card by any authorized body as such and should be taken only has bench mark to measure your success. Also note that these rates are applicable for medium and large software companies. Small company rate cards are very irregular and governed by a single owner of the company. So the above rate card is not applicable for small company. Many people do get mind blowing salaries even with small experience which again the score card does not reflect.

Points to remember

√ One of the first questions asked during interview is "Can you say something about yourself"?

√ Can you describe about your self and what you have achieved till now?

√ Why do you want to leave the current company?

√ Where do you see yourself after three years?

√ What are your positive and negative points?

√ How much do you rate yourself in JAVA in one out of ten?

√ Are you looking for onsite opportunities? (Be careful do not show your desperation of abroad journeys)

√ Why have you changed so many jobs? (Prepare a decent answer do not blame companies and individuals for your frequent change).

√ Never talk for more than 1 minute straight during interview.

√ Do not mention client names in resume. If asked say that it's confidential which will bring out qualities like honesty. Who knows the interviewer will be impressed by this one sentence.

√ When you make your resume keep your recent projects at the top.

√ Find out what the employer is looking for by asking him questions at the start of interview and best is before going to interview. Example if a company has projects on web application employer will be looking for JSP , Servlets and JDBC.

√ Can you give brief about your family background?

√ As you are fresher do you think you can really do this job?

√ Have you heard about our company ? Say five points about our company? Just read at least once what company you are going for?

√ Can you describe your best project you have worked with?

√ Do you work on Saturday and Sunday?

√ Which is the biggest team size you have worked with?

√   Can you describe your current project you have worked with?

√   How much time will you need to join our organization? What's notice period for your current company?

√   What certifications have you cleared?

√   Do you have pass port size photos, last year mark sheet, previous companies employment letter, last months salary slip, pass port and other necessary documents.

√   What is the most important thing that motivates you?

√   Why you want to leave the previous organization?

√   Which type of job gives you greatest satisfaction?

√   What is the type of environment you are looking for?

√   Do you have experience in project management?

√   Do you like to work as a team or as individual?

√   Describe your best project manager you have worked with?

√   Why should I hire you?

√   Have you been ever fired or forced to resign?

√   Can you explain some important points that you have learnt from your past project experiences?

√   Have you gone through some unsuccessful projects, if yes can you explain why did the project fail?

√   Will you be comfortable with location shift? If you have personal problems say no right at the first stage.... or else within two months you have to read my book again.

√   Do you work late nights? Best answer if there is project deadline yes. Do not show that it's your culture to work during nights.

√   Any special achievements in your life till now...tell your best project which you have done best in your career.

√   Any plans of opening your own software company...Beware do not start pouring your bill gate's dream to him.....can create a wrong impression.

Interview rating Sheet

In the CD we have provided Interview rating excel sheet. This sheet will help you in providing insight of really how much you are ready for JAVA, .NET or SQL Server Interviews. In the sheet we have seven sections:

√   Guidelines

√   JAVA

√   Java results

√   .NET

√   .NET Results

√   SQL Server

√   SQL Server results

The guidelines sheet defines the guidelines for the rating. For every question you can give one to five rating. Ratings are rated using the following guidelines:

0 - You have no idea about the question

1 - You know only the definition.

2 - You know the concept but not the depth of the subject.

3 - You know the concept and have partial knowledge about the concept.

4 - You know the concept and have in depth knowledge about the subject. But it's possible that you will stumble in some in depth question.

5 - You are an expert and no one can touch you in this.

The remaining six sections are questions and results. For instance we have the JAVA sections and the JAVA results section. JAVA section will take in the rating inputs for every questions and JAVA result will show the output. Same hold true for .NET and SQL Server.

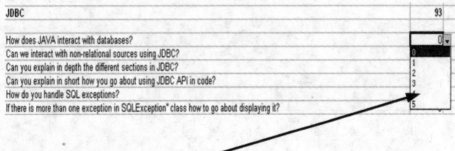

0 -You have no idea about the question
1- You know only the definition.
2- You Know the concept but not the depth of the subject.
3- You know the concept and have partial knowledge about the concept.
4 - You know the concept and have in depth knowledge about the subject. But its possible that you will stumble in some in depth question.
5 - You are a expert and no one can touch you in this.

Figure 0.4: Choose rating

For every question you need to select ratings.

So go through every question and see how good you are. Definitely you do not have any one to govern you but finally you have to clear the interview so be fair and know your results before hand.

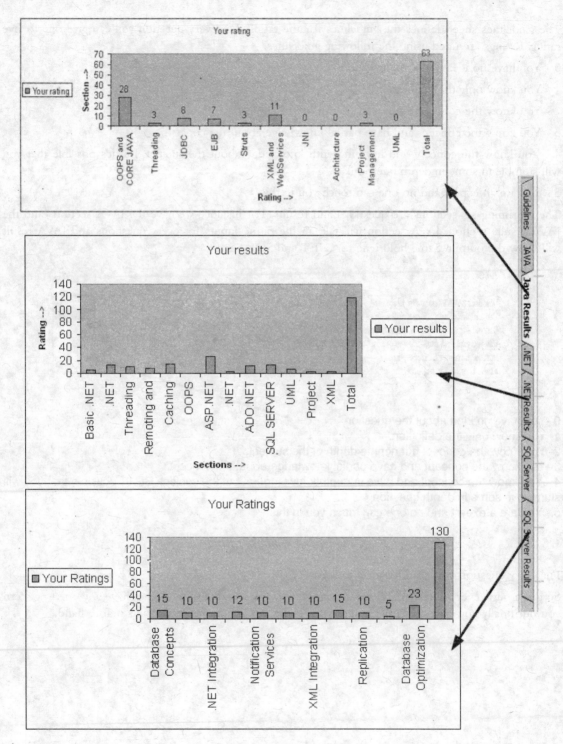

Figure 0.5: Rating values

Contents

2. Threading   62

3. JDBC   68

4.   Servlets and JSP   89

5. EJB   120

12. Project Management   **195**

13. Database   **237**

16. SQL Server Interview Questions 283

1

OOPS AND CORE JAVA

(B) What is JVM (Java Virtual Machine)?

Twist: What are Java Byte Codes?

JVM stands for Java Virtual Machine. It's an abstract computer or virtual computer which runs the compiled java programs. Actually JVM is a software implementation which stands on the top of the real hardware platform and operating system. It provides abstraction between the compiled java program and the hardware and operating system.

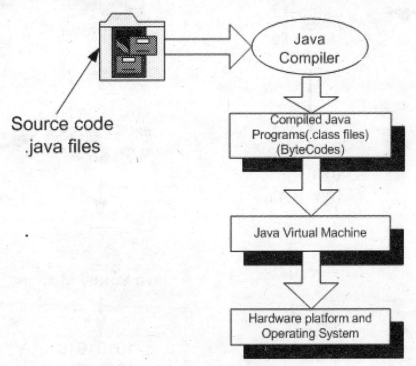

Figure 1.1: Java Virtual Machine

So the compiled program does not have to worry about what hardware and operating system he has to run in, it's all handled by the JVM and thus attaining portability. All Java programs are compiled in to bytecodes. JVM can only understand and execute Java bytecodes. You can visualize Java bytecodes as machine language for JVM. Java compiler takes the .java files and compiles it to a "bytecode" file with .class file extension. Compiler generates one class file for one source file.

(B)   What is JIT (Just-in-Time) Compilation?

> Note: *Before we can get in to what is JIT we need to get some basic compiler fundamentals.*

There are two basic ways languages are compiled:

√   Compiled Languages

√   Interpreted Languages

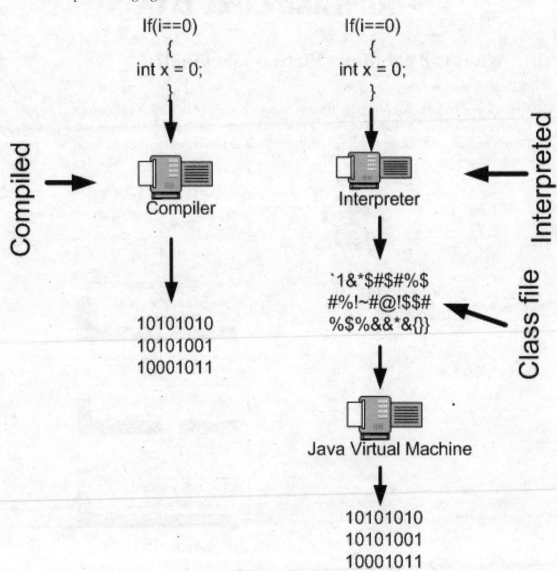

Figure 1.2: Compiled and Interpreted

Machine understands only binary language. So finally source code has to be compiled in binary format. Compiled and interpreter varies from the way they generate the binary files. You can see from the above figure on the left hand side we have the compiled way of generating the binary and on the right hand side we have the interpreted way. In the compiled way the compiler directly generates the binary file from the source code. While in the interpreted way it generates the class file which is then run by the virtual machine. That means the binary file is generated during runtime.

Now lets try to answer what is JIT?. When JVM compiles the class file he does not compile the full class file in one shot. Compilation is done on function basis or file basis. Advantage gained from this is that heavy parsing of original source code is avoided. Depending on need basis the compilation is done. This type of compilation is termed as JIT or Just-in-Time compilation.

(B)   What is Object Oriented Programming?

It is a problem solving technique to develop software systems. It's a technique to think real world in terms of objects. Object maps the software model to real world concept. These objects have responsibilities and provide services to application or other objects.

(B)   What's a Class?

A class describes all the attributes of objects, as well as the methods that implement the behavior of member objects. It's a comprehensive data type which represents a blue print of objects. It's a template of object.

(B)   What's an Object?

It's a basic unit of a system. An object is an entity that has attributes, behavior, and identity. Objects are members of a class. Attributes and behavior of an object are defined by the class definition.

(A)   What's the relation between Classes and Objects?

They look very much same but are not same. Class is a definition, while object is instance of the class created. Class is a blue print while objects are actual objects existing in real world. Example we have class CAR which has attributes and methods like Speed, Brakes, Type of Car etc.Class CAR is just a prototype, now we can create real time objects which can be used to provide functionality. Example we can create a Maruti car object with 100 km speed and urgent brakes.

(B)   What are different properties provided by Object-oriented systems?

Twist: Can you explain different properties of Object Oriented Systems?

> *Note: Difference between abstraction and encapsulation is one of the favorite interview question and quiet confusing as both the terminology look alike. Best is if you can brainstorm with your friends or do a little reading.*

Following are characteristics of Object Oriented System's:

Abstraction

It allows complex real world to be represented in simplified manner. Example color is abstracted to RGB. By just making the combination of these three colors we can achieve any color in world. It's a model of real world or concept.

Encapsulation

The process of hiding all the internal details of an object from the outside world.

Communication

When application wants to achieve certain task it can only be done using combination of objects. A single object can not do the entire task. Example if we want to make order processing form. We will use Customer object, Order object, Product object and Payment object to achieve this functionality. In short these objects should communicate with each other. This is achieved when objects send messages to each other.

Object lifetime

All objects have life time. Objects are created, initialized, necessary functionalities are done and later the object is destroyed. Every object have there own state and identity, which differ from instance to instance.

Class hierarchies (Inheritance and aggregation)

Twist: What's difference between Association, Aggregation and Inheritance relationships?

In object oriented world objects have relation and hierarchies in between them. There are basically three kind of relationship in Object Oriented world:

Association

This is the simplest relationship between objects.Example every customer has sales. So Customer object and sales object have a association relation between them.

Aggregation

This is also called as composition model. Example in order to make a "Accounts" class it has use other objects example "Voucher"," Journal" and "Cash" objects. So accounts class is aggregation of these three objects.

Inheritance

Hierarchy is used to define more specialized classes based on a preexisting generalized class. Example we have VEHICLE class and we can inherit this class make more specialized class like CAR, which will add new attributes and use some existing qualities of the parent class. Its shows more of a parent-child relationship .This kind of hierarchy is called inheritance.

Polymorphism

When inheritance is used to extend a generalized class to a more specialized class, it includes behavior of the top class (Generalized class).The inheriting class often implement a behavior that can be somewhat different than the generalized class, but the name of the behavior can be same. It is important that a given instance of an object use the correct behavior, and the property of polymorphism allows this to happen automatically.

(B)   How do you implement inheritance in Java?

Short answer from interview point of view inheritance is implemented by using "EXTEND" keyword. As discussed in the previous basic definitions of OOP's inheritance is used to define more specialized class below the hierarchy. To understand this better lets do a small project to get the actual feel of the same.

Below is the project structure of the "Inheritance" project. It has the three classes:

√   **"ClsAdd.java"**

This class has a basic subroutine which adds two numbers.

√   **"ClsSpecialAdd.java"**

This class inherits from "ClsAdd.java" and overrides the subroutine which does the basic addition. It changes the basic addition functionality by adding an extra adjustment value of "20".

√   **"ClsRun.java"**

This is the class which has the "public static void main (String [] args)" method. It's the main class which will run the whole show by creating the objects of "ClsAdd" and "ClsSpecialAdd" and executing the "Add" method.

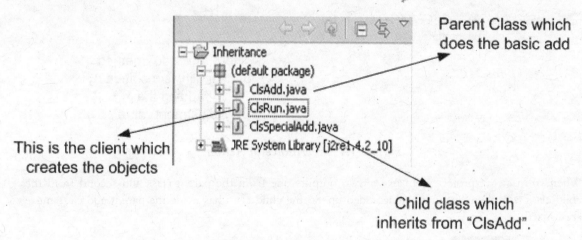

Figure 1.3: Project File structure of inheritance structure

```
public class ClsAdd

{
// This method does simple addition
public int Add(int num1,int num2)
{
    return num1 + num2;
}


}
```

⬇ Inheritance

```
public class ClsSpecialAdd extends ClsAdd
{
// This method inherits from the parent class and adds the adjustment value
    public int Add(int num1, int num2)
    {
        int intAdjustValue = 20;
        return num1 + num2 + intAdjustValue;
    }

}
```

Here the "Add" method functionality is modified by adding the "AdjustmentValue".

Figure 1.4: Inheritance in Action

When you run the project you can see two outputs one from the parent class and second from the child class with the adjustment value added up. So the child class has made the parent add class more specialized.

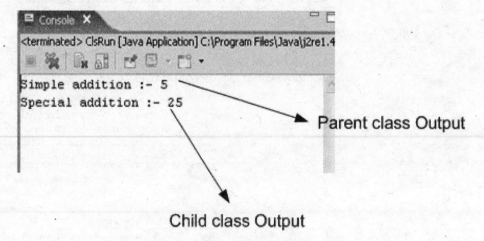

Figure 1.5: Output from Inheritance Project

(B)   How can we implement polymorphism in Java?

Twist: How can we implement overloading in Java?

Polymorphism is the capability of an action or method to do different things based on the object that it is acting upon. There are two types of polymorphism:

√   Method Polymorphism through overloading.

√   Object polymorphism by inheritance / interfaces.

Method Polymorphism through overloading

Let's try to understand this concept by a small sample. In CD you can find the "Polymorphism" folder which has two files "clsPolymorphism.java" and "clsTestRun.java".

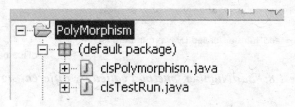

Figure 1.6: Polymorphism Explorer

"ClsTestRun.java" is the driver which has the main method, while "ClsPolymorphism" class has the actual stuff which demonstrates polymorphism. Below is the snippet of what "Clspolymorphism.java" looks like.

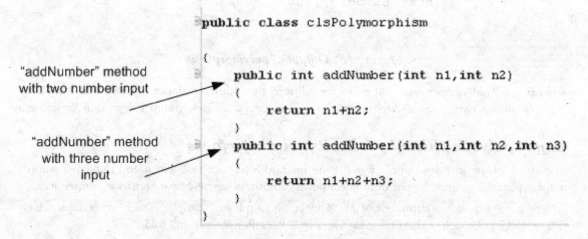

Figure 1.7: Snippet of "Clspolymorphism.java"

It has "addNumber" function which is overloaded with two types of signatures. One takes two number (n1 and n2) and other takes three (n1, n2 and n3).

```
public class clsTestRun
{
    public static void main(String[] args)
    {
        // TODO Auto-generated method stub

        // Created object for polymorphism
        clsPolymorphism objclsPolymorphism = new clsPolymorphism();
        // Two numbers input results
        System.out.println("Two numbers input :- " + objclsPolymorphism.addNumber(10,10));
        // Three numbers input results
        System.out.println("Three numbers input :- " + objclsPolymorphism.addNumber(10,10,10));
    }
}
```

"addNumber" called by two numbers

"addNumber" called by three numbers

Figure 1.8: "addNumber" method called by different signatures

Below is the output when we run the program.

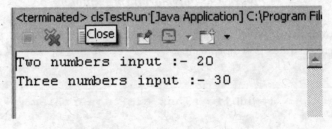

Figure 1.9: Output of polymorphism

You can see "addNumber" method performed differently in different inputs. "Poly" means multi and "morph" means change. So "addNumber" method is having multiple outputs depending on different inputs.

Object polymorphism by inheritance / interfaces

The above polymorphism sample was on the method level, but real worth and implementation of polymorphism concept is by objects. Object polymorphism is possible by inheritance or interfaces.

So let's make a quick walk through of an "Objectpolymorphism" sample. The below sample which I will be walking through is also provided in CD in "ObjectPolymorphism" folder.

There are four java files in "Objectpolymorphism" sample project:

√   ClsAdd.java

√   ClsSpecialAdd.java

√   ClsSpecialAddandDivide.java

√   ClsTestRun.java

Below is how the "objectPlymorphism" project looks like with four files.

Figure 1.10: Object polymorphism explorer

"clsTestRun.java" is class which will have the "main" method which will be executed on the first instance. Below is the relationship between the other three classes. "ClsAdd" is the main parent class and "clsSpecialAdd" and "clsSpecialAddandDivide" derives from "ClsAdd" class.

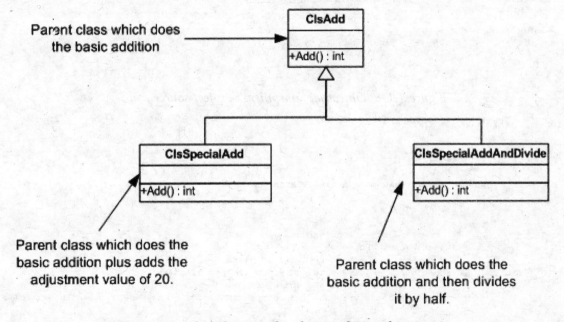

Figure 1.11: Class diagram for object polymorphism project.

Below is the source code explanation.

√   "ClsAdd" only adds the two numbers and returns the results.

√   "ClsSpecialAdd" adds the numbers and also adds adjustment value of 20.

√   "ClsSpecialAddandDivide" adds the numbers and divides it by 2.

Finally we will walk through "clsTestRun" class which will demonstrate polymorphism using the above three classes. Below is the code snippet. "ClsTestRun" first creates object of all the three classes.

```
public class ClsAdd
{
// This method does simple addition
public int Add(int num1,int num2)
{
    return num1 + num2;
}

}
```

```
public class ClsSpecialAdd extends ClsAdd
{
// This method inherits from the parent class and adds the adjustment value
    public int Add(int num1, int num2)
    {
        int intAdjustValue = 20;
        return num1 + num2 + intAdjustValue;
    }
}
```

```
public class ClsSpecialAddAndDivide extends ClsAdd
{
// This method inherits from the parent class
// It adds two numbers and divides it by 2.
    public int Add(int num1, int num2)
    {
        return (num1 + num2)/2;
    }
}
```

Figure 1.12: "Objectpolymorphism" project source code.

```
public class clsTestRun {

    /**
     * @param args
     */
    public static void main(String[] args)
    {
        // TODO Auto-generated method stub

        // Create object of the parent class
        ClsAdd objClsAddParent = new ClsAdd();
        // Create object of the special add class
        ClsSpecialAdd objClsSpecialAdd = new ClsSpecialAdd();
        // Create object of the add and divide class
        ClsSpecialAddAndDivide objClsSpecialAddAndDivide = new ClsSpecialAddAndDivide();

        // call the parent object
        System.out.println("Simple addition :- " + objClsAddParent.Add(2,3));
        // set the parent object to the child special add and call the
        // add method
        objClsAddParent = objClsSpecialAdd;
        System.out.println("Special addition :- " + objClsAddParent.Add(2,3));

        // set the parent object to the child special add and divide class
        // and call the add method
        objClsAddParent = objClsSpecialAddAndDivide;
        System.out.println("Special addition :- " + objClsAddParent.Add(6,6));
    }

}
```

Object creation

Parent object reference changed dynamically to the child objects.

Figure 1.13: "clsTestRun" for "objectpolymorphism" project

You can see in the code we have set both the child object references to parent object and called the add method respectively. Depending on which child is referenced by the parent object the child object method is called. For instance when we referred "ClsSpeicalAdd" object it added the two numbers adding the adjustment value. So depending on what object the parent object is referring the actions is taking place which is nothing but polymorphism.

Below is the output you can see both the child classes are called by the parent object.

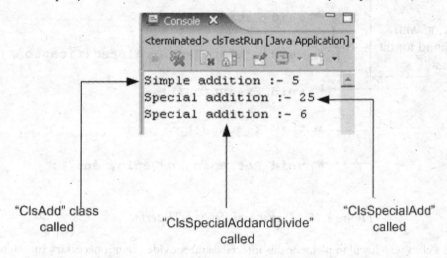

Figure 1.14: Output results of "Objectpolymorphism"

(B) What's an interface and how will you go about implementing an interface?

An interface is a named collection of method definitions, without implementations. Interface defines a protocol of behavior for a class. So if "Class1" is adhering to an interface and "Class2" wants to communicate with "Class1" then it should follow the same interface which "Class1" is following". In short it defines a contract to the external consumer of the class i.e. if you want use me then you need to follow these interfaces.

So let's run through a sample in order to understand the interface concept.

In the below sample we want to develop a class which will make us run through software development phases in a proper order. So first let's decide an interface which will have all the necessary vocabulary so that we do not miss anything.

So below is the interface with six phases of software life cycle. Preparing this interface is a one time exercise. Now any time we want to do a project regarding software development life cycle we just have to implement this interface. So we can say interfaces define vocabulary and contract.

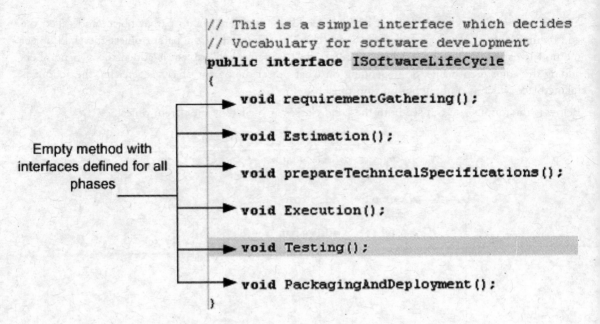

Figure 1.15: "ISoftwareLifeCycle" interface

Now let's make a class which will implement this interface and provide us with necessary functionalities. This class does not do anything special but will just display the name of the phase.

Interfaces are implemented using "implements" keyword. You can see the best thing about using interfaces is that the shell is predefined (in this case it's the "ISoftwareLifeCycle"). Programmer who is coding "clsSoftware" class does not have to think about what different phases exists for software but rather just implement the "ISoftwareLifeCycle" interface. In big projects where you have a huge programmer group coding it's much possible that every one will not follow same naming conventions and method names. So the best way is to define an interface and let the programmers implement the interface and write the implementation. Due to this approach every programmer is implementing the same interface it brings in consistency of method and naming conventions through out the project.

```
public class clsSoftware implements  SoftwareLifeCycle
{
        public void Estimation()
        {
                // TODO Auto-generated method stub
                System.out.println(" Start Estimation ");
        }

        public void Execution()
        {
                // TODO Auto-generated method stub
                System.out.println(" Start Execution ");
        }

        public void PackagingAndDeployment()
        {
                // TODO Auto-generated method stub
                System.out.println(" Start Packaging ");
        }

        public void prepareTechnicalSpecifications() {
                // TODO Auto-generated method stub
                System.out.println(" Start Technical Specifications ");
        }

        public void requirementGathering() {
                // TODO Auto-generated method stub
                System.out.println(" Start Requirement Gathering ");
        }

        public void Testing()
        {
                // TODO Auto-generated method stub
                System.out.println(" Start Testing ");
        }

        public void startProject()
        {
                requirementGathering();
                Estimation();
                prepareTechnicalSpecifications();
                Execution();
                Testing();
                PackagingAndDeployment();
        }

}
```

Interface is implemented by "implements" keyword.

Just displayed the name of the phase

This method runs all the implemented method in a proper sequence

Figure 1.16: Class "ClsSoftware" implementation

In "ClsSoftware" class we also have a "StartProject" method which calls all the phases in a proper order. If you run the project using eclipse you will get the following output.

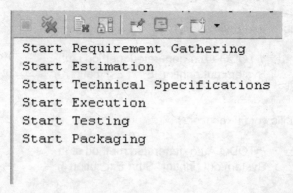

```
Start Requirement Gathering
Start Estimation
Start Technical Specifications
Start Execution
Start Testing
Start Packaging
```

Figure 1.17: Output from the interface project.

If you want to apply interface to class you can automate it by clicking on "Extract Interface" menu.

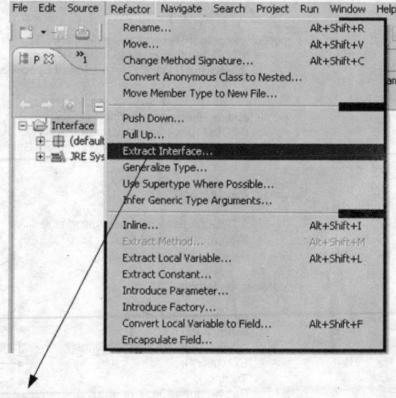

Use the extract interface to automatically
generate interface generation for a class.

Figure 1.18: Click on "Extract Interface" for automating process

(B)   What is an Abstract class?

Abstract class defines an abstract concept which can not be instantiated and comparing to interface it can have some implementation while interfaces can not. Below are some points for abstract class:

√   We can not create object of abstract class it can only be inherited in a below class.

√   Normally abstract classes have base implementation and then child classes derive from the abstract class to make the class concrete.

Ok let's try to get the abstract class fundamentals just to make sure that you do not stumble in interview. Abstract classes normally represent concept. Just to make it precise it represents half implemented concepts. What does that mean fundamentally?. You can have concept like food but you can not have an instance of the same. You can have instance of cheese, milk etc. So food represents an abstract concept while cheese, milk etc represent the actual instance. In your project you can have a general concept called as "Transaction" but then further your project can make the "Transaction" class more concrete by saying "Bank Transaction" or "Ledger Transaction" class. So you would like to model the "Transaction" class but not create objects of the same. It makes more sense to create "Bank Transaction" class object or "Ledger Transaction" class objects.

In order to understand abstract class fundamentals lets do a sample project. You can get the sample project in CD in "\Sourcecode\Abstract" folder. Below is the class diagram of the project. "clsAbstractPerson" class represents a person. It has three methods "Numberoflegs", "NumberofEyes" and "Sex". Now conceptually all humans have two legs and two eyes, but sex is something which can vary from person to person. So what we do is we write implementation for "numberofEyes" method and "numberOfLegs" method and leave the "Sex" method implementation to subclasses.

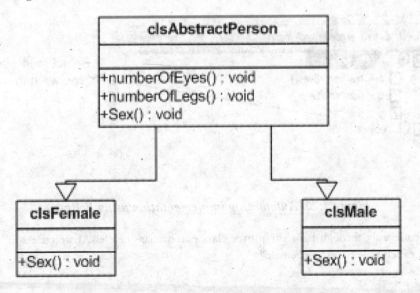

Figure 1.19: Class diagram for abstract project

We have made two subclasses "clsFemale" and "clsMale" which will provide us concrete implementation for "Sex" method. So let's make a code walk through for all of the classes defined in the class diagram.

Note: *If you want the method names to included automatically in the subclasses you click on*
       "Override/Implement methods" menu which is present in the main "Source" menu as shown
       in figure below. You will then be prompted with a dialog box as to which method from the
       parent should be overridden. For the current "Abstract" project we only need to check the "Sex"
       method as that's the only method we will need to override.

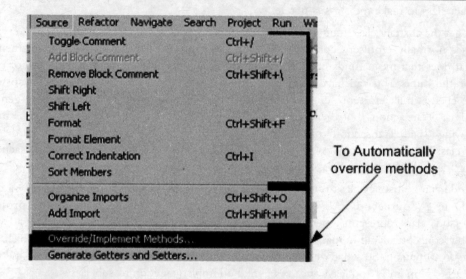

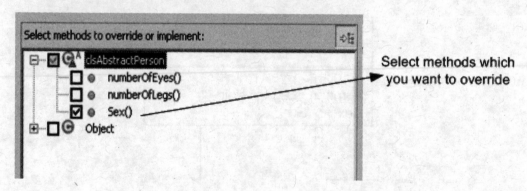

Figure 1.20: Automating implementation using Eclipse

Below is the code walk through for all the three class parent class i.e. "clsAbstractPerson" and the two
child classes i.e. "clsMale" and "clsFemale".

```
abstract class clsAbstractPerson

    public void numberOfEyes()
    {
        System.out.println("Two Eyes");
    }

    public void numberOfLegs()
    {
        System.out.println("Two Legs");
    }

    public void Sex()
    {
        // This implementation will defined at the lower
        // class level
    }
}
```

```
public class clsFemale extends clsAbstractPerson
{

    public void Sex()
    {
        System.out.println("This is a female implementation");
    }
}
```

```
public class clsMale extends clsAbstractPerson
{

    public void Sex()
    {
        System.out.println("This is a male implementation");
    }
}
```

Figure 1.21: Code walk through for abstract class

```
public class clsRun
{

    public static void main(String[] args)
    {
        clsMale objclsMale = new clsMale();
        clsFemale objclsFemale = new clsFemale();

        System.out.println("--------------------");
        objclsMale.numberOfEyes();
        objclsMale.numberOfLegs();
        objclsMale.Sex();
        System.out.println("--------------------");
        objclsFemale.numberOfEyes();
        objclsFemale.numberOfLegs();
        objclsFemale.Sex();
        System.out.println("--------------------");
    }
}
```

```
--------------------
Two Eyes
Two Legs
This is a male implementation
--------------------
Two Eyes
Two Legs
This is a female implementation
--------------------
```

Figure 1.22: Output of "Abstract" project

Nothing special has been done in the "Sex" method implementation other than just displaying the whether its "Female" or "Male" implementation according to the class. You can now visualize the concept of using "Abstract" class. In this situation "Person" is a concept but it can not have instance as there is no point in creating an object of "Person". It's a half made class which does not have "Sex" implementation. Conceptually "Person" can be either female or male. But later when subclasses inherit the "ClsAbstractPerson" class they provide a true implementation by providing functionality for the "Sex" method. It sounds sense for creating objects for "clsFemale" or "clsMale" class.

"ClsRun" class is the driver which creates objects for both classes "clsMale" and "clsFemale" and calls all the three methods. You can see the output "Eyes" and "Legs" implementation remain same for both the classes but "Sex" implementation varies. So basically abstract class "clsAbstractPerson" provides conceptual implementation but later the concrete classes give more detail implementation and complete meaning to the class.

(B)   What are Abstract methods?

Abstract class can contain abstract methods. Abstract methods do not have implementation. Abstract methods should be implemented in the subclasses which inherit them. So if an abstract class has an abstract method class inheriting the abstract class should implement the method or else java compiler will through an error. In this way, an abstract class can define a complete programming interface thereby providing its subclasses with the method declarations for all of the methods necessary to implement that programming interface.

Abstract methods are defined using "abstract" keyword. Below is a sample code snippet.

```
abstract class myAbstractGraphics
{
        abstract void draw();
}
```

Any class inheriting from "myAbstractGrpahics" class should implement the "draw" method or else the java compiler will throw an error.

> *Note:* *One way the interviewer would like to confuse you is if we do not implement a abstract method will*
> *the program compile.*

(B)   What's the difference between "Abstract" classes and "Interfaces"?

Difference between Abstract class and Interface is as follows:

√   Abstract class can only be inherited while interfaces can not be it has to be, implemented.

√   Interface cannot implement any methods, whereas an abstract class can have implementation.

√   Class can implement many interfaces but can have only one super class.

√   Interface is not part of the class hierarchy while Abstract class comes in through inheritance.

√   Unrelated classes can implement the same interface.

(I)   What's difference between Static and Non-Static fields of a class?

Non-Static values are also called as instance variables. Each object of the class has its own copy of Non-Static instance variables. So when a new object is created of the same class it will have completely its own copy of instance variables.

While Static values have only one copy of instance variables and will be shared among all the objects of the class.

Here's a small practical stuff we will do to understand the concept. Let's create a small sample project to demonstrate the static and non-static concepts. In CD, in the source code folder there is a sample provided for the same in "StaticNonStatic" folder. Below is the file structure. Basically the project has two main classes "clsStaticNonStatic.java" and "ClsTestRun.java". We will be explaining the above two classes in the coming sections.

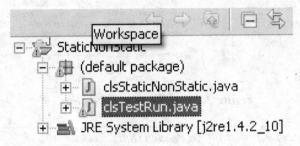

Figure 1.23: Static and Non-Static Project Files

"clsStaticNonStatic.java" is the core class it has two variable declarations as shown in figure below.

```
public class clsStaticNonStatic
{
public static int intStat;   ──────▶  Static variable declaration

public int intNonStat;       ──────▶  Non-Static variable declaration

}
```

Figure 1.24: clsStaticNonStatic java class.

"ClsTestRun.java" is the class who will run create objects of "clsStaticNonStatic.java" and run it. Below is the figure which has "clsTestRun.java" in action. It does nothing special but creates four objects and increments the static and non-static properties. In the below figure at the left hand side you can see the static variables values are preserved as they are. So the "intStat" value goes up to "4" and "intNonStat" has value "1".

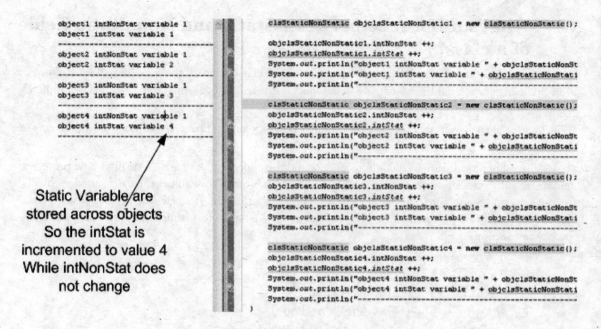

Figure 1.25: clsTestrun.java class

Note: *You can find the sample project in "StaticNonStatic" folder.*

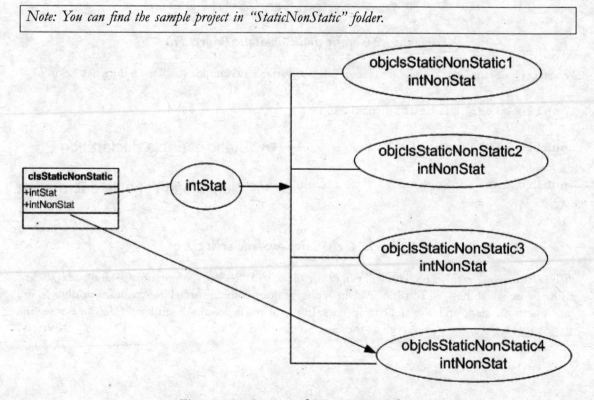

Figure 1.26: Static and Non-Static Values

The above figure shows how "Static" and "NonStatic" properties are shared across object. You can see "intStat" property is shared across objects and "intNonStat" have there own local copy.

(I)   What are inner classes and what's the practical implementation of inner classes?

Inner classes are nested inside other class. They have access to outer class fields and methods even if the fields of outer class are defined as private.

```java
public class Person
{
    class clsName
    {
        // inner class defines the required structure
        String first;
        String last;
    }
    // array of name objects
    clsName personArray[] = {new clsName(), new clsName(), new
    clsName()};
}
```

Normally inner classes are used for data structures like one shown above or some kind of helper classes.

(B)   What are packages?

Packages group related classes and interfaces together and thus avoiding any name conflicts. From OOP's point of view packages are useful for grouping related classes together. Classes are group together in a package using "package" keyword.

Below is a sample snippet for a package which groups "Class1" and "Class2" in one package "Package1".

```java
package Package1;
public class Class1
{
    public void displayClassName()
    {
        System.out.println(" I am class1 from Package1");
    }
}
public class Class2
{
    public void displayClassName()
    {
        System.out.println(" I am class2 from Package1");
    }
}
```

When we want to use the above "package1" in project we need to use the import keyword.

```
import Package1.*;
public class clsRun
{
    public static void main(String[] args)
    {
        Package1.Class1 objp1Class1 = new Package1.Class1();
        objp1Class1.displayClassName();
    }
}
```

Note: You can add a package using eclipse using the wizard as shown below.

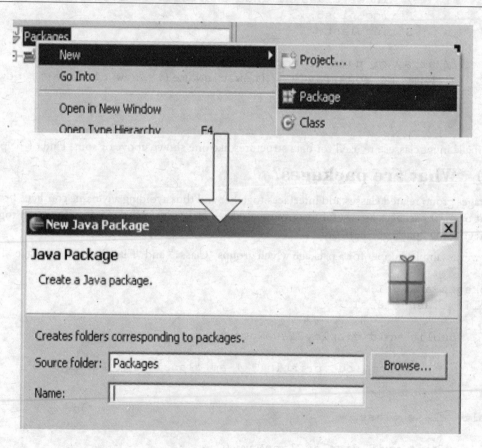

Figure 1.27: Adding package using eclipse wizard

In order to make concepts more clear there is a sample package project shipped in CD in "package" folder. Below is the solution of the package project. There two packages "Package1" which has "Class1" class and "Package2" which has again a class by name "Class1".

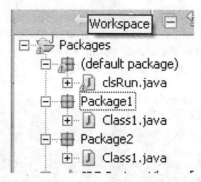

Figure 1.28: Solution for package project

```java
import Package1.*;
import Package2.*;

public class clsRun {

    /**
     * @param args
     */
    public static void main(String[] args)
    {
        Package1.Class1 objp1Class1 = new Package1.Class1();
        objp1Class1.displayClassName();

        Package2.Class1 objp2Class1 = new Package2.Class1();
        objp2Class1.displayClassName();

    }

}
```

Figure 1.29: "clsRun" class for package project

In "clsRun" class we have created objects of "Class1" class which exist in "package1" as well as "package2". There are two things which is important to be noted one is the "import" keyword at the top of the class and second is both objects are created using "PackageName.Classname" . For instance "objp1class1" object is created using "Package1.Class1". You can see that we can have class with same name but they lie in different packages. For instance in the above example "Class1" name is give two files but they lie in different packages.

Normally in big projects where we have huge amount of classes its better to group them logically together so that the project can be manageable.

(B)   What is a constructor in class?

Constructor has the same name as the class in which it resides and from syntax point of view it looks similiar to a method. Constructor is automatically called immediately after the object is created, before the new operator completes. Constructors have no return type, not even void. This is because the implicit return type of a class' constructor is the class type itself. It is the constructor's job to initialize the internal state of an object so that the code creating an instance will have a fully initialized, usable object immediately. Below is a snippet of constructor code:

Constructor does
not return anything

```
class clsMaths {
   double PI;


   // This is the constructor for the maths constant class.
   clsMaths()
   {
   PI = 3.14;
   }


   void MakeMyCircle(int intRadius)
   {
      double dblCircle = 0;
      dblCircle =  PI * intRadius * intRadius;
      System.out.println(" Circle radius is " + dblCircle);
   }
}
```

Figure 1.30: Constructor in action

Above snippet shows declaration for constructor in "clsMaths" class. We have initialized the PI value to "3.14".

Note: Same sample has been provided in "Constructor" folder in CD.

(I)   Can constructors be parameterized?

Yes we can have parameterized constructor which can also be termed as constructor overloading. Below is a code snippet which shows two constructors for "clsMaths" class one with parameter and one with out.

```
class clsMaths
{
     double PI;
     // This is the constructor for the maths constant class.
     clsMaths()
     {PI = 3.14;}
     clsMaths(int pi)
     {
          PI = pi;
     }
}
```

(I)   What is the use of "instanceof" keyword?

"instanceof" keyword is used to check what is the type of object. For instance in the below code snippet we are trying to check is "object1" of the same type as "object2".

> *if(object1 instanceof object2)*

(B)   What are Native methods in Java?

There may be times when you want to call subroutines which are written in some other language other than Java like C++, VB6 etc.

(B)   How do refer to a current instance of object?

You can refer the current instance of object using "this" keyword. For instance if you have class which has "color" property you can refer the current object instance inside any of the method using "this.color".

(I)   Explain in depth Garbage collector?

Garbage collection is the process of automatically freeing objects that are no longer referenced by the program. This frees the programmer from having to keep track of when to free allocated memory, thereby preventing many potential bugs. Thus making programmers more productive as they can now put more effort in coding rather than worrying about memory management.

The only disadvantage of garbage collector is it adds overheads. Because the JVM (Java virtual machine) has to keep a constant track of the objects which are not referenced and then free these unreferenced objects on fly. This whole process has a slight impact on the application performance. But garbage collector has a good algorithm and it runs in its own thread thus having a least impact on the application performance but still, it has some impact.

(I)   How does the garbage collector determine that the object has to be marked for deletion?

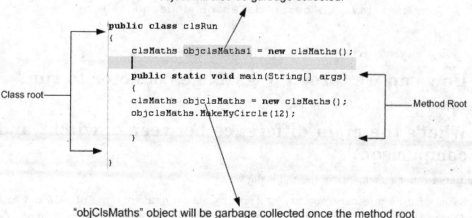

Figure 1.31: "root" and "reach" in garbage collection

GC has defined set of "roots" and "object reach from the roots". Ok let's try to understand this statement. "roots" can be a method, class etc. So if the "method" or "class" root has access to the objects then the object can not be garbage collected. Lets try to understand root and reach from the below code snippet.

In the above snippet we have two roots one is the class root i.e. "clsRun" class itself and second method root "main" method. We have two objects at both levels of roots "objClsMaths1" object is in class root while "objClsMaths" object is on method root. Once the "main" method execution is completed object "objClsMaths" object will be marked for garbage collection. Once object of "clsRun" class is destroyed then "objClsMaths1" object will marked for garbage collection.

"Mark" and "Sweep" algorithm is done for removing unused objects from memory. "Mark" and "Sweep" refer to two phases before an unused object is garbage collected. In "Mark" phase the garbage collector runs through all objects and marks object as unused depending on the roots reach to the object. In the "Sweep" phase unmarked objects are freed, and the resulting memory is made available to the executing program.

(B)   Can you explain "finalize()" method?

Sometimes the object needs to perform some action before the object is destroyed. For instance if an object is holding some non-Java resource such as a file handle which you might want to make sure are released before the object is destroyed. For such conditions Java provides a mechanism called finalization. By using finalization, you can define specific actions that will occur when an object is just about to be reclaimed by the garbage collector.

You can add a finalizer to a class by simply defining the "finalize()" method. JVM calls that method whenever it is about to recycle an object of that class. Inside the "finalize()" method you can specify those actions that must be performed before an object is destroyed. GC runs periodically checking for objects that are no longer referenced. Right before an asset is freed, the Java run time calls the "finalize()" method on the object.

Below is the snippet for finalize method

```
protected void finalize()
{
        // Your non java resource deletion code goes here
}
```

Protected access prevents access to "finalize()" by code defined outside its class.

(I)   How can we force the garbage collector to run?

Garbage collector can be run forcibly using "System.gc()" or "Runtime.gc()"

(B)   What's the main difference between "Switch" and "If" comparison?

Switch differs from if statements in the following way:

√   Switch can only test for equality, whereas it can evaluate any type of Boolean expression. That is, the switch looks only for a match between the value of the expression and one of its case constants.

√   Switch statements are more efficient that if statements.

When Java compiler compiles a switch statement it looks at the case constants and creates a jump table that it will use for selecting the path of execution depending on the value of the expression. So if you are comparing large group of values switch will be faster than sequence of if-elses. Compiler knows that the case constants are all the same type and simply must be compared for equality with the switch expression. The compiler has no such knowledge of a long list for if expressions.

In the below code snippet we are displaying the number in words. If its "1" then display "one" and if its "2" display "two. For "if" condition it scans through the entire if" conditions but in switch statement it directly jumps to the logic after looking at the lookup table.

```java
for (int i=0;i < intNumbers.length+1;i++)
{
    if (i==1)
    {
        displayString(" One ");
    }
    else if(i==2)
    {
        displayString(" Two ");
    }
}
displayString(" Displaying Numbers using SWITCH / CASE Statements ");
for (int i=0;i < intNumbers.length+1;i++)
{
    switch(i)
    {
    case 1:
        displayString("One");
        break;
    case 2:
        displayString("Two");
        break;
    }
}
```

If condition will compare for conditions

Does not evaluate all case statement directly jumps to the condition. For instance in this case the value is 2 it jumps to the second case statement.

Figure 1.32: Difference between SWITCH and IF statements

Note: Sample for "Switch and If" condition is provided in "SwitchAndIf" folder in CD.

(I)   What's the use of JAVAP tool?

"javap" disassembles compiled Java files and spits out representation of the Java program. This is a useful option when the original source code is not available.

(B)   What are applets?

Applets are small applications that are accessed from web server, automatically installed and run from the browser. Once an applet arrives on the client it has limited access to resources thus ensuring security for the end user. An applet is controlled by the software that runs it. Usually, the underlying software is a browser, but it can also be applet viewer. If you run the applet source code from eclipse it runs inside an applet viewer. All applets should inherit from applet class.

Below are sequences of events which occur in applet:

The init Method: The init method is called when the applet is first loaded. Init method can be used to initialize color, fonts or any type of one type operation needed for the applet.

The start Method: The start method is called when user visits a browser with an applet on it. In start method applet spawns a thread in which it runs the paint method.

paint(): is called every time when applet has to re-display everything. paint() event can occur due to various reasons some of the reasons are:

√   When browser running the applet is covered or uncovered by some other window.

√   When browser running the applet is minimized and maximized.

√   paint() is also called when the applet begins execution.

Applet must always redraw its output when paint() method is called. paint() accepts graphics object as a input parameter you can see the same in the figure below. To just add something about this object it actually contains the graphics context. Graphic context determines the graphics environment in which the applet will be running and applet will use the same context to display output on the browser.

The stop and destroy Methods: The stop method stops the applet user goes to a different web page.

The destroy method is called when the browser exits. This is the place we can put in cleaning up of threads or any resource which is not a java resource.

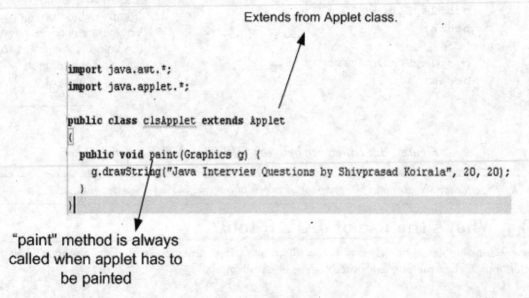

Figure 1.33: applet in action.

In order to make your fundamental stronger there is a small program on applet which displays my name of the book. You can get the above code of applet in CD in "applet" folder.

(B) In which package is the applet class located?

Applet classes are located in "java.applet" package.

(I) What are native interfaces in Java?

> *Note: This can be answered in one liner to just make sure that you get enough grasp of native interfaces we have one topic which is completely dedicated to JNI.*

(I) what are Class loader's?

JAVA was designed thinking platform independency in mind. So from loading libraries point of view it should not rely only on file systems. In short it's not necessary that you should be able to load libraries which are in only file systems but also from other sources like FTP, HTTP etc. So JAVA went one step further you can load classes from across network or from any other source like FTP, HTTP etc. In order to attain this Class loaders came in to picture. Class loader is the class responsible for finding and loading classes at runtime. You can either use different class loaders or you can make a custom one.

(I) what is Bootstrap, Extension and System Class loader?

> *Twist: Can you explain primordial class loader?*

There three types of class loaders:

√ BootStrap Class loader also called as primordial class loader.

√ Extension Class loader.

√ System Class loader.

Let's now try to get the fundamentals of these class loaders.

Bootstrap Class loader

Bootstrap class loader loads those classes which are essential for JVM to function properly. Bootstrap class loader is responsible for loading all core java classes for instance java.lang.*, java.io.* etc. Bootstrap class loader finds these necessary classes from "jdk/jre/lib/rt.jar". Bootstrap class loader can not be instantiated from JAVA code and is implemented natively inside JVM.

Extension Class loader

The extension class loader also termed as the standard extensions class loader is a child of the bootstrap class loader. Its primary responsibility is to load classes from the extension directories, normally located the "jre/lib/ext" directory. This provides the ability to simply drop in new extensions, such as various security extensions, without requiring modification to the user's class path.

System Class loader

The system class loader also termed application class loader is the class loader responsible for loading code from the path specified by the CLASSPATH environment variable. It is also used to load an application's entry point class that is the "static void main ()" method in a class.

(I)   Can you explain the flow between bootstrap, extension and system class loader?

Ok below is a simple class lets get in to details of how the class will be loaded.

Import Koirala.Interview.Java;

```
public class mySimpleClass
{
      public static void main(String[] args)
      {
            String myStr = "I am going to get a job";
            System.out.println(myStr);
      }
}
```

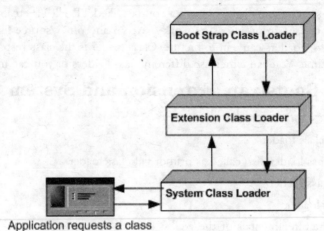

Figure 1.34: Flow between class loaders

The above class uses "String" class that means it has reference to "java.lang.String". JVM will request the system class loader to load "java.lang.String". But before he tries to load it will delegate to extension class loader. Extension class loader will pass it to Boot strap class loader. Now Boot Strap class loader does not have any parent so it will try to load "java.lang.String" using "rt.jar". Now the Boot strap will return the class back using the same chain to the application.

Now lets see how "Import Koirala.Interview.Java;" is loaded using the class loaders. For the import statement JVM will make a call to the system class loader who will delegate the same to the extension class loader which will delegate the same to the boot strap class loader. Boot strap loader will not find "Koirala.Interview.Java" and return nothing to the extension class loader. Extension class loader will also check the same in its path and will not find anything thus returning nothing to the system class loader. System class loader will use its class path and load the class and return the same to the JVM who will then return it to the application.

> *Note: In the coming question we will be answering three question in on shot.*

(I)   Can you explain how can you practically do dynamic loading?

(I)   What is Reflection API in Java ?

(I)   What's the difference between static and dynamic class loading ?

```
public class clsDynamicLoading
{
public static void main(String[] args) throws Exception
{
// Load the class
Class toRun = Class.forName("Interview.Questions.Java");    <---- 1
// Call the find main method of the class
Method mainMethod = findMain(toRun);    <---- 2
// Invoke the method
mainMethod.invoke(null, new Object[] { toRun });    <---- 3
}
// This method finds the main method of the class
private static Method findMain(Class clazz) throws Exception
{
Method[] methods = clazz.getMethods();
    for (int i=0; i<methods.length; i++)
    {
    if (methods[i].getName().equals("main"))
    return methods[i];
    }

    return null;
}}
```

Figure 1.35: Dynamic class loading in action

Above is the code snippet to implement dynamic class loading. In the above code snippet we also have marked the steps in order. First thing we need to do is load the class which is done by using "Class.forName". In the second step we just try to find out the main method and get the method reference using "getMethods()" collection. Finally invoke the method using "invoke".

In static loading we use the "new" keyword to create object. "myObj obj = new myObj();". In short we need to know from the start what type of object we will be creating. While in dynamic class loading we need to know the string name of the class and then everything else will be dynamically loaded.

Dynamic class loading is only possible due to Reflection API Interface. Reflection API is a member of core java.lang package. The methods provided by the Reflection API obtain information about a class, such as the fields, constructors, methods, and super classes of the class. In addition, you can obtain the interfaces implemented by the class. You can notice in the above sample how we inspected the methods in the class.

Note: You can find dynamic class loading sample project in the "\Source" folder.

(B)   How can you copy one array in to a different array?

System.arraycopy(myOldArray, 0, myNewArray, 0, length);

(B)   Can you explain the core collection interfaces?

There are six interfaces and come under two different inheritance group one which comes under the collection interface root and the other in the map interface root.

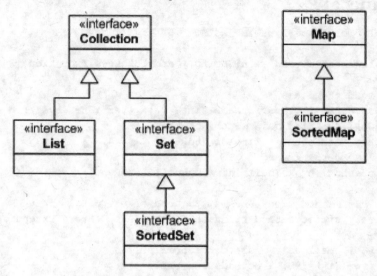

Figure 1.36: Collection Interface hierarchy

Below are the details of core collection interface.

Collection

It's the base of all collection classes. It provides a unified way to manipulate collection objects. Collection has group of object called as elements. These elements can be accessed and manipulated using Iterator.

List

In List interface the elements are arranged sequentially. Elements can be inserted in to any location and you can also insert duplicate elements. In order to access the elements you need to use the "ListIterator". Using "ListIterator" you can move back and forth which makes it unique as compared to other iterators.

Set

It represents a collection but no duplicates are allowed in this case.

SortedSet

It extends the Set interface and sorts the set in ascending order.

Map

Map stores association between keys and value pairs. So given a key you can easily find the value. One thing important to note is they do not implement iterable interface. But yes you can obtain a collection view of the map which allows you loop using for loop.

SortedMap

It Extends Map so that the keys are maintained in ascending order.

(I) Can you explain in brief the collection classes which implement the collection interfaces?

Class	Description
AbstractCollection	Implements most of the Collection interface.
AbstractList	Extends AbstractCollection and implements most of the List interface.
AbstractQueue	Extends AbstractCollection and implements parts of the Queue interface. New feature in J2SE 5.
AbstractSequentialList	Extends AbstractList for use by a collection that uses sequential rather than random access of its elements.
LinkedList	Implements a linked list by extending AbstractSequentialList.
ArrayList	Implements a dynamic array by extending AbstractList.
AbstractSet	Extends AbstractCollection and implements most of the Set interface.
EnumSet	Extends AbstractSet for use with enum elements.
HashSet	Extends AbstractSet for use with a hash table.
LinkedHashSet	Extends HashSet to allow insertion-order iterations.
PriorityQueue	Extends AbstractQueue to support a priority-based queue.
TreeSet	Implements a set stored in a tree. Extends AbstractSet.

Figure 1.37: Standard collection classes

(B) What's the difference between standard JAVA array and ArrayList class?

ArrayList support dynamic arrays that can grow depending on demand. But traditional JAVA arrays are of fixed length once they are created.

(B) What's the use of "ensureCapacity" in ArrayList class?

ArrayList are designed so that they can grow depending on demand. But there is a cost attached to the same. The cost of allocating and reallocating memory. You can prevent this reallocation by increasing the capacity at once. This can be attained by "ensureCapacity" method. Below is the syntax:

```
void ensureCapacity(int cap)
```

(I)   How can we obtain an array from an ArrayList class?

You can convert from arraylist to traditional arrays using "toArray()" below is the code snippet for the same.

```
ArrayList<Integer> myArrayList = new ArrayList<Integer>();
// add in to the arraylist collection
myArrayList.add(1);
myArrayList.add(2);
// Get the array.
Integer tempArray[] = new Integer[myArrayList.size()];
tempArray = myArrayList.toArray(tempArray);
```

> *Note: This is a small home work to the readers write a simple program and sees how you can use "ArrayList". As this is an interview question book I have not got in to sample code for arraylist.*

(B)   What is "LinkedList" class for?

It provides link-list data structure. Below is the code snippet which shows LinkedList class in action.

```
public static void main(String args[])
{
LinkedList list1 = new LinkedList();
list1.add("Shiv");
list1.add("Raju");
list1.add("Vishna");
list1.add("Sanjana");
list1.add("Simran");
System.out.println("Contents of the list:" +list1);
list1.removeLast();
list1.removeFirst();
System.out.println("The list after removing the first and last item:" +list1);
list1.addFirst("Priya");
System.out.println("Contents of the list after adding:" +list1);
Object value = list1.get(2);
list1.set(2,(String)value +" is my wife");
System.out.println("After alteration " +list1);
list1.add(2,"Harisingh");
System.out.println("The list after adding in a specific location:" +list1);
}
```

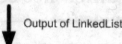

Output of LinkedList

```
Contents of the list:[Shiv, Raju, Vishna, Sanjana, Simran]
The list after removing the first and last item:[Raju, Vishna, Sanjana]
Contents of the list after adding:[Priya, Raju, Vishna, Sanjana]
After alteration [Priya, Raju, Vishna is my wife, Sanjana]
The list after adding in a specific location:[Priya, Raju, Birma, Vishna is my wife, Sanjana]
```

Figure 1.38: LinkedList sample code and output

We can add elements to the beginning or the end of the list using the below code snippet:

> *void addFirst(Object objlst)*
>
> *void addLast(Object objlst)*

objlst is the element added to the list.

In order to get the first and the last element of the linked list we can use the getFirst() and getLast() methods respectively. Below is the code snippet for the same:

> *Object getFirst()*
>
> *Object getLast()*

In order to delete the first and the last element of the list we can use the removeFirst() and removeLast() methods, respectively. Below is the code snippet for the same:

> *Object removeFirst()*
>
> *Object removeLast()*

> *Note:* *You can find the above code for LinkedList in "\Source Code\LinkedLIst" folder.*

(B) Can you explain HashSet class in collections?

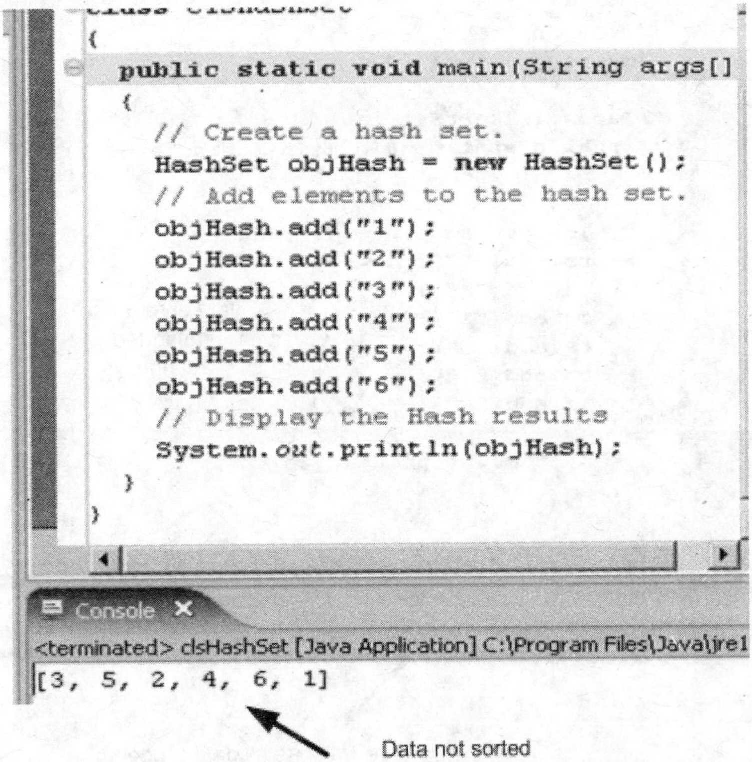

```
class clsHashSet
{
    public static void main(String args[]
    {
        // Create a hash set.
        HashSet objHash = new HashSet();
        // Add elements to the hash set.
        objHash.add("1");
        objHash.add("2");
        objHash.add("3");
        objHash.add("4");
        objHash.add("5");
        objHash.add("6");
        // Display the Hash results
        System.out.println(objHash);
    }
}
```

```
Console  X
<terminated> clsHashSet [Java Application] C:\Program Files\Java\jre1
[3, 5, 2, 4, 6, 1]
```

Data not sorted

Figure 1.39: HashSet Sample code

HashSet extends AbstractSet and implements the Set interface. It creates a collection that uses a hash table for storage. Hash table stores information by using a mechanism called hashing. Information of the key is used to determine a unique value termed hash code. This hash code is then used as an index for data associated with the key is stored. This happens automatically and you will never need to know the hash code value. Also, your code can't directly index the hash table.

The biggest advantage of hashing is that execution time of add( ), contains( ), remove( ), and size( ) to remain same even when the collection are large in size. Hash set does not guarantee sorting. You can see from the below code snippet that data is not sorted.

> *Note:* *You can fine the source code for the same in "\SourceCode\Hashset" folder in CD.*

(I)   what is LinkedHashSet class?

LinkedHashSet extends HashSet class but it does not add any extra members as such. LinkedHashSet maintains list of entries in the order in which they are inserted. So when you iterate through a LinkedHashSet class elements will be returned in the order they are inserted. In order to just see how LinkedHashSet works you can try the HashSet code with LinkedHashset you should get the order as "[1, 2, 3, 4, 5, 6]".

(I)   what is a TreeSet class?

TreeSet creates a collection that uses a tree for storage. Items in collection are stored in ascending order. TreeSet are good choice for storing large amount of data. Below is a small snippet which shows "TreeSet" in action.

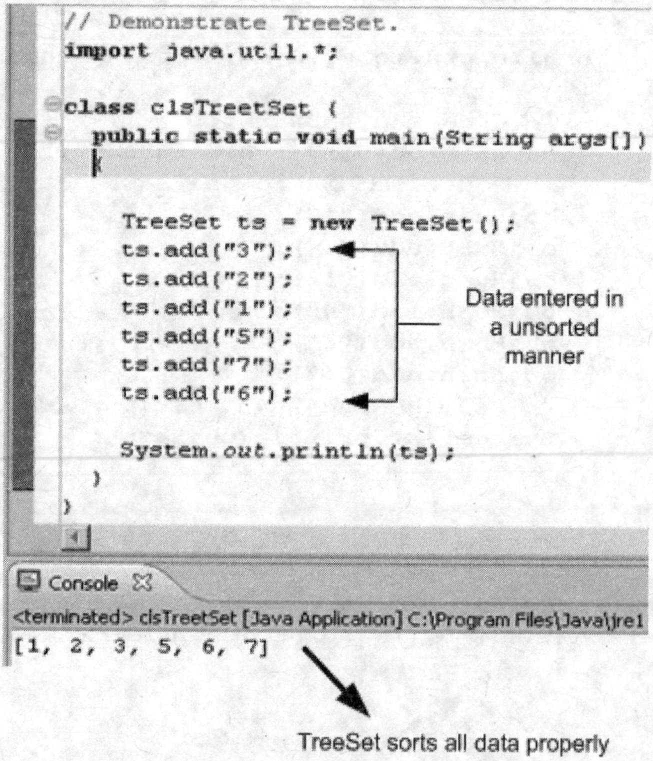

Figure 1.40: TreeSet collection in action

> Note: You can find "TreeSet" code in "TreeSet" directory.

(I)   what's the use of Comparator Interface?

By default JAVA sorts collection in ascending order. We can use the Comparator Interface to specify a sort order. Comparator interface provides compare() method which compares two elements. Below is the syntax snippet for the same:

> int compare(Object o1, Object o2)

Below is a sample code which shows how to use the comparator interface. It sorts using the string length. In order to achieve this we have created two classes clsComparator and clsMain. clsComparator implements the Comparator interface and implements the compare method with out custom comparison. clsMain is the entry point and has the void main method. We can see object of clsComparator is passed to the TreeSet object.

```java
import java.util.*;

public class clsComparator
implements Comparator
{public int compare(Object arg0, Object arg1)
{
String str1,str2;
str1 = (String)arg0;
str2 = (String) arg1;
        if (str1.length() < str2.length())

                return 1;
        }
        if (str1.length() > str2.length())
        {return -1;}
        else
        {
                return 0;
        }
}}

import java.util.*;
public class clsMain
{
    public static void main(String[] args)
    {
        TreeSet ts = new TreeSet(new clsComparator());
        ts.add("ShivXXXX");
        ts.add("ShivXXXXXXX");
        ts.add("ShivXXXXX");
        ts.add("ShivXXXXX");
        Iterator i = ts.iterator();
        while(i.hasNext())
        {
        Object el = i.next();
        System.out.println(el +"");
        }
}}
```

Comparison based on length of string

Comparator based as argument

Sorted the data based on length of string

```
ShivXXXXXXX
ShivXXXXX
ShivXXXX
ShivXXXX
```

Figure 1.41: Comparator in action

Note: *You can find the above code snippet in "Comparator" folder.*

(B)   How can we access elements of a collection?

You can access the elements using Iterator or ListIterator. For sample you can look at the above comparator sample which uses iterator to display the details. You can also use for-each to loop.

(B)   What is Map and SortedMap Interface?

Map is an object that stores associations between keys and values, or key/value pairs. Given a key, you can find its value. Keys and values are stored as objects. Keys always have to be unique but the values may be duplicated. Some maps can accept null key and null values. Maps don't implement the Iterable interface. So that means you cannot iterate through a map using a for-each. But collection-view of a map allows getting around the sort coming of iteration.

Sorted Map ensures that the entries are maintained in ascending order based on the keys. You can also use the comparator specify some custom sort order.

(B)   Have you used any collection algorithm?

Note: *During interview you only need to mention few of them. But for the sake of just grabbing some in your mind I have listed all. Just see which you have used and say the same during interview.*

static <T> boolean addAll(Collection <? super T> c, T ... elements)

Inserts the elements specified by elements into the collection specified by c. Returns true if the elements were added and false otherwise.

static <T> int binarySearch(List<? extends T> list, T value, Comparator<? super T> c)

Searches for value in list ordered according to c. Returns the position of value in list, or a negative value if value is not found.

static <T> int binarySearch(List<? extends Comparable<? super T>> list, T value)

Searches for value in list. The list must be sorted. Returns the position of value in list, or a negative value if value is not found.

static <E> Collection<E> checkedCollection(Collection<E> c, Class<E>t)

Returns a run-time type-safe view of a collection. An attempt to insert an incompatible element will cause a ClassCastException.

static <E> List<E> checkedList(List<E> c, Class<E> t)

Returns a run-time type-safe view of a List. An attempt to insert an incompatible element will cause a ClassCastException.

static <K, V> Map<K, V> checkedMap(Map<K, V> c, Class<K> keyT, Class<V> valueT)

Returns a run-time type-safe view of a Map. An attempt to insert an incompatible element will cause a ClassCastException.

static <E> List<E> checkedSet(Set<E> c, Class<E> t)

Returns a run-time type-safe view of a Set. An attempt to insert an incompatible element will cause a ClassCastException.

static <K, V> SortedMap<K, V> checkedSortedMap(SortedMap<K, V> c, Class<K> keyT, Class<V> valueT)

Returns a run-time type-safe view of a SortedMap. An attempt to insert an incompatible element will cause a ClassCastException.

static <E> SortedSet<E> checkedSortedSet(SortedSet<E> c, Class<E>t)

Returns a run-time type-safe view of a SortedSet. An attempt to insert an incompatible element will cause a ClassCastException.

static <T> void copy(List<? super T> list1, List<? extends T> list2)

Copies the elements of list2 to list1.

static boolean disjoint(Collection<?> a, Collection<?> b)

Compares the elements in a to elements in b. Returns true if the two collections contain no common elements (i.e., the collections contain disjoint sets of elements). Otherwise, returns true.

static <T> List<T> emptyList( )

Returns an immutable, empty List object of the inferred type.

static <K, V> Map<K, V> emptyMap( )

Returns an immutable, empty Map object of the inferred type.

static <T> Set<T> emptySet( )

Returns an immutable, empty Set object of the inferred type.

static <T> Enumeration<T> enumeration(Collection<T> c)

Returns an enumeration over c. (See "The Enumeration Interface," later in this chapter.)

static <T> void fill(List<? super T> list, T obj)

Assigns obj to each element of list.

static int frequency(Collection<?> c, Object obj)

Counts the number of occurrences of obj in c and returns the result.

static int indexOfSubList(List<?> list, List<?> subList)

Searches list for the first occurrence of subList. Returns the index of the first match, or –1 if no match is found.

static int lastIndexOfSubList(List<?> list, List<?> subList)

Searches list for the last occurrence of subList. Returns the index of the last match, or –1 if no match is found.

static <T> ArrayList<T> list(Enumeration<T> enum)

Returns an ArrayList that contains the elements of enum.

static <T> T max(Collection<? extends T> c, Comparator<? super T> comp)

Returns the maximum element in c as determined by comp.

static <T extends Object & Comparable<? super T>> T max(Collection<? extends T> c)

Returns the maximum element in c as determined by natural ordering. The collection need not be sorted.

static <T> T min(Collection<? extends T> c, Comparator<? super T> comp)

Returns the minimum element in c as determined by comp. The collection need not be sorted.

static <T extends Object & Comparable<? superT>> T min(Collection<? extends T> c)

Returns the minimum element in c as determined by natural ordering.

static <T> List<T> nCopies(int num, T obj)

Returns num copies of obj contained in an immutable list. num must be greater than or equal to zero.

static <T> boolean replaceAll(List<T> list, T old, T new)

Replaces all occurrences of old with new in list. Returns true if at least one replacement occurred. Returns false, otherwise.

static void reverse(List<T> list)

Reverses the sequence in list.

static <T> Comparator<T> reverseOrder(Comparator<T> comp)

Returns a reverse comparator based on the one passed in comp. That is, the returned comparator reverses the outcome of a comparison that uses comp.

static <T> Comparator<T> reverseOrder( )

Returns a reverse comparator, which is a comparator that reverses the outcome of a comparison between two elements.

static void rotate(List<T> list, int n)

Rotates list by n places to the right. To rotate left, use a negative value for n.

static void shuffle(List<T> list, Random r)

Shuffles (i.e., randomizes) the elements in list by using r as a source of random numbers.

static void shuffle(List<T> list)

Shuffles (i.e., randomizes) the elements in list.

static <T> Set<T> singleton(T obj)

Returns obj as an immutable set. This is an easy way to convert a single object into a set.

static <T> List<T> singletonList(T obj)

Returns obj as an immutable list. This is an easy way to convert a single object into a list.

static <K, V> Map<K, V> singletonMap(K k, V v)

Returns the key/value pair k/v as an immutable map. This is an easy way to convert a single key/value pair into a map.

static <T> void sort(List<T> list,Comparator<? super T> comp)

Sorts the elements of list as determined by comp.

static <T extends Comparable<? super T>> void sort(List<T> list)

Sorts the elements of list as determined by their natural ordering.

static <T> void swap(List<T> list, int idx1, int idx2)

Exchanges the elements in list at the indices specified by idx1 and idx2.

static <T> Collection<T>synchronizedCollection(Collection<T> c)

Returns a thread-safe collection backed by c.

static <T> List<T> synchronizedList(List<T> list)

Returns a thread-safe list backed by list.

static <K, V> Map<K, V> synchronizedMap(Map<K, V> m)

Returns a thread-safe map backed by m.

static <T> Set<T> synchronizedSet(Set<T> s)

Returns a thread-safe set backed by s.

static <K, V> SortedMap<K, V> synchronizedSortedMap(SortedMap<K, V> sm)

Returns a thread-safe sorted map backed by sm.

static <T> SortedSet<T> synchronizedSortedSet(SortedSet<T> ss)

Returns a thread-safe set backed by ss.

static <T> Collection<T> unmodifiableCollection(Collection<? extends T> c)

Returns an unmodifiable collection backed by c.

static <T> List<T> unmodifiableList(List<? extends T> list)

Returns an unmodifiable list backed by list.

static <K, V> Map<K, V> unmodifiableMap(Map<? extends K, ? extends V> m)

Returns an unmodifiable map backed by m.

static <T> Set<T> unmodifiableSet(Set<? extends T> s)

Returns an unmodifiable set backed by s.

static <K, V> SortedMap<K, V> unmodifiableSortedMap(SortedMap<K, ? extends V> sm)

Returns an unmodifiable sorted map backed by sm.

static <T> SortedSet<T> unmodifiableSortedSet(SortedSet<T> ss)

Returns an unmodifiable sorted set backed by ss.

(B)   Why do we use collections when we had traditional ways for collection?

Before the collection framework JAVA provided ad hoc classes such as Dictionary, Vector, Stack and Properties to store and manipulate group of objects. Following are the main reason why collection framework is more desirable than the traditional JAVA collection objects:

√   Traditional objects did not have the unifying theme. The way you access VECTOR is different from Properties. Due to this ADHOC approach software is not easily extendable and adaptable. One of the unifying themes in the new JAVA collection is the iterator interface. It gives a unifying way for looping through JAVA collections.

√   Ready made algorithms are one of the important features of the JAVA collection. Algorithms operate on collections and are defined as static methods within the Collections class. Thus, they are available for all collections. Each collection class need not implement its own versions. The algorithms provide a standard means of manipulating collections.

√   Implementation of dynamic arrays, linked lists, trees, and hash tables are done in efficient manner. In case of traditional JAVA collection you will need to code all these implementation by yourself.

(B)   Can you name the legacy classes and interface for collections?

Below are the legacy classes and interfaces for JAVA:

Dictionary

Dictionary is represents a key/value storage repository and operates in very similiar fashion like Map. Given a key and value, you can store the value in a Dictionary object. Once the value is stored, you can retrieve it by using its key. Thus, like a map, a dictionary can be thought of as a list of key/value pairs. Although not currently deprecated, Dictionary is classified as obsolete, because it is fully replaced by Map.

Hashtable

Hashtable stores key/value pairs in a hash table. When using a Hashtable, you specify an object that is used as a key, and the value that you want linked to that key. The key is then hashed, and the resulting hash code is used as the index at which the value is stored within the table. You can visual HashMap as replacement for Hashtable.

Properties

Properties is a child class of Hashtable. It is specially used to maintain lists of values in which the key and the value is String. The Properties class is used by many Java classes. For instance type of object returned by System.getProperties( ) when obtaining environmental values is type of Properties class. One of the most useful aspects of Properties is that the information contained in a Properties object can be easily stored to or loaded from disk with the store( ) and load( ) methods. At any time, you can write a Properties object to a stream or read it back.

Stack

Stack is a subclass of Vector that implements a standard last-in, first-out stack.

Vector

Vector implements a dynamic array. Though similar to ArrayList it has one main differences Vector is synchronized. Which mean any thread using Vector is thread safe.

(B)   What is Enumeration Interface?

Enumeration interface defines the methods by which you can enumerate the elements in a collection of objects. In JAVA collection it's now replaced by Iterator.

(I)   what's the main difference between ArrayList / HashMap and Vector / Hashtable?

Vector / HashTable are synchronized which means they are thread safe. Cost of thread safe is performance degradation. So if you are sure that you are not dealing with huge number of threads then you should use ArrayList / HashMap.But yes you can still synchronize List and Map's using Collections provided methods:

List OurList = Collections.synchronizedList (OurList);

Map OurMap = Collections.synchronizedMap (OurMap);

(I)   Are String object Immutable, Can you explain the concept?

When we create a string object that means you are creating a string which can not be changed. So once you have created a string object you can not change the value of string. You must be thinking but I can always change the value. Yes but when you assign a value it creates a new object and the first object is still in memory. Lets try to understand the same by the below code snippet.

```
public class clsString
{
    public static void main(String[] args)
    {
        String str;           ———————▶ Declare the string object

        str= "FirstString";   ———————▶ Creates new object

        str="SecondString";   ———————▶ Creates new object
    }
}
```

Figure 1.42: Strings in Action

In the above code we have assigned the string with two values. So there are two objects of string instances created in the above statement. First statement declares the string object at this point no object is created. As soon as you assign a value to the str a object is created and assigned to it. That means in the second step when you assign value "FirstString" value it creates a new instance. In the third step when you assign "SecondString" value it creates a new instance and assigns it to str. But the first instance is still in memory. It's only that str is now referring to the new instance of string object.

(I)   what is a StringBuffer class and how does it differs from String class?

StringBuffer is a peer class of String that provides almost all functionality of strings. String represents fixed-length, immutable character sequences. Comparatively StringBuffer represents mutable, growable and writeable character sequences. But StringBuffer does not create new instances as string so it's more efficient when it comes to intensive concatenation operation. Below is a simple code which shows clearly the efficiency of StringBuffer object.

```
public class clsStringBuffer
{
    public static void main(String[] args)
    {
        // Using the string object
        String strValue = "Count from 1 to 10 using String";
        for (int i=0;i<10;i++)
        {
            strValue = strValue + "\n" + i ;
        }
        System.out.println(strValue);

        // Using string buffer object
        StringBuffer strBuffer = new StringBuffer();
        strBuffer.append("Count from 1 to 10 using StringBuffer");
        for (int i=0;i<10;i++)
        {
            strBuffer.append("\n" + i) ;
        }
        System.out.println(strBuffer);
    }
}
```

Creates 10 objects of string class

Creates only one object of stringbuffer

Figure 1.43: String and StringBuffer Comparison

When we loop using String class we are creating 10 objects. But with StringBuffer only one object is created.

(I)   what is the difference between StringBuilder and StringBuffer class?

It is very much similar to StringBuffer except for one difference: it is not synchronized, which means that it is not thread-safe. The advantage of StringBuilder is good performance. In case of multithreading, you must use StringBuffer rather than StringBuilder.

(B)　What is Pass by Value and Pass by reference? How does JAVA handle the same?

In Pass by Value the function or subroutine receives a copy of variable. The function or the method can not change variable values.

In pass By ref the function or subroutine receives a pointer of the variable. And any changes to variable value are also visible outside the function or subroutine. Lets try to understand the concept from the below snippet code.

```
// Pass by value
int x = 10;
PassByValueMethod(x);
System.out.println(x);     ◄──── This prints 10
// Pass by reference
clsValue y = new clsValue();                        public class clsValue
y.i = 10;                          clsValue code snip    {
PassByReference(y);
System.out.println(y.i);   ◄──── This prints 20        public int i;
//Testing is it really pass by reference                }
clsValue z = new clsValue();
z.i = 10;
PassByReferenceTest(z);
System.out.println(z.i);   ◄────This prints 10
}
private static void PassByValueMethod(int i) ◄──── This does not modify the value
{i = 20;}
private static void PassByReference(clsValue x) ◄──── This modifies the value
{x.i = 20;}
private static void PassByReferenceTest(clsValue x) ◄──── This does modify the value
{
    x = new clsValue();
    x.i = 20;
}}
```

Figure 1.44: Pass by Value and reference in action

Note:　You can find the above source code in "PassByValRef" folder in the CD.

There are two methods "PassByValueMethod" and "PassByReference" method. When we pass value to "PassByValueMethod" it does not return a changed value for the variable. When we pass value to "PassByReference" method (here we have passed object of "clsValue") it changes the value of property "i". Now that we know the fundamentals of "Pass by Value" and "Pass by Reference" lets try to see the same from JAVA perspective.

"JAVA is strictly Pass by Value. So if it's either primitive data type or an object JAVA always passes by value"

Hmmm i know what's going on in your mind if JAVA is pass by value why did "PassByReference" method change the value. Have a look at "PassByReferenceTest" its prints "10" and not "20". Even when we have changed the object reference it still reflects the old object value. In short object references are passed by value. So put it in your head in JAVA everything is "Pass By Value".

(I)   What are access modifiers?

Access modifiers decide whether a method or a data variable can be accessed by another method in another class or subclass.

Java provides four types of access modifiers:

Public: Can be accessed by any other class anywhere.

Protected: Can be accessed by classes inside the package or by subclasses (that means classes who inherit from this class).

Private: Can be accessed only within the class. Even methods in subclasses in the same package do not have access.

Default: (Its private access by default) accessible to classes in the same package but not by classes in other packages, even if these are subclasses.

(I)   what is Assertion?

Assertion includes a Boolean expression. If the Boolean expression evaluates to false AssertionError is thrown. Assertion helps a programmer to debug the code effectively. Assertion code is removed when the program is deployed. Below is a code snippet which checks if inventory object is null.

```
Inventory objInv = null;
// ...
// Get your inventory object reference here
// ...
// Use assert to check if the object is null
// by any chance
assert objInv != null;
```

(I)   Can you explain the fundamentals of deep and shallow Cloning?

Many times in project you need to create exact copy of the object and operate on them. To do this there two ways of doing it Shallow clone and Deep clone. When an object is Shallow cloned the parent object or the top level object and its members are duplicated. But any lower level objects are not duplicated. Rather references of these objects are copied. So when an object is shallow cloned and you modify any of it child classes it will affect the original copy. When an object is deep cloned the entire object and its aggregated objects are also duplicated.

Below is the diagram which explains things in a clear and pictorial manner.

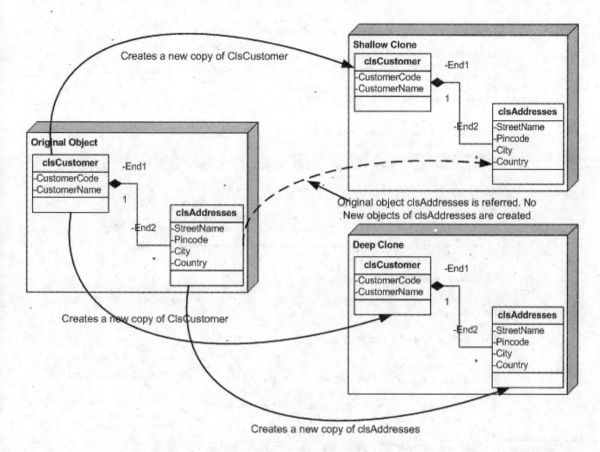

Figure 1.45: Deep clone and Shallow clone in action

In the above diagram there are three blocks the first block is the original object, second block is the Shallow clone and the third is Deep clone block. Here the object to be cloned is a simple Customer class which has multiple addresses. Now when you shallow clone it, you can see the top class clsCustomer is duplicated but clsAddresses still refers to the original object. But in case of Deep clone complete new copy is created of the whole structure.

(I)   How do we implement Shallow cloning?

In order to implement shallow cloning we need to implement cloneable interface and override the clone method with implementation. You can look in to the below code snippet.

```
public class clsExampleClone implements Cloneable
{
    int myNum;
    // Array aggregated inside the object
    Integer [] myArray;                                  Implements cloneable interface
    // Constructor loads array of iteger values
    clsExampleClone (int nElements)
    {
        myNum = nElements;
        myArray = new Integer[myNum];
        Random ran = new Random ();
        for (int i=0; i < myNum; i++)
        {myArray[i] = new Integer (ran.nextInt (10000));}
    }
    // Override the clone object with Implementation
    public Object clone ()
    {                                          Also put implementation by
        try                                    overriding the clone method
        {
            return super.clone ();  ──────────────── Note the clone syntax
        }
        catch (CloneNotSupportedException e)
        {throw new Error ("Clone Error");}
    }
                                                        Get the object using
                                                        the clone method
public class clsRun
{
    public static void main (String [] args)
    {                                                  ┌──────────────────────────────────┐
        // Create a clone                              │ Original value of Myarray[0] = 111111│
        clsExampleClone ex   = new clsExampleClone (5);│ Copy value of Myarray[0] = 111111    │
        // Create a copy of clone using the clone method└──────────────────────────────────┘
        clsExampleClone copy = (clsExampleClone)ex.clone ();
        ex.myArray[0] = new Integer (111111);                   It has changed the
        // Displaying both original and copy values             original object value
        System.out.println ("Original value of Myarray[0] = " + ex.myArray[0]);
        System.out.println ("Copy value of Myarray[0] = " + copy.myArray[0]);
    }
}
```

Create a new array
with some value

Figure 1.46: Shallow cloning in action

In the above code snippet we have defined a class clsExampleClone which implements the Cloneable interface. We have also provided implementation for the clone method. It just returns the parents clone object. Once we have defined this object we created the same in void main and you can see even though we have cloned the object it still refers to original array and modifies the original object values.

Note: You can find the above code in "ShallowClone" folder.

(I)   How do we implement deep cloning?

Deep cloning can be done by two ways:

All objects implement a clone method

Every object is responsible for cloning itself via its clone () method. So when the parent is called it makes calls to all the referenced objects inside the class and calls its clone method.

Serialization

This is the best way to do deep cloning and not to mention best answer in interview of how to implement deep cloning. There are three steps to do deep cloning using serialization:

√   Ensure that all classes in the object are serializable

√   Create output stream for writing the new object and input stream for reading the same.

√   Pass the object you want to copy to the output stream.

√   And finally read the object using the input stream.

Below is the code snippet which implements all the above steps.

```java
// returns a deep copy of an object
static public Object GetDeepCopy(Object myOldObj) throws Exception
{
    ObjectOutputStream objoutstream = null;
    ObjectInputStream objinstream = null;
    try
    {
        // Create a output stream
        ByteArrayOutputStream bos = new ByteArrayOutputStream();
        objoutstream = new ObjectOutputStream(bos);          // Create a output stream

        // Serialize you original object in to the output stream
        objoutstream.writeObject(myOldObj);
        objoutstream.flush();                    // Serialize the object using writeobject method

        // To read the object create a inputstream
        ByteArrayInputStream bin = new ByteArrayInputStream(bos.toByteArray());
        objinstream = new ObjectInputStream(bin);

        // and read the complete object
        return objinstream.readObject();}        // Use the inputstream to read the same

    catch(Exception e)
    {throw(e);}
    finally
    {
        objoutstream.close();
        objinstream.close();
    }
}
```

Figure 1.47: Deep cloning

In the above code snippet note the three important steps which have been marked for simplicity.

Note: *You can get the above code in "DeepCloning" folder. Define a complex object and try to create a deep cloned object from the function.*

(I)   What's the impact of private constructor?

Private constructors prevent a class from being explicitly instantiated by callers.

(I)   What are the situations you will need a constructor to be private?

Below are some of the situations when you will need a constructor to be private:

√   To implement singleton pattern. That means only one instance of the object need to be running.

√   When classes contain static methods. It makes sense that no object of the class need to be created.

√   If classes have only constants.

(I)   Can you explain final modifier?

Below are some important points to be noted for final modifiers:

√   Final access modifiers apply to class, method and variables.

√   So depending on what you are applying the final context changes.

√   Final class can not be sub classed.

√   A final variable cannot be modified once it has been assigned a value. They play the same role as constant variables.

√   You can not change a final object reference variable. But you can change the object data.

(I)   What are static Initializers?

Static initializer block is a method with no name (sounds funny hmm), no arguments, and no return type. It doesn't need a name, because there is no need to refer to it from outside the class definition. The code in a static initializer block is executed by the JVM when the class is loaded. You can use the static initializer block to initialize static variables or do some class level initialization. Static initializer block runs only once irrespective of how many instances you create of the object.

```
public class clsStaticInit
{
    static
    {
        System.out.println("Inside Static");    ──▶ First execution
    }
    public static void main(String args[])
    {
        System.out.println("Inside Main");    ──▶ Second execution
    }
}
```

                          │ Output
                          ▼

```
Inside Static
Inside Main
```

Figure 1.48: Static Initializers in action

Above is the code snippet which shows how static initializers work. The first thing which will execute is the static initializer block and then the void main method. One of the important point to keep in mind is it runs before the constructor.

> *Note: You can find the above code sample in "StaticInitializers" folder. Feel free to test it using constructor.*

(I) If we have multiple static initializer blocks how is the sequence handled?

You can have more than one static initializer block in your class definition, and they can be separated by other code such as method definitions and constructors. The static initializer blocks will be executed in the order in which they appear in the source code.

(B) Define casting? What are the different types of Casting?

Changing the type of the value from one type to other is termed as casting. For instance look at the below code snippet in which we are trying to cast integer value to double data type.

```
int i;
double d;
i = 10;
d = i; // we are trying to assign a int value to double
```

There are two types of casting explicit and implicit. To explicitly cast an expression prefix the expression with type name as shown in the code snippet below.

```
Button mybtn = (Button) (myVector.elementAt(9));
```

In some situations JAVA runtime changes the type of an expression with out performing a cast. For instance in the below code snippet my inventory object is type casted and stored as type Object.

```
myVectorSales.add(objInventory);
```

(B) Can you explain Widening conversion and Narrowing conversion?

When you try to move a big value data type to a small data type variable it leads to narrowing conversion. Below is the code snippet which explains in detail of how the conversion happens. In the below code we are trying to move double to an integer data type. Because integer data type is smaller than double data type it looses its decimal portion. So the below code will display the integer value as "3".

```
public class clsCasting
{
    public static void main(String[] args)
    {
        double dbl = 3.2;
        int i;
        i = (int)dbl;
        System.out.println(i);
    }}
```

This will print 3. That means you have lost
the decimal portion of the original value.

Figure 1.49: Casting of narrowing conversion

Widening conversion is exactly vice versa of the same in which try to move small data type value to big one. In this case no conversion happens and neither have we loosed data. Below is the conversion tree which says when Widening conversion will happen and when narrowing conversion will be done.

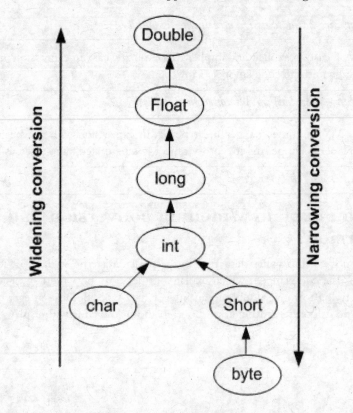

Figure 1.50: Conversion tree

So if we try to move up the tree that means if we try move char to int, int to long, float to double widening conversion will happen. If we try to move down the tree like int to char, double to int narrowing conversion will happen and probably also data loss. We need to specify explicit casting only if narrowing conversion is taking place. Doing that we say to the compiler that we are aware of the data loss which can happen.

(I)   Can we assign parent object to child objects?

Let us first try to understand the question in a more precise manner. Glance the below class diagram which depicts a typical hierarchical relation ship between two wheelers. So can we move an object of Cycle to object of two wheeler?. Answer is yes we can do it by type casting the parent to child type. Again the law of conversion hierarchy applies here. In the below figure you can see the two arrows one which points from top to down and the other vice-versa.

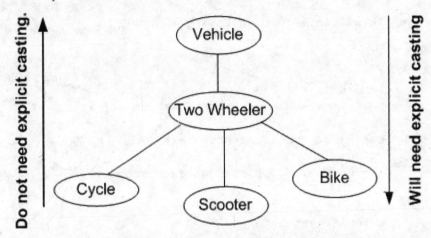

Figure 1.51: Object casting hierarchy

So if you are moving from down the hierarchy to the top you do not need to do explicit casting. That means if you move cycle object to two wheeler compiler will not throw error. But if you try to move two wheeler to cycle it will throw an error if you have not defined explicit casting of the object type. Below is the sample pseudo code which shows how things work.

```
TwoWheeler T;
Cycle C = new Cycle();
// Moving child object to the parent
T = C; // Will work and compile fine
// Moving Parent to child
C = T // Will throw a error
// Moving Parent to child with type casting
C = (Cycle)T // Will work properly
```

(B)   Define exceptions?

An exception is an abnormal condition that arises in a code sequence at run time.

(B)   Can you explain in short how JAVA exception handling works?

Basically there are four important keywords which form the main pillars of exception handling: try, catch, throw and finally. Code which you want to monitor for exception is contained in the try block. If any exception occurs in the try block its sent to the catch block which can handle this error in a more rational manner. To throw an exception manually you need to call use the throw keyword. If you want to put any clean up code use the finally block. The finally block is executed irrespective if there is an error or not. Below is a small error code snippet which describes how the flow of error goes.

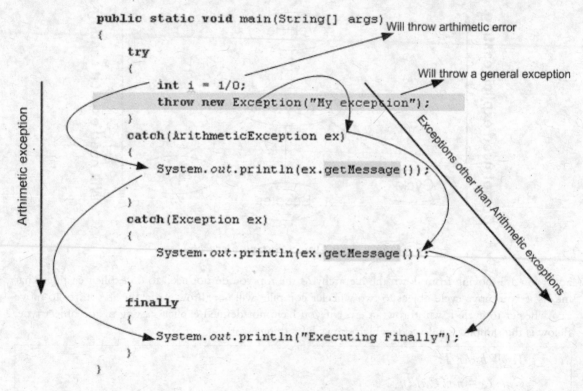

Figure 1.52: JAVA exception in action

In the try block we have two exceptions raised one (1/0) which will throw an exception error and the other will use the throw clause to throw a general exception error. Arithmetic exception will flow from try block to the arithmetic catch block and then execute the finally block. But the general exception will flow from the try block, then to the exception catch block and then execute the finally block. In short the finally block always execute. It's the best place to put your clean up code in finally block as it is executed irrespective that there is an error or not.

(B) Can you explain different exception types?

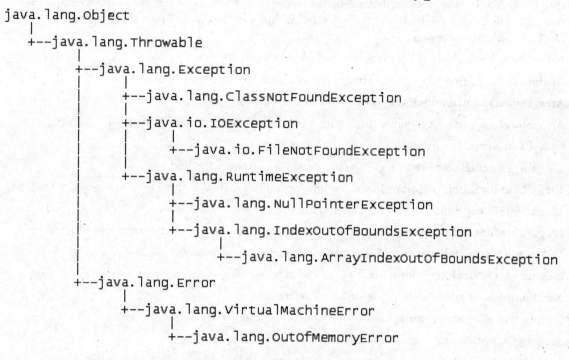

```
java.lang.object
  |
  +--java.lang.Throwable
       |
       +--java.lang.Exception
       |    |
       |    +--java.lang.ClassNotFoundException
       |    |
       |    +--java.io.IOException
       |    |    |
       |    |    +--java.io.FileNotFoundException
       |    |
       |    +--java.lang.RuntimeException
       |         |
       |         +--java.lang.NullPointerException
       |         |
       |         +--java.lang.IndexOutOfBoundsException
       |              |
       |              +--java.lang.ArrayIndexOutOfBoundsException
       |
       +--java.lang.Error
            |
            +--java.lang.VirtualMachineError
                 |
                 +--java.lang.OutOfMemoryError
```

Figure 1.53: JAVA exception hierarchy

Above is the diagram which gives you a picture of how the exception classes' hierarchy is. All exception types are subclasses of Throwable. Throwable is at the top of the exception class hierarchy. Immediately below Throwable are two subclasses that partition exceptions into two distinct branches. One branch is headed by Exception. This class is used for exceptional conditions that user programs should catch. This is also the class that you will subclass to create your own custom exception types. There is an important subclass of Exception, called RuntimeException. Exceptions of this type are automatically defined for the programs that you write and include things such as division by zero and invalid array indexing.

The other branch is topped by Error, which defines exceptions that are not expected to be caught under normal circumstances by your program. Exceptions of type Error are used by the Java run-time system to indicate errors having to do with the run-time environment, itself. Stack overflow is an example of such an error.

(B) Can you explain checked and unchecked exceptions?

Exceptions generated from runtime are called unchecked exceptions, since it is not possible for the compiler to determine that your code will handle the exception. Exception classes that descend from RuntimeException and Error classes are unchecked exceptions. Examples for RuntimeException are illegal cast operation, inappropriate use of a null pointer, referencing an out of bounds array element. Error exception classes signal critical problems that typically cannot be handled by your application. Examples are out of memory error, stack overflow, failure of the Java VM.

Thrown exceptions are referred to as checked exceptions. The compiler will confirm at compile time that the method includes code that might throw an exception. Moreover the compiler requires the code that calls such a method to include this call within a try block, and provide an appropriate catch block to catch the exception.

Below are some unchecked exceptions:

ArithmeticException: Arithmetic error, such as divide-by-zero.

ArrayIndexOutOfBoundsException: Array index is out-of-bounds.

ArrayStoreException: Assignment to an array element of an incompatible type.

ClassCastException: Invalid cast.

IllegalArgumentException: Illegal argument used to invoke a method.

IllegalMonitorStateException: Illegal monitor operation, such as waiting on an unlocked thread.

IllegalStateException: Environment or application is in incorrect state.

IllegalThreadStateException: Requested operation not compatible with current thread state.

IndexOutOfBoundsException: Some type of index is out-of-bounds.

NegativeArraySizeException: Array created with a negative size.

NullPointerException: Invalid use of a null reference.

NumberFormatException: Invalid conversion of a string to a numeric format.

SecurityException: Attempt to violate security.

StringIndexOutOfBounds: Attempt to access index outside the bounds of a string.

Below are some checked exceptions:

ClassNotFoundException: Class not found.

CloneNotSupportedException: Attempt to clone an object that does not implement the Cloneable interface.

IllegalAccessException: Access to a class is denied.

InstantiationException: Attempt to create an object of an abstract class or interface.

InterruptedException: One thread has been interrupted by another thread.

NoSuchFieldException: A requested field does not exist.

NoSuchMethodException: A requested method does not exist.

(I)   Can we create our own exception class?

Just define a subclass of Exception and then you can override methods to provide custom functions.

(A)   What are chained exceptions?

The chained exception feature allows you to associate another exception with an exception. This second exception describes the cause of the first exception. Consider a situation in which you are getting null exception because of permission issues. You would like to know if this exception is associated with some other exception.For chained exceptions there are two constructors and two methods. The constructors are shown here:

> Throwable(Throwable causeExc)
>
> Throwable(String msg, Throwable causeExc)

In the first form, causeExc is the exception that causes the current exception. That is, causeExc is the underlying reason that an exception occurred. The second form allows you to specify a description at the same time that you specify a cause exception.

```
static void demo()
{
// create an exception
NullPointerException nullerror = new NullPointerException("First layer");
// add a cause
nullerror.initCause(new ArithmeticException("Arthimetic"));     Main exception
throw nullerror;
}

public static void main(String args[])     Set the main cause of exception
{
    try
    {
        demo();
    }

    catch(NullPointerException e)
    {
    // display First layer exception
    System.out.println("Caught: " + e);

    // Display the cause of exception
    System.out.println("Original cause: " + e.getCause());
}}
```

```
Caught: java.lang.NullPointerException: First layer
Original cause: java.lang.ArithmeticException: Arthimetic
```

The top layer exception   The main cause of error.

Figure 1.54: Chained exception in action

Above is the code snippet which shows chained exception in action. We have defined a method by name demo. In demo we have thrown a null pointer error. But after that we set the main cause of error using initcause as arthimetic exception. You can also see the display. You can get the main cause of error using getCause method.

(B)   What is serialization?

Serialization is a process by which an object instance is converted in to stream of bytes. There are many useful stuff you can do when the object instance is converted in to stream of bytes for instance you can save the object in hard disk or send it across the network.

(I)   How do we implement serialization actually?

In order to implement serialization we need to use two classes from java.io package ObjectOutputStream and ObjectInputStream. ObjectOutputStream has a method called writeObject, while ObjectInputStream has a method called readObject. Using writeobject we can write and readObject can be used to read the object from the stream. Below are two code snippet which used the FileInputStream and FileOutputstream to read and write from harddisk.

```
private void SaveObject(myObject obj) throws IOException
{
        //open a FileInputStream associated with the data
        String filePath = "c:\my.obj";
        FileOutputStream fos = new FileOutputStream(filePath);
        // Associate the fileobject with the outputstream
        ObjectOutputStream oos = new ObjectOutputStream(fos);
        // write the object to the outputstream
        oos.writeObject(obj);
        // close and clear all objects
        oos.close();
        fos.close();
        fos =null;
        oos = null;
}
private myobject getObject(string fullfilepath) throws IOException,
ClassNotFoundException
{
        myobject obj = null;
        // open the file and read the same in file inputstream
        FileInputStream fis = new FileInputStream(fullfilepath);
        //Read in the data from the object
        ObjectInputStream ois = new ObjectInputStream(fis);
        obj = (myobject)ois.readObject();
        ois.close();
        fis.close();
        return obj;
}
```

(A)   What's the use of Externalizable Interface?

When performance becomes a important criteria, then you can serialize using the java.io.Externalizable interface instead of the Serializable interface. Externalizable requires that you write the details of reading and writing the object's state to the byte stream. The ObjectOutputStream class no longer simplifies this process. You must use the methods readExternal and writeExternal method to write the object in to stream and read from stream.

(B)   What is JAVAdoc utility?

Javadoc parses comments in JAVA source files and produced HTML pages for the same. Below is the syntax for the same

> *javadoc [options] [packagenames] [sourcefiles] [@files]*

Arguments can be in any order.

Options Command-line options that is doctitle, windowtitle, header, bottom etc

Packagenames: A series of names of packages, separated by spaces, such as java.lang java.lang.reflect java.awt. You must separately specify each package you want to document. Javadoc uses -sourcepath to look for these package names. Javadoc does not recursively traverse subpackages.

sourcefiles: A series of source file names, separated by spaces, each of which can begin with a path and contain a wildcard such as asterisk (*). The path that precedes the source file name determines where javadoc will look for it. (Javadoc does not use -sourcepath to look for these source file names.)

@files: One or more files that contain packagenames and sourcefiles in any order, one name per line.

(I)   what are JAVAdoc doclets?

Doclets helps us to specify the content and format for Javadoc tool. By default Javadoc uses the standard doclet provided by sun. But you can supply your own customized output for Javadoc.

(I)   What is Auto boxing and unboxing?

This is a newly added feature in J2SE 5.0. Auto boxing is the process in which primitive type is automatically boxed in to equivalent type wrapper. There is no need to explicitly do casting for the same. Auto boxing is vice versa of the same. Value of the boxed object is converted in to primitive data type. You can see in the below code snippet we have two samples of Auto boxing and Unboxing.

```
// this will auto box a int to a Integer object automatically
Integer objint = 100;
// this will auto unbox. That means move a integer object to a primitive
data type
int i = objint;
```

> *Note: Auto boxing and unboxing does prevent lot of errors. So programmer may be tempted to use this feature extensively. For instance the below code would be more efficient if primitive data type was used.*

```
// the below example shows a bad use of autoboxing and unboxing
Double dbla, dblb, dblc;
dbla = 11;
dblb = 22;
dblc = Math.sqrt(dbla*dbla + dblb*dblb);
```

> *Note: In the coming question we will be answering three question in on shot.*

(I)   How much subclasses you can maximum in Inheritance?

In one of my old JAVA projects I had an inheritance depth of five. Believe me I never liked that code. It's bad to have a huge inheritance depth. A maintainable inheritance depth should be maximum

5. Anything above that is horrible. There is no limit as such specified anywhere that there is some limit on the inheritance sub classing (In case you come across mail me at shiv_koirala@yahoo.com). But depending on environments you will get stack over flow error for large inheritance depth.

(I)   Can you explain transient and volatile modifiers?

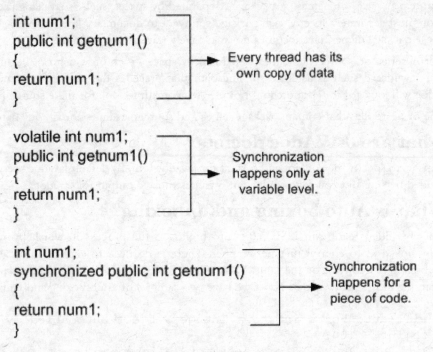

Figure 1.55: Volatile keyword in action

To understand the concept we have three variations defined above.

√   Simple variable.

√   Variable declared as volatile.

√   And method which is synchronized. You will understand why we are talking about synchronized methods when the fundamental is about volatile.

Before we start dealing with the above fundamentals lets try to understand the concept of main memory in java. Main memory is a memory which at any moment has the correct value of variable. So when variables are updated its possible that value in main memory can be different from the value of the actual variables. In short it's possible that for a given moment of time which can be very small the main memory and the variable value can be different. Ok now that we know about the main memory fundamentals lets go ahead with the above three cases and then try to understand the concept of volatile variables.

For the first case i.e. simple variable every thread will have its own local copy. At any given moment of time it's possible that the variable data is not as same as the main memory.

For the second case because the variable is defined as volatile it is not allowed to have a local copy of a variable that is different from the value currently held in "main" memory. Effectively, a variable declared volatile must have its data synchronized across all threads, so that whenever you access or update the variable in any thread, all other threads immediately see the same value. Of course, it is likely that volatile variables have a higher access and update overhead than "plain" variables, since the reason threads can have their own copy of data is for better efficiency.

Ok now you must definitely have a question if volatile variables are for this then what's does the synchronized keyword do?. Volatile only synchronizes the value of one variable between thread memory and "main" memory, synchronized synchronizes the value of all variables between thread memory and "main" memory, and locks and releases a monitor to boot. Clearly synchronized is likely to have more overhead than volatile.

2
Threading

(B) What's difference between thread and process?

A thread is a path of execution that run on CPU, a process is a collection of threads that share the same virtual memory. A process has at least one thread of execution, and a thread always run in a process context. A process is a collection of virtual memory space, code, data, and system resources. A thread is code that is to be serially executed within a process. A processor executes threads, not processes. One more significant difference between process and thread is every process has its own data memory location but all related threads can share same data memory and have their own individual stacks. Thread is a light weighted process, collection of threads become process.

(B) What is thread safety and synchronization?

Thread safe is used to describe a method that can run safely in multithreaded environments allowing accessing to data in a safe and efficient way. Thread safety is achieved by synchronization. Synchronization assures that the object data is not accessed by multiple threads at the same time.

(I) What is semaphore?

Semaphore is an object which helps two threads to communicate with one another in order to synchronize there operation.

(I) What are monitors?

Monitor is a body of code which can be executed by only one thread at a time. If any other thread tries to get access at the same time, it will be suspended until the current thread releases the Monitor.

(B) What's the importance of synchronized blocks?

Synchronized blocks implement the concept of monitors described in the first answer. Below is the code snippet of the synchronized block.

> *Note: Feel free to experiment with the below code snippet. You can find the same in CD in "Synchronization" folder.*

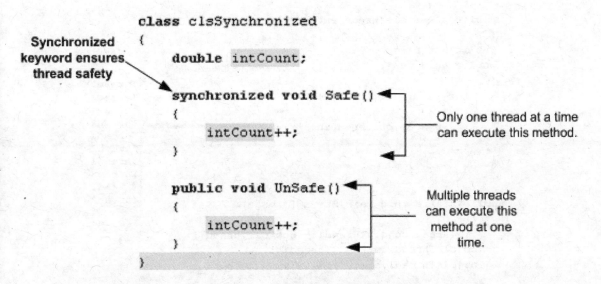

Figure 2.1: Synchronization in action

In the above code we have two methods Safe and Unsafe. You can see how the Safe method is using the Synchronized keyword thus ensuring that multiple threads do not execute this method. On the other hand you can see the UnSafe method is not thread safe as it's defined like a normal method.

(B) How do we create threads?

There are two ways to create a thread.

extend the java.lang.Thread class.

Create a class which extends the thread class. When the class is instantiated, the thread and object are created together and the object is automatically bound to the thread. By calling the object's start() method, the thread is started and immediately calls the object's run() method.

implement the java.lang.Runnable interface

Create the thread and supply it an object with a run() method. This object will be permanently associated with the thread. The object's run() method will be invoked when the thread is started. This method of thread creation is useful if you want many threads sharing an object.

Let's make a code walk through of both the ways of creating threads. Below is a sample code which inherits from thread class. Then creates object of the class and calls start.

```
public class clsThread extends Thread
{
public String str;
public void run()
{
     for(int i =0;i<=10;i++)
     {
          System.out.println(str);
     }
}
```

↑ Extends the thread class

→ Output

```
Thread1
Thread2
Thread2
Thread1
Thread2
Thread1
Thread2
Thread1
Thread2
Thread1
Thread2
```

```
public static void main(String[] args)
{
     clsThread objclsThread1 = new clsThread();
     objclsThread1.str = "Thread1";
     objclsThread1.start();

     clsThread objclsThread2 = new clsThread();
     objclsThread2.str= "Thread2";
     objclsThread2.start();
}
```

Two new
thread started

Figure 2.2: Create thread using inheritance

Next is the code snippet which creates thread using the runnable interface. You can see the class is implements the runnable interface. And later this class is tied up with thread object.

```
public class clsThreadRunnable implements Runnable
{
     String str;
     public clsThreadRunnable(String strval)
     {
          str = strval;
     }
     public void run()
     {
          System.out.println( str );
     }
     public static void main( String[] args )
     {
          clsThreadRunnable threadedClass1 = new clsThreadRunnable("Thread1");
          Thread t1 = new Thread(threadedClass1);
          t1.start();

          clsThreadRunnable threadedClass2 = new clsThreadRunnable("Thread2");
          Thread t2 = new Thread(threadedClass2);
          t2.start();
     }
}
```

Implemented the runnable interface

```
Thread1
Thread2
```

Class is associated with the thread

Figure 2.3: Create thread using Runnable

Note: Both the above code snippets you can find in "ThreadByInheritance" and "ThreadByRunnable" folders.

(I)   what's the difference in using runnable and extends in threads?

Below are some of the main differences between threads using runnable interface and by extending the thread class.

√   Thread is a class and Runnable is an interface in java.

√   If a class is not extending another class we can use either extending Thread class or implementing Runnable interface. If our class is already extending another class we can't extend Thread class because java doesn't support multiple inheritance so we have left only one choice that is implementing Runnable interface.

√   When you extend a thread each of your threads has a unique object associated with it, whereas with Runnable, many threads share the same object instance.

(B)   Can you explain Thread.sleep?

Thread.sleep() is a static method of the Thread class that causes the currently executing thread to delay for a specified number of milliseconds. Below is the code snippet:

```
try
{
      Thread.sleep ( 1000 );
}
catch ( InterruptedException e ) {}
```

(B)   How to stop a thread?

thread.stop;

(I)   What is wait() and notify() ?

By using wait() and notify(), a thread can give up its hold on a lock at an arbitrary point, and then wait for another thread to give it back before continuing. By executing wait() from a synchronized block, a thread gives up its hold on the lock and goes to sleep.Later, when the necessary event happens, the thread that is running it calls notify() from a block synchronized on the same object. Now the first thread wakes up and begins trying to acquire the lock again.

(I)   Can you explain how Scheduling and Priority works in threads?

Every thread has priority.If, at any time, a thread of a higher priority than the current thread becomes runnable, it preempts the lower priority thread and begins executing. By default, threads at the same priority are scheduled round robin, which means once a thread starts to run

In order to set thread priority below is the code snippet:

```
Thread mythread = new MyThread("my");
mythread.setPriority( Thread.NORM_PRIORITY + 1 );
mythread.start();
MIN_PRIORITY :- Minimum priority
NORM_PRIORITY :- Normal priority
MAX_PRIORITY :- Maximum priority
```

(B)   Can you explain Yielding in threading?

It causes the currently executing thread object to temporarily pause and allow other threads to execute.

(I)   what are daemon threads?

Daemon threads are designed run in background. One example of a daemon thread is the garbage collector thread. You can use setDaemon() to mark a thread as daemon.

(I)   How do we implement singlethreaded model in servlets?

Lets try to understand how servlets work in multi-threaded environments.In most circumstances only a single servlet instance will exist in the servlet container. That means for every request a new object will not be created. But all the method call like the service(),doget(),dopost() etc are executed inside their own thread. So any local variables declared inside these methods will not be shared across requests. That means all the local variables are thread safe. But any variable declaration for example instance variables will be shared across request. You can see in the below code HitCount variable will be shared across request which means its not thread safe.

```
public class ThreadServlet extends HttpServlet
{
        // Not thread safe
        private int HitCount;
        public void doGet(HttpServletRequest req, HttpServletResponse res)
        throws ServletException
        {
                ...
        }
}
```

So in order to assure the concurrency issue we need to make the servlet single threaded. This can be achieved by using the SingleThreadModel {} interface. So at any moment of time two threads will not be executing the same servlet instance which gurantees thread safety.

```
public class ThreadServlet extends HttpServlet
 implements SingleThreadModel
{
```

```
     // thread safe
     private int HitCount;
     public void doGet(HttpServletRequest req, HttpServletResponse res)
     throws ServletException
     {
          ...
     }
}
```

3

JDBC

(B) How does JAVA interact with databases?

Twist: What is JDBC?

JAVA interacts with database using a common database application programming interface called as JDBC. JDBC allows a developer to write applications that is database independent. So the developer will be interacting with JDBC API rather than getting in to complications of the database.JDBC allows you to write Java code, and leave the platform (database) specific code to the driver. JAVA was designed to be platform independent and JDBC takes java one step ahead making java database code database independent. That means if you use JDBC for connectivity for SQL Server you can run the same code with out changing for ORACLE.

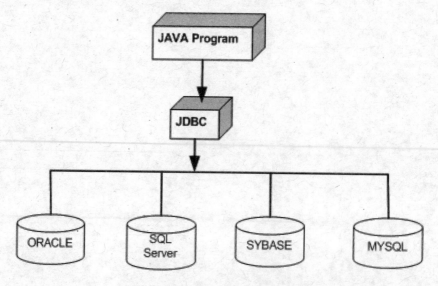

Figure 3.1: JDBC as a layer

(B) Can we interact with non-relational sources using JDBC?

Yes

(I) Can you explain in depth the different sections in JDBC?

There are four major components in JDBC. Below is the diagram which shows the four major sections and the way they interact to achieve the final "resultset".

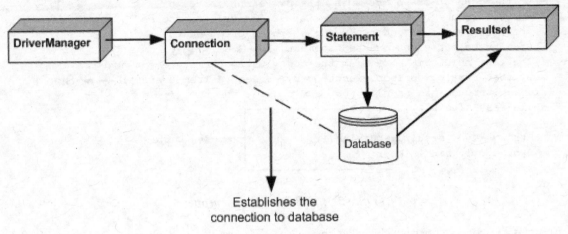

Figure 3.2: JDBC in detail

Driver manager section creates the connection object. Connection object create the statement object with the required SQL which is then executed against the database. And finally database gives the result back in the resultset.

(B) Can you explain in short how you go about using JDBC API in code?

Let's make a sample walk through of a JDBC code and try to understand the fundamentals. This book will use "postgreSQL" database to understand the database concept. You can also find the setup installation in the CD supplied. I have created the following object in "postgreSQL" to understand the fundamentals:-

√   Database "interview".

√   Table "users".

√   Column "name" with varchar(10).

In this example we will make a simple select to the "users" table in "interview" database.

```
// URL for where the database is
String url = "jdbc:postgresql://localhost:5432/interview";
// Load the postgres driver
try{Class.forName("org.postgresql.Driver");}          ➤ Step 1

catch( Exception e ){System.out.println("Failed to load mSQL driver.");return;}

                                                        Step 2
try {                                                     ↑
// Get the connection object using the drivermanager class
  Connection con = DriverManager.getConnection(url, "postgres", "pass@1234!@#$");
  // create a statement object using the connection object
  Statement select = con.createStatement();      ➤ Step 3
  // get the resultset by firing the query using the statement object
  ResultSet result = select.executeQuery("Select * from users");  ➤ Step 4
  // loop through the resul object and display the name field
  while(result.next())
  {
    String key = result.getString(1);                    ➤ Step 5
    System.out.println(key);
  }
```

Figure 3.3: JDBC database snippet

Above is the code snippet which makes the select. You can also find the same in CD in "JDBC" folder. Basically there are four steps to connect to database using JDBC (Same is highlighted in the above figure):

√   **Step1:** Load the driver of the database. Currently we are using "postgreSQL" so we will be using "org. postgresql.Driver".

√   **Step2:** Call the "DriverManager" class to create the connection object. In order to created the connection object we need to give the URL where the database is located with proper credentials. Currently my database is "interview" with userid as "postgres" and password as "pass@1234!@#$".

√   **Step3:** We call the connection object to give back the statement object. Statement object will be used to fire the sql.

√   **Step4:** Using the statement object we fire the SQL and get the resultset object.

√   **Step5:** We just looped and displayed the values.

> *Note: The above code snippet is provided with the CD but please note you will need to create database, tables and probably change the userid and password accordingly to make the code working.*

(I)   How do you handle SQL exceptions?

Twist: (A) Can you explain "SQLException" class in detail?

Twist: (A) what is SQL State in SQL Exceptions?

Any database related errors are thrown as "SQLException"type errors. So if you want to catch any database related error below is the code snippet to go about it:

```
try
{
      //JDBC code
}
catch(SQLException sqlex)
{
      System.err.println(sqlex);
}
```

There are three important information which you can obtain from the "SQLException" class:-

Exception message

Using "sqlex.getMessage();" you can get a descriptive string display of the error message. The error description varies from driver to driver depending how vendor has implemented it. So if you are using SQL Server driver you will get different error messages and using ORACLE driver you will get different message for the same type of error.

SQL State

SQL state is a string that contains a state as defined by the X/Open SQL standard. It can be obtained from the SQLException by calling the "sqlex.getSQLState();" method. SQL State is a five character string which has two parts. The first two characters define the class of the state and the three characters later define subclass of the error code. Below figure can show you the difference.

Class	Subclass	Description
01		*Success with warning*
	002	Disconnect error
	004	String data, right truncation
	006	Privilege not revoked

01 002

Figure 3.4: SQL State code structure

Above shows a small table section for the error code i.e "Success with warning". Actually the error code table is huge do look in to documentation for more depth. The only point we wanted to highlight is the way the SQL State code structure is. For instance in the above the SQL State code represents a warning of disconnect error. When do we really want to use SQL State?. There are situations where you will like your program to recover or to do more customize handling. For instance in the above scenario we get a disconnect error and we would like our program to connect to some other server. In short SQL State can be useful when we want our program to act depending on the severity of the error.

Vendor Error code

This returns us vendor specific error code which can be useful in case the driver itself has some errors. This value is obtained using "getErrorCode()" method.

Using the above three information you can really show some in depth information to the end user.

(A)   If there is more than one exception in SQLException" class how to go about displaying it?

If there are more than one exception in a try "SQLException" class maintain a collection of exceptions. We can use the "getNextException()" method to loop through all the errors. Below is the code snippet for the same.

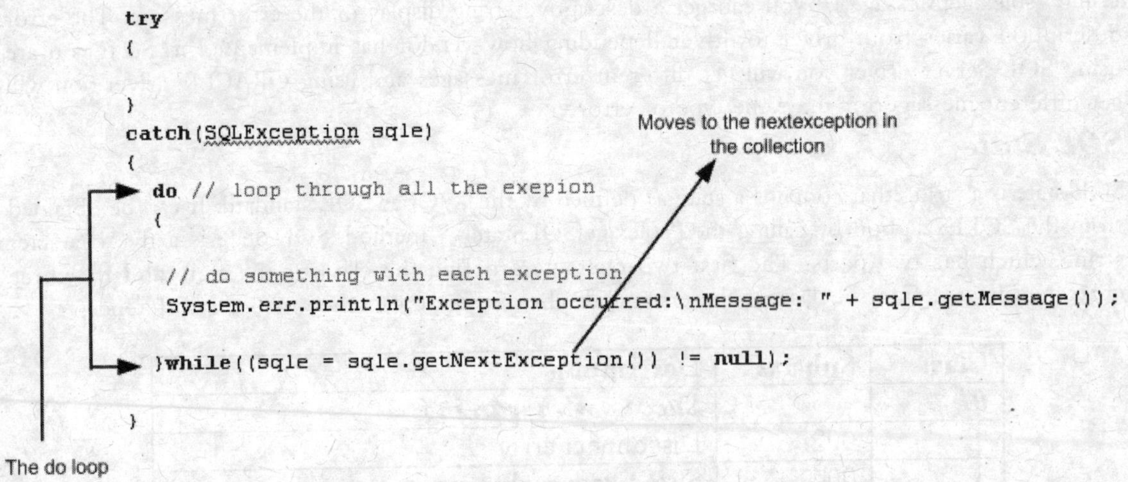

```
try
{

}
catch(SQLException sqle)                          Moves to the nextexception in
{                                                    the collection
    do // loop through all the exepion
    {

        // do something with each exception
        System.err.println("Exception occurred:\nMessage: " + sqle.getMessage());

    }while((sqle = sqle.getNextException()) != null);

}
```

The do loop

Figure 3.5 : "getNextException()" in action

(I) Explain Type1, Type2, Type3 and Type4 drivers in JDBC?

All JDBC drivers are divided in to four types as defined below:

√   **Type1:** JDBC-ODBC bridge.

√   **Type2:** Native-API/ Partially Java Driver.

√   **Type3:** Net-Protocol/ All-Java driver.

√   **Type3:** Native-protocol/ All-Java driver.

Let's make a walkthrough for all the drivers and try to understand there principle.

JDBC-ODBC Bridge

JDBC-ODBC Bridge is a type 1 JDBC driver which converts JDBC operations in to C language ODBC API's and then ODBC calls are then passed to appropriate ODBC driver. Below figure shows in detail how JDBC-ODBC driver control flows.

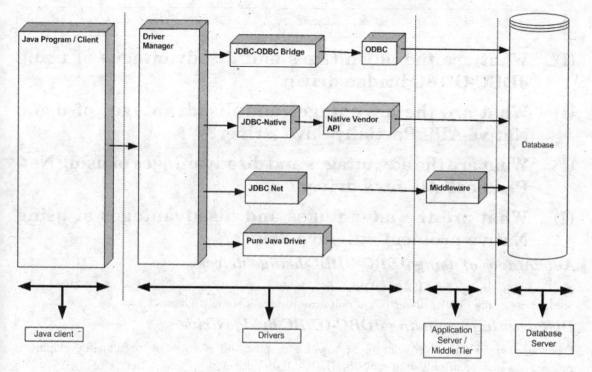

Figure 3.6: JDBC Architecture diagram

Native-API/ Partially Java Driver

Type 2 driver resides on the client along with the JAVA application. This driver communicates directly with the database server. It requires the driver binary code to be present on the JAVA client application. They do offer very much significant performance improvement than JDBC ODBC Bridge but again the main drawback is the driver must be installed on the client machine.

Net-Protocol/ All-Java driver

Type 3 drivers are the right choice for three-tiered approach and they can only be implemented with three-tier architecture. There are two portions of Type 3 drivers one is the small JDBC driver who is responsible to pass the SQL commands to the application server. Second section is the middle ware or so called the application server which passes the request to database. Middle ware section can be type 1, type 2 JDBC driver or a native code.

Native-protocol/ All-Java driver

This is the most used type of driver in JAVA world and the also has best performance as it talks with the database directly. Type 4 drivers are completely written in JAVA. Using Type4 we can move towards platform independence and avoid any kind of deployment issues. But because this kind of driver is very specific to particular database vendor it can be available only by the RDBMS or DBMS vendor as they have more depth about the protocol. The one big issue is if you are changing the database you need to also change the driver which means you need to change the connection string to load the driver. But the connection string change is a small issue if you design your application architecture carefully you can really make it configurable.

Note: *Below there are four questions, we will try to answer all of them in shot.*

(I) **What are the advantages and disadvantages of using JDBC-ODBC bridge driver?**

(I) **What are the advantages and disadvantages of using Native-API/ Partially Java Driver?**

(I) **What are the advantages and disadvantages of using Net-Protocol/ All-Java driver?**

(I) **What are the advantages and disadvantages of using Native-protocol/ All-Java driver?**

Advantages of using JDBC-ODBC bridge driver

The one good thing about JDBC-ODBC driver is you get to work huge number of ODBC drivers. Some times really ODBC driver is the only way to access some databases.

Disadvantages of using JDBC-ODBC bridge driver

Developers prefer this driver only for prototyping purpose and avoid them for actual development. Below are some significant drawbacks of JDBC-ODBC drivers:

√   If you are using ODBC driver you are limited to the limitations of the ODBC driver.

√   There can be performance issues as you go through two layers JDBC and ODBC.

√   JDBC ODBC has problems for multi-threading applications as some of the ODBC drivers do not support the same.

Advantages of using Native-API/ Partially Java Driver:

√   Has better performance than JDBC ODBC as it makes direct calls to the vendor API.

Dis-advantages of using Native-API/ Partially Java Driver:

√   Vendor API has to be installed on the client's machine.

√   Lot of inconsistency in code as we are dealing with different vendor API.

Advantages of using Net-Protocol/ All-Java driver:

√   The driver lies in the middle tier so do not need vendor API on the client machine.

√   If you are targeting for large number of users, performance benefits, three tier architecture, scalability and portability this the best choice.

√   As we have middle tier we can do caching and load balancing.

Disadvantages of using Net-Protocol/ All-Java driver:

√   Need to do database specific coding on the middle tier.

Advantages of using Native-protocol/ All-Java driver:

√   As there not intermediate layers for type 4 they have good performance compared to other drivers.

√   No need to install anything on the client.

Disadvantages of using Native-protocol/ All-Java driver:

√   Different drivers are needed for different databases.

(I)   Define meta-data?

Meta-data is data about data. For instance meta-data for a database are schemas, catalogs, tables and columns.

> *Note: Below there are three questions, we will try to answer all of them in shot.*

(I)   What is DatabaseMetaData?

(A)   Can you explain "ConnectionFactory" class?

(A)   I want to display tables of a database how do I do it?

"DatabaseMetaData" object provides information about database. Below is the code snippet for the same:

> *DatabaseMetaData dbmd = connection.getMetaData();*

"DatabaseMetaData" provides the following information:

√   Users in database, functions and stored procedures.

√   Limitation of database like maximum length of the database.

√   What features are not supported by database and what not?

√   Schema, catalogs, tables, and columns

Below is the code snippet of how to use the "DatabaseMetaData" object. I have made inline comment so that we can understand it line by line. If you note in previous questions we used "DriverManager.getConnection()" to get the connection. But in order to retrieve meta-data we need to get the connection object using the "ConnectionFactory" class.

```
// Connection factory provides connection to the database
Connection dbconn = ConnectionFactory.getConnection();
// Get the meta data object from the connection object
DatabaseMetaData dbmetadata = dbconn.getMetaData();
// Use the meta data object to display database meta data like
productname, version ,
// driver name , does it support ANSI92 etc.
System.out.println("Database           name=["        +
dbmetadata.getDatabaseProductName()+ "]");
System.out.println("version=[" + dbmetadata.getDatabaseProductVersion()
+ "]");
System.out.println("Driver name=[" + dbmetadata.getDriverName() + "]");
System.out.println("ANSI92 =[" + dbmetadata.supportsANSI92EntryLevelSQL()
+ "]");
```

> *Note: Just to get little practical, here's a small assignment which you can do, connect to a database and get all the table names in the database using metadata object. I am sure if you do this sample you will get crystal clarity of "DatabaseMetaData" class and how useful it is. Just for hint purpose below is the code snippet.*

```
DatabaseMetaData dbmdmetadata = databaseConnection.getMetaData();
String[] strtableTypes = new String[] {"TABLE"};
ResultSet    tablesmetadata    =    dbmdmetadata.getTables(
null,null,null,strtableTypes);
Vector vtables = new Vector();
String TableMetaData;
while(tablesmetadata.next())
{
     TableMetaData = tablesmetadata.getString("TABLE_NAME");
     vtables.add(TableMetaData);
}
```

(I)   Define "ResultSetMetaData"?

If you want to get Meta data information about a result set you can use the "ResultSetMetaData" object. It contains types and properties of the column in the result set. Below is code snippet which displays column name, type and whether the column allows nulls or not. I have also provided inline comments so that every line of code in the snippet can be understood.

```
// Get the connection using the connection factory
connmetadata = ConnectionFactory.getConnection();
// get the Statement object
stmtmetadata = connmetadata.createStatement();
String sql = "select * from Mytable";
// get the recordset object from the statement object
recordset = stmtmetadata.executeQuery(sql);
// create the resultsetmetadata object using the recordset object
ResultSetMetaData rsmetadata = recordset.getMetaData();
int numcol = rsmetadata.getColumnCount();
// browse through all the columns to display there properties
for (int i = 1; i <= numcol; i++)
{
     // Display the column name
     System.out.println("Name: " + rsmetadata.getColumnName(i));
     // Display the column type
     System.out.println("Type: " + rsmetadata.getColumnType(i));
     // Display will the column allow nulls to be displayed
     System.out.print("Nullable : ");
     switch (rsmetadata.isNullable(i))
     {
          case ResultSetMetaData.columnNoNulls:
```

```
        System.out.println("This columns does not allow nulls to
    be displayed");
            break;
    case ResultSetMetaData.columnNullable:
    System.out.println("This column allows nulls to be
    displayed");
            break;
    }
}
```

(B) What is the difference between "ResultSet" and "RowSet"?

(A) Can "ResultSet" objects be serialized?

(A) Explain "ResultSet", "RowSet", "CachedRowset", "JdbcRowset" and "WebRowSet"?

Below are the major points of difference:

√ "ResultSet" is a connected architecture while "RowSet" is a disconnected architecture.

√ As "ResultSet" is a connected architecture we can not serialize the object while "RowSet" can be serialized.

√ "RowSet" object is a Java bean while "ResultSet" is not. In the below diagram you can see "RowSet" interface also derives from "BaseRowSet" interface. "BaseRowSet" interface has all the ingredients to make it a Java bean.

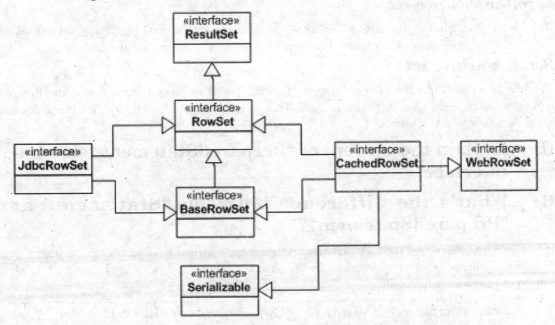

Figure 3.7: Interface diagram for "Resultset" and "RowSet"

As "RowSet" is a disconnected from database it needs to maintain Meta data for columns. "RowSet" can also provide scrollable resultsets or updatable resultsets even if the JDBC driver is not supporting the same. Java client can get a "RowSet" manipulate the same and finally send all the results to the database at one go. Sun has provided three implementation of "RowSet" as below:

CachedRowSet: Disconnected rowset always keeps the data in memory. It is scrollable and can also be serialized. It's an ideal choice where we want to pass data between tiers or to do batch updates. "CachedRowSet" are disconnected so can be used for huge number of updates. Get the "CachedRowSet" object manipulate all your data and send the whole bunch of manipulated data in on go to the Database.

JDBCRowSet: It's opposite to "CachedRowSet". It maintains a connection to the database while the client has reference to it. So it's a connected architecture as compared to CachedRowSet.

WebRowSet: "WebRowSet" is a extension of "CachedRowSet". But the added feature is it can produce XML presentation of the data cached. If you are thinking of exposing your data through web services or to provide data to thin client which are written in different language other than JAVA. Best bet if you want to pass data in XML format over HTTP protocol.

The above diagram shows the complete relationship between all the interface and classes.

(I)   what are the different types of resultset?

"ResultSet" is an object that contains the results of SQL query. That means it contains the rows that satisfy the conditions of the query.

There are three basic types of resultsets:

Forward-only results set

These types of resultset are non-scrollable and moves only forward.

Scroll-insensitive set

Resultset is scrollable so the cursor can move forward, backward, to a particular row etc. While the resultset is open it does not show any changes done to the underlying database.

Scroll-sensitive set

Resultset is scrollable so the cursor can move forward, backward, to a particular row etc. Resultset is sensitive to changes when it is open or used. That means if any values are modified in the database it's propagated to the resultset.

(I)   Explain the concept of "PreparedStatement "statement interface?

(I)   What's the difference between "Statement" and "PreparedStatement"?

In the previous questions we had executed SQL using "Statement" object. Let's try to go deep what actually happens when we execute the SQL using "Statement". Below is a simple SQL which will be executed from the code.

```
String mySimpleSql = "INSERT INTO MyTable(Name) VALUES (" + "Shiv"+ ")";
MyResult = statement.executeUpdate(mySimpleSQL);
```

When the above SQL is translated it looks something like this below.

> INSERT INTO MyTable(Name) VALUES ('Shiv');

If any new data is inserted in to "MyTable" below is the new SQL. But if you notice nothing has changed considerably other than the values i.e. "Shiv" is changed to "Raju".

> INSERT INTO MyTable(Name) VALUES ('Raju');

Even though we see nothing has changed still the database has to parse, check syntax and generate code for the same. Sometimes in complicated SQL statement with huge joins you can see the parsing, syntax checking and code generation is more than executing the actual SQL statement. So if we can some how tell the database that this SQL is going to get executed multiple times but the only change is the data it can really speed up the SQL turn around time. That can be done by using "PreparedStatement" interface. Below is the code snippet with inline explanation of the same

```
// create a SQl Statement note the "?" which tells that the valueswill
be determined later
String mySimpleSql = "INSERT INTO MyTable(Name,Age) VALUES(?,?)";
// create the prepared statement object using the MySimpleSQl
PreparedStatement                myPreparedStatement              =
connection.prepareStatement(MySimpleSql);
// First data input
// Set the name value
myPreparedStatement.setString(1, "Shivprasad Koirala");
// Set the Age value
myPreparedStatement.setInt(2, 28);
// Finally execute the SQL
myPreparedStatement.executeUpdate();
// Clear all parameter value and be ready for next data input
myPreparedStatement.clearParameters();
// Second data input no need to prepare SQL Statement again
// Set the name value
myPreparedStatement.setString(1, "Raju Koirala");
// Set the Age value
myPreparedStatement.setInt(2, 24);
// finally execute the SQL
myPreparedStatement.executeUpdate();
```

(I)　How can we call stored procedure using JDBC?

(I)　Can you explain "CallableStatement" interface in detail?

> *Note: "CallableStatement" is not supported by the current postgres driver so if you want to practice the same try oracle driver.*

"CallableStatement" interface is used to execute stored procedure. Following are the four basic steps:

Get the connection object from the "ConnectionFactory" class.

> *conn = ConnectionFactory.getConnection();*

Prepare the SQL statement as shown below. Note the "?" which is given in the input and return values. Get statement object from the connection object using "prepareCall" method.

> *String sql = "{ ? = call spgetusers(?) }";*
>
> *stmt = conn.prepareCall(sql);*

Set the value using the column index. In this case my table has only one field so used the index "1".

> *stmt.setString(1, "Shiv");*

Finally execute the store procedure with data.

> *stmt.executeUpdate();*

Finally below is small code snippet of the above explained fundamentals.

```java
import java.sql.*;
import connections.*;
import java.util.*;
public class InsertUsers {
    public static void main(String[] args) {
        Connection conn = null;
        CallableStatement stmt = null;
        try {
            conn = ConnectionFactory.getConnection();
            String sql = "{ ? = call spgetusers(?) }";
            stmt = conn.prepareCall(sql);
            stmt.setString(1, "Shiv");
            stmt.executeUpdate();
            // if no exception is thrown, the new user is added
            successfully
            System.out.println("User is added to the database");
        } catch (Exception e)
        {
            System.out.println("User can not be added to the
            database");
            e.printStackTrace();
        }
        finally
        {
            ConnectionFactory.close(stmt);
            ConnectionFactory.close(conn);
        }
    }
}
```

(I)   How do you get a resultset object from stored procedure?

Call the "getObject" method of the "Statement" as shown in the code snippet below.

> *MyResultSet rset = (MyResultSet) Mystmt.getObject(1);*

(A)   How can we do batch updates using "CallableStatement" Interface?

There are times when you want to send batch updates to stored procedure rather than making call now and then for every update. This can be attained by "CallableStatement" interface. Below is the code snippet for the same. Let's make a walk through of each step to understand the fundamental.

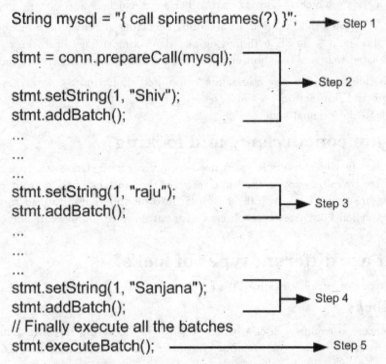

Figure 3.8: Batchupdate using stored procedure

Step1 is our usual statement which we have discussed many times in our previous questions. It prepares the SQL statement with the stored procedure name. We call the "prepareCall" function to get the statement object and then keep on adding the data using the "addBatch" method as seen in Step2, Step3 and Step4. Keep a note until we are adding the data i.e. till step4 no statements are sent to the database. In Step5 all the data inputs are finally sent to the database.

(I)   Define transactions?

Transaction can be defined as a one event or a series of event that must all complete successfully. If one or more event fails then the whole event should be rolled back. For instance when you go to a bank you do the following event in order to deposit money from one account to other account:

√   Login with your "userid" and "password".

√   Deduct the amount from your account.

√   Deposit it to the other account.

If any of the events above fail everything should be rolled back.

(I)   what is ACID in transaction?

(I)   what are the four essential properties of a transaction?

A transaction is proper if it fulfils ACID properties. These four properties are as below:-

Atomicity: This rule states if one part of the transaction fails then the entire transaction should fail.

Consistency: This rule states that only valid data should be written to database. Any invalid data should roll back the whole transaction. If the transaction executes successfully then it should take database from one state which is consistent to other state which is also consistent.

Isolation: This rule states that multiple transactions occurring at the same time should not impact each other. If "shiv" and "raju" is withdrawing and depositing money both the transaction should operate in an isolated manner. Isolation ensures that transactions do not affect each other.

Durability: This rule states that any transaction committed should not be lost. It's ensured through database backups and transaction logs in database. So that if there is a problem at any point we can restore back to the original state.

(I)   Explain concurrency and locking?

There are situations in which multiple users need to interact with database at the same. There can be situations where two users access the same resource. For instance in a customer table two users at the same time are trying to update the customer information. This can lead to quiet confusion. This situation is called concurrency problems. Concurrency problems can be solved by proper locking.

(I)   What are different types of locks?

There are four types of major locks in JDBC:

Exclusive Locks

A transaction places an exclusive lock on data when it is modifying the data. This lock prevents other transactions from reading or updating the locked data. The data remains locked until the transaction is committed or rolled back.

Shared Locks

Shared locks permit other transactions to read the locked data but prevent these transactions from modifying the data. The isolation level of transactions involved in the locking process determines the duration of the lock.

Read Locks

A read lock is a lock placed on a resource that is being read or accessed by a transaction. Read lock prevents other transaction to read or update the data which is locked by a read lock.

Update Locks

Update lock prevents any other transaction to update data. When a transaction tried to update data update lock converts to an exclusive lock.

(A)   What are the different types of levels of resource on which locks can be placed?

(A)   Define lock escalation?

(A)   What is Table level and Row level locking?

There are three types of locking level for a resource:-

√   Table level locking

√   Page level locking

√   Row level locking

When a system is configured for a row level locking database decides whether he should apply lock at a row level or a table level on different parameters. For instance if you execute a query against a single row it will place row level lock. But in case you are selecting more than one row database will go for table level lock or page lock. Page is the memory which holds part of the table or the whole table. For instance if we issue a SQL query like "Select count(*) from table1" its possible that it can place a table level lock as this SQL touch bases all the rows of the table. But again it depends this escalation depends on what type of database you are using. For instance if you are using ORACLE it will not place a table lock. Migration from one level of locking to other is called as Lock escalation.

(B)   What are the problems that can occur if you do not implement locking properly?

Following are the problems that occur if you do not implement locking properly:

Lost Updates

Lost updates occur if you let two transactions modify the same data at the same time, and the transaction that completes first is lost. You need to watch out for lost updates with the READ UNCOMMITTED isolation level. This isolation level disregards any type of locks, so two simultaneous data modifications are not aware of each other. Suppose that a customer has due of 2000$ to be paid. He pays 1000$ and again buys a product of 500$.Lets say that these two transactions are now been entered from two different counters of the company. Now both the counter user starts making entry at the same time 10:00AM.Actually speaking at 10:01 AM the customer should have 2000-1000+500 = 1500$ pending to be paid. But as said in lost updates the first transaction is not considered and the second transaction overrides it. So the final pending is 2000$+500$ = 2500$.....I hope the company does not loose the customer.

Non-Repeatable Read

Non-repeatable reads occur if a transaction is able to read the same row multiple times and gets a different value each time. Again, this problem is most likely to occur with the READ UNCOMMITTED isolation level. Because you let two transactions modify data at the same time, you can get some unexpected results. For instance, a customer wants to book flight, so the travel agent checks for the flights availability. Travel agent finds a seat and goes ahead to book the seat.

While the travel agent is booking the seat, some other travel agent books the seat. When this travel agent goes to update the record, he gets error saying that "Seat is already booked". In short the travel agent gets different status at different times for the seat.

Dirty Reads

Dirty reads are a special case of non-repeatable read. This happens if you run a report while transactions are modifying the data that you're reporting on. For example there is a customer invoice report which runs on 1:00 AM in afternoon and after that all invoices are sent to the respective customer for payments. Lets say one of the customer has 1000$ to be paid. Customer pays 1000$ at 1:00 AM and at the same time report is run. Actually customer has no money pending but is still issued an invoice.

Phantom Reads

Phantom reads occur due to a transaction being able to read a row on the first read, but not being able to modify the same row due to another transaction deleting rows from the same table. Lets say you edit a record in the mean time somebody comes and deletes the record , you then go for updating the record which does not exist....Panic. The only isolation level that doesn't allow phantoms is SERIALIZABLE, which ensures that each transaction is completely isolated from others. In other words, no one can acquire any type of locks on the affected row while it is being modified.

(B)   What are different transaction levels?

> *Twist: what are different types of locks?*

Transaction Isolation level decides how is one process isolated from other process. Using transaction levels you can implement locking. There are four transaction levels:

Read Committed

The shared lock is held for the duration of the transaction, meaning that no other transactions can change the data at the same time. Other transactions can insert and modify data in the same table, however, as long as it is not locked by the first transaction.

Read Uncommitted

No shared locks and no exclusive locks are honored. This is the least restrictive isolation level resulting in the best concurrency but the least data integrity.

Repeat Table Read

This setting disallows dirty and non-repeatable reads. However, even though the locks are held on read data, new rows can still be inserted in the table, and will subsequently be read by the transaction.

Serializable

This is the most restrictive setting holding shared locks on the range of data. This setting does not allow the insertion of new rows in the range that is locked; therefore, no phantoms are allowed.

(B)   What is difference between optimistic and pessimistic locking?

In pessimistic locking transaction locks the record as soon as it selects the row to update. While in optimistic locking it is only locked when the actual updating takes place. Let's try to understand the concept by the figure below.

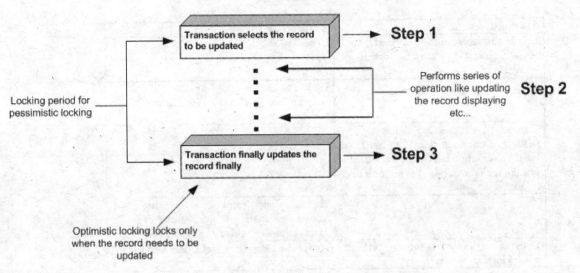

Figure 3.9: Optimistic and Pessimistic locking

To update any record minimum three steps need to be executed as shown in figure above. Step1 select the record which needs to be updated, Step2 perform the necessary operation on the record and Step3 update the record. In pessimistic locking we lock the record right from Step1 to Step3 that means as soon as you select the record is locked and keeps it locked until you complete the operation. No other transaction can access the same until you release the lock. While in optimistic locking you do not lock the record for the complete cycle but only when you are actually updating the record. You can see from the figure above pessimistic locking have longer locking life time than optimistic so it has least amount of concurrency.

So in order a row is locked as soon as it is selected you can use the select query something as shown below.

SELECT column1 FROM Table1 WHERE column1=2 FOR UPDATE

The FOR UPDATE clause puts a lock on the row thus ensuring no other transaction can update the same until the transaction is completed.

In order to implement optimistic locking we do something like this in the SQL update.

UPDATE Table1 SET column1=3 WHERE column1=4 and column4='ss'

In the above query we are trying to update column1 from 4 to 3. So when we actually want to update, we just make a check before the update are the old values same or has some thing changed. This can be done by putting a comparison on the where clause of the update query. For instance in the above SQL update column1 had value 4 and column4 had value "ss" so we make a compare before update to ensure that nothing has changed. If anything has changed the update will not happen thus ensuring safe concurrency.

(B) What are deadlocks?

Deadlocks occur when two transactions are each blocked waiting for the other transaction to complete. In order to get a clear understanding of how dead lock occurs lets look at the sequence of events in the below table.

Transaction A	Transaction B
Update customer name from "cust1" to "cust2". Now it is blocked for further updates.	
	Update customer name from "cust1" to "cust3". Now it's blocked for further updates.
Transaction A attempts to update customer name from "cust1" to "cust2" but the transaction is blocked because it waiting for Transaction B to commit or rollback.	
	Transaction B attempts to update customer name from "cust1" to "cust3" but wait for Transaction A to either commit or rollback.
Both transactions wait for each other to release the respective locks thus moving to a dead lock situation	

◄── Dead lock

Figure 3.10: Dead lock in action

In the above table both transactions "A" and "B" are trying to update the customer table with there respective values. That means Transaction "A" wants to update customer name from "cust1" to "cust2" while transaction B wants to update it to "cust3". Later when actually transaction A goes to update the values it finds himself in a blocking situation as Transaction B is trying to do the same. And on the other end Transaction B also goes in to blocking stage as Transaction A is trying to update the customer name. This situation is termed as dead lock.

So what happens in such kind of dead locks.....hmmm a good database design will help you get you out of this situation. If you planned your database locking well this will not be situation it will roll back one of the transactions and make road for other thus let you come out from the chicken and egg situation.

(A)   How can we set transaction level through JDBC API?

We can set and get transaction level using two API's of JDBC "setTransactionIsolation()" and "getTransactionIsolation()". You can see the code snippet for the declaration of both the API's.

```
public void setTransactionIsolation(int level) throws SQLException;
public int getTransactionIsolation() throws SQLException;


Connection connection = ConnectionFactory.getConnection();
connection.setTransactionIsolation(1);
```

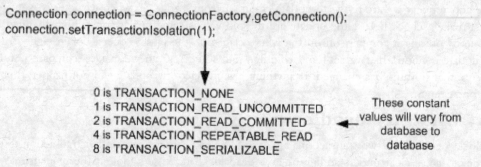

```
0 is TRANSACTION_NONE
1 is TRANSACTION_READ_UNCOMMITTED
2 is TRANSACTION_READ_COMMITTED
4 is TRANSACTION_REPEATABLE_READ
8 is TRANSACTION_SERIALIZABLE
```

These constant values will vary from database to database

Figure 3.11: Setting transaction level using JDBC

Once we have reference to the "Connection" object we can use the "setTransactionIsolation()" method to set the transaction level. You need to pass the appropriate transaction level constant to the method. For instance we have set the above connection to transaction level to "Read uncommitted".

(I) Can you explain transaction control in JDBC?

Transaction control can be provided by Connection class of the JDBC driver. By default every SQL is treated as a transaction and the transaction is committed when the SQL statement is complete. When JDBC driver fires a SQL a new transaction is started and it's committed when the SQL is completed. This is the default behavior for JDBC drivers. But definitely you want to control the commit and roll back of the transaction. For that you need make the connection object's auto commit property as false. Below is the code snippet for the same:

```
Connection conn =
DriverManager.getConnection ("jdbc:oracle:oci8:@ora8idev","username","
password");
conn.setAutoCommit (false);
```

After this you can either use conn.commit(); to commit or conn.rollback(); to rollback a transaction. Below table has list of common transaction related method and properties in the connection object.

Method	Description
void setAutoCommit(boolean)	Sets the autocommit mode to true (commit transaction automatically, the default setting) or false (require explicit transaction commit).
void commit()	Commits the current transaction. All changes made since the last commit or rollback is made permanent. Any database locks are released.
void rollback()	Returns the database to the state that existed after the last successful commit, usually prior to the start of the current transaction. Any database locks are released.
void close()	Close the Connection. This also closes any Statements and ResultSets that have not been closed. Whether this commits or rolls back the transaction is database-dependent. The JDBC specification does not require a particular behavior.
boolean isClosed()	Returns true if the method close() has been called on the Connection

Figure 3.12: Transaction properties and methods related to connection object

(A) What are Savepoints in a transaction?

JDBC 3.0 introduced a new concept called as "Savepoint".Using save points you can mark one or more places in transaction and some time later you can perform rollback to one of those "Savepoint". Below code snippet will give a clear idea of how save points can be used

```
Savepoint recordSavepoint1 = null;
Savepoint recordSavepoint2 = null;

// Do some transaction operation
recordSavepoint1 = connection.setSavepoint("Insert complete One");  ◄——— Step 1

..

..

..

// Do some transaction operation
recordSavepoint2 = connection.setSavepoint("Insert complete Two");  ◄——— Step 2

..

..

connection.rollback(recordSavepoint1);  ◄——— Step 3

..

..

..

connection.rollback(recordSavepoint2);  ◄——— Step 4

..

..

connection.rollback();  ◄——— Step 5

..

..

..

connection.commit();  ◄——— Step 6
```

Figure 3.13 : - Snippet code for Savepoint's

In the above code snippet we have defined two save points Step1 and Step2. After that we can rollback
to a particular save point using rollback. For instance step3 and step4 show how we can rollback to a
particular save point. You can also rollback every thing using our traditional commit and rollback as
shown in step5 and step6.

Note: In order to define a savepoint we need to define "Savepoint" data type.

4

Servlets and JSP

(B) What are Servlets?

Servlets are small program which execute on the web server. They run under web server environment exploiting the functionalities of the web server.

(B) What are advantages of servlets over CGI?

In CGI for every request there is a new process started which is quiet an overhead. In servlets JVM stays running and handles each request using a light weight thread. In CGI if there are 1000 request then 1000 CGI program is loaded in memory while in servlets there are 1000 thread and only one copy of the servlet class.

(B) Can you explain Servlet life cycle?

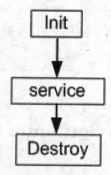

Figure 4.1: Servlet Life cycle

There are three methods which are very important in servlet life cycle i.e. "init", "service" and "destroy". Server invokes "init ()" method when servlet is first loaded in to the web server memory. Servlet reads HTTP data provided in HTTP request in the "service ()" method. Once initialized servlet remains in memory to process subsequent request. So for every HTTP request "service ()" method of the servlet is called. Finally when server unloads the "servlet ()" from the memory it calls the "destroy" method which can be used to clean up any resource the servlet is consuming.

(B) What are the two important API's in for Servlets?

Two important packages are required to build servlet "javax.servlet" and "javax.servlet.http". They form the core of Servlet API. Servlets are not part of core Java but are standard extensions provided by Tomcat.

(B)   Can you explain in detail "javax.servlet" package?

javax.servlet package has interfaces and classes which define a framework in which servlets can operate. Let's first make a walk through of all the interfaces and methods and its description.

Interfaces in javax.servlet

Servlet Interface

This interface has the init( ), service( ), and destroy( ) methods that are called by the server during the life cycle of a servlet.

Following are the method in Servlet interface:

void destroy( ): Executed when servlet is unloaded from the web server memory.

ServletConfig getServletConfig(): Returns back a ServletConfig object that contains initialization data.

String getServletInfo( ): Returns a string describing the servlet.

init method: Called for first time when the servlet is initialized by the web server.

void service() method: Called to process a request from a client.

ServletConfig Interface

This interface is implemented by the servlet container. Servlet can access any configuration data when its loaded. The methods declared by this interface are summarized here:

Following are the methods in ServletConfig interface:

ServletContext getServletContext(): Gives the servlet context.

String getInitParameter(String param): Returns the value of the initialization parameter named param.

Enumeration getInitParameterNames(): Returns an enumeration of all initialization parameter names.

String getServletName( ): Returns the name of the invoking servlet.

(I)   What's the use of ServletContext?

ServletContext Interface

It gives information about the environment. It represents a Servlet's view of the Web Application.Using this interface servlet can access raw input streams to Web Application resources, virtual directory translation, a common mechanism for logging information, and an application scope for binding objects.

Following are the methods defined in ServletContext Interface

Object getAttribute(String attr): Returns the value of the server attribute named attr.

String getMimeType(String file): Gives MIME type for a file.

String getRealPath(String vpath): Gives the actual physical path for a virtual path.

String getServerInfo( ): You can get the server information using this function.

void log(String s): Used to write to server log.

void log(String s, Throwable e): Writes s and the stack trace for e to the servlet log.

void setAttribute(String attr, Object val): Sets the attribute specified by attr to the value passed in val.

ServletRequest Interface

The ServletRequest interface is implemented by the servlet container. It gives data regarding client request.

Following are the methods defined in ServletRequest Interface

Object getAttribute(String attr): Returns the value of the attribute named attr.

String getCharacterEncoding( ): Returns the character encoding of the request.

int getContentLength( ): Gives the size of the request. If no size is there then it returns -1.

String getContentType( ): Returns the type of the request. A null value is returned if the type cannot be determined.

ServletInputStream getInputStream( ): Returns a ServletInputStream that can be used to read binary data from the request.

String getParameter(String pname): Returns the value of the parameter named pname.

Enumeration getParameterNames( ): Returns an enumeration of the parameter names for this request.

String[ ] getParameterValues(String name): Returns an array containing values associated with the parameter specified by name.

String getProtocol( ): Gives back protocol description.

BufferedReader getReader( ): Returns a buffered reader that can be used to read text from the request.

String getRemoteAddr(): Returns client IP address.

String getRemoteHost(): Returns client host name.

String getScheme( ): Return what's the transmission protocol HTTP , FTP etc.

String getServerName(): Returns the name of the server.

int getServerPort(): Returns the port number.

ServletResponse Interface

The ServletResponse interface is implemented by the servlet containerUsed to give response back to the client.

Following are the methods defined in ServletResponse Interface

String getCharacterEncoding(): Returns back character encoding.

ServletOutputStream getOutputStream(): Returns a ServletOutputStream that can be used to write binary data to the response.

PrintWriter getWriter(): Returns a PrintWriter that can be used to write character data to the response.

void setContentLength(int size): Sets the content length for the response to size.

void setContentType(String type): Sets the content type for the response to type.

GenericServlet Class

The GenericServlet class provides implementations of the basic life cycle methods for a servlet. GenericServlet implements the Servlet and ServletConfig interfaces.

> void log(String s)

> void log(String s, Throwable e)

Here, s is the string to be appended to the log, and e is an exception that occurred.

Now let's revise through different classes.

ServletInputStream Class

This class extends InputStream. It is implemented by the servlet container and provides an input stream that a servlet developer can use to read the data from a client request. It defines the default constructor. In addition, a method is provided to read bytes from the stream.

int readLine(byte[ ] buffer, int offset, int size) :- Here, buffer is the array into which size bytes are placed starting at offset. The method returns the actual number of bytes read or –1 if an end-of-stream condition is encountered.

ServletOutputStream Class

The ServletOutputStream class extends OutputStream. It is implemented by the servlet container and provides an output stream that a servlet developer can use to write data to a client response. A default constructor is defined. It also defines the "print()" and "println()" methods, which output data to the stream.

Servlet Exception Classes

javax.servlet defines two exceptions. The first is ServletException, which indicates that a servlet problem has occurred. The second is unavailableException, which extends ServletException. It indicates that a servlet is unavailable.

(I)   How do we define an application level scope for servlet?

(B)   What's the difference between GenericServlet and HttpServlet?

HttpServlet class extends GenericServlet class which is an abstract class to provide HTTP protocol-specific functionalities. Most of the java application developers extend HttpServlet class as it provides more HTTP protocol-specific functionalities. You can see in HttpServlet class doGet (), doPOst () methods which are more targeted towards HTTP protocol specific functionalities. For instance we can inherit from GenericServlet class to make something like MobileServlet. So GenericServlet class should be used when we want to write protocol specific implementation which is not available. But when we know we are making an internet application where HTTP is the major protocol its better to use HttpServlet.

(B)   Can you explain in detail javax.servlet.http package?

The javax.servlet.http package inherits from "javax.servlet" package and supplies HTTP protocol specific functionalities for JAVA developers. If you are aiming at developing HTTP application you will find "javax.servlet.HTTP" more comfortable than "javax.servlet".

So let's revisit through the interfaces and methods

HttpServletRequest Interface

Below are the lists of methods in HttpServletRequest Interface:

String getAuthType( ): Returns the type of authentication.

Cookie[ ] getCookies( ): Returns the collection of cookies for the request.

long getDateHeader(String field): Returns the value of the date header field named field.

String getHeader(String field): Returns the value of the header field named field.

Enumeration getHeaderNames( ): Returns an enumeration of the header names.

int getIntHeader(String field): Returns the int equivalent of the header field named field.

String getMethod( ): What type of method does this request have POST , GET etc.

String getPathInfo( ): Returns any path information that is located after the servlet path and before a query string of the URL.

String getPathTranslated( ): Returns any path information that is located after the servlet path and before a query string of the URL after translating it to a real path.

String getQueryString( ): Returns any query string in the URL.

String getRemoteUser( ): Returns the name of the user who issued this request.

String getRequestedSessionId( ): Returns the ID of the session.

String getRequestURI( ): Returns the URI.

StringBuffer getRequestURL( ): Returns the URL.

String getServletPath( ): Returns that part of the URL that identifies the servlet.

HttpSession getSession( ): Returns the session for this request. If a session does not exist, one is created and then returned.

HttpSession getSession(boolean new): If new is true and no session exists, creates and returns a session for this request. Otherwise, returns the existing session for this request. This section is explained in more detail in further questions.

boolean isRequestedSessionIdFromCookie( ): Returns true if the cookie has the session id.

boolean isRequestedSessionIdFromURL( ): Gives true if the URL has session id.

boolean isRequestedSessionIdValid( ): Return true if the session is valid in the current context.

HttpServletResponse Interface

The HttpServletResponse interface is implemented by the servlet container. It enables a servlet to formulate an HTTP response to a client. Several constants are defined. These correspond to the different status codes that can be assigned to an HTTP response.

Below are the methods and functions for the interface

> void addCookie(Cookie cookie): Adds cookie to the HTTP response.

String encodeURL(String url): Determines if the session ID must be encoded in the URL identified as url. If so, returns the modified version of URL. Otherwise, returns URL. All URLs generated by a servlet should be processed by this method.

String encodeRedirectURL(String url): Determines if the session ID must be encoded in the URL identified as url. If so, returns the modified version of URL. Otherwise, returns URL. All URLs passed to sendRedirect( ) should be processed by this method.

void sendError(int c): Sends the error code c to the client.

void sendError(int c, String s): Sends the error code c and message s to the client.

void sendRedirect(String url): Redirects the client to url.

void setDateHeader(String field, long msec): Adds field to the header with date value equal to msec (milliseconds since midnight, January 1, 1970, GMT).

void setHeader(String field, String value): Adds field to the header with value equal to value.

void setIntHeader(String field, int value): Adds field to the header with value equal to value.

void setStatus(int code): Sets the status code for this response to code.

HttpSession Interface

HTTP protocol is a stateless protocol and this interface enables to maintain sessions between requests.

Object getAttribute(String attr): Returns the value associated with the name passed in attr. Returns null if attr is not found.

Enumeration getAttributeNames( ): Returns an enumeration of the attribute names associated with the session.

long getCreationTime( ): Returns the time (in milliseconds since midnight, January 1, 1970, GMT) when this session was created.

String getId( ): Returns the session ID.

long getLastAccessedTime( ): Returns the time (in milliseconds since midnight, January 1, 1970, GMT) when the client last made a request for this session.

void invalidate(): Invalidates this session and removes it from the context.

boolean isNew( ): Returns true if the server created the session and it has not yet been accessed by the client.

void removeAttribute(String attr): Removes the attribute specified by attr from the session.

void setAttribute(String attr, Object val): Associates the value passed in val with the attribute name passed in attr.

HttpSessionBindingListener

The HttpSessionBindingListener interface is implemented by objects that need to be notified when they are bound to or unbound from an HTTP session. The methods that are invoked when an object is bound or unbound are

> void valueBound(HttpSessionBindingEvent e)

> void valueUnbound(HttpSessionBindingEvent e)

Here, e is the event object that describes the binding.

Cookie Class

The Cookie class encapsulates a cookie. A cookie is stored on a client and contains state information. Cookies are valuable for tracking user activities. For example, assume that a user visits an online store. A cookie can save the user's name, address, and other information. The user does not need to enter this data each time he or she visits the store.

A servlet can write a cookie to a user's machine via the addCookie( ) method of the HttpServletResponse interface. The data for that cookie is then included in the header of the HTTP response that is sent to the browser.

The names and values of cookies are stored on the user's machine. Some of the information that is saved for each cookie includes name of the cookie, value of the cookie, expiration date of the cookie and domain/path of the cookie.

The expiration date determines when this cookie is deleted from the user's machine. If an expiration date is not explicitly assigned to a cookie, it is deleted when the current browser session ends. Otherwise, the cookie is saved in a file on the user's machine.

The domain and path of the cookie determine when it is included in the header of an HTTP request. If the user enters a URL whose domain and path match these values, the cookie is then supplied to the Web server. Otherwise, it is not. There is one constructor for Cookie. It has the signature shown here:

Cookie(String name, String value): Here, the name and value of the cookie are supplied as arguments to the constructor. The methods of the Cookie class are

Object clone( ): Returns a copy of this object.

String getComment( ): Returns the comment.

String getDomain( ): Returns the domain.

int getMaxAge( ): Returns the maximum age (in seconds).

String getName( ): Returns the name.

String getPath( ): Returns the path.

boolean getSecure( ): Returns true if the cookie is secure. Otherwise, returns false.

String getValue( ): Returns the value.

int getVersion( ): Returns the version.

void setComment(String c): Sets the comment to c.

void setDomain(String d): Sets the domain to d.

void setMaxAge(int secs): Sets the maximum age of the cookie to secs. This is the number of seconds after which the cookie is deleted.

void setPath(String p): Sets the path to p.

void setSecure(boolean secure): Sets the security flag to secure.

void setValue(String v): Sets the value to v.

void setVersion(int v): Sets the version to v.

HttpServlet Class

The HttpServlet class extends GenericServlet. It is commonly used when developing servlets that receive and process HTTP requests.

void doDelete(HttpServletRequest req, HttpServletResponse res) throws IOException, ServletException: Handles an HTTP DELETE.

void doGet(HttpServletRequest req, HttpServletResponse res) throws IOException, ServletException: Handles an HTTP GET.

void doOptions(HttpServletRequest req, HttpServletResponse res) throws IOException, ServletException: Handles an HTTP OPTIONS.

void doPost(HttpServletRequest req, HttpServletResponse res) throws IOException, ServletException: Handles an HTTP POST.

void doPut(HttpServletRequest req, HttpServletResponse res) throws IOException, ServletException: Handles an HTTP PUT.

void doTrace(HttpServletRequest req, HttpServletResponse res) throws IOException, ServletException: Handles an HTTP TRACE.

long getLastModified(HttpServletRequest req): Returns the time (in milliseconds since midnight, January 1, 1970, GMT) when the requested resource was last modified.

void service(HttpServletRequest req, HttpServletResponse res) throws IOException, ServletException: Called by the server when an HTTP request arrives for this servlet. The arguments provide access to the HTTP request and response, respectively.

HttpSessionEvent Class

HttpSessionEvent encapsulates session events. It extends EventObject and is generated when a change occurs to the session.

HttpSession getSession( )

It returns the session in which the event occurred.

The HttpSessionBindingEvent Class

The HttpSessionBindingEvent class extends HttpSessionEvent. It is generated when a listener is bound to or unbound from a value in an HttpSession object. It is also generated when an attribute is bound or unbound. Here are its constructors:

> HttpSessionBindingEvent(HttpSession session, String name)

> HttpSessionBindingEvent(HttpSession session, String name, Object val)

Here, session is the source of the event, and name is the name associated with the object that is being bound or unbound. If an attribute is being bound or unbound, its value is passed in Val.

String getName( ): The getName( ) method obtains the name that is being bound or unbound. Its constructor is shown here:

HttpSession getSession( ): The getSession( ) method, shown next, obtains the session to which the listener is being bound or unbound:

Object getValue( ): The getValue( ) method obtains the value of the attribute that is being bound or unbound. It is shown here:

(B)   What's the architecture of a Servlet package?

In the previous questions we saw all the servlet packages. But the basic architecture of the servlet packages is as shown below.

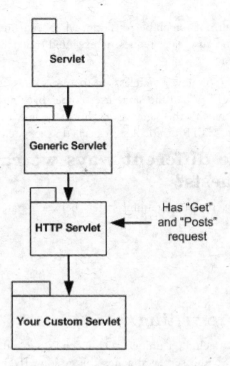

Figure 4.2: Servlet package in action

At the top of all is the main servlet interface which is implemented by the generic servlet. But generic servlet does not provide implementation specific to any protocol. HTTP servlet further inherits from the generic servlet and provides HTTP implementation like "Get" and "Post". Finally comes our custom servlet which inherits from HTTP Servlet.

(B) Why is HTTP protocol called as a stateless protocol?

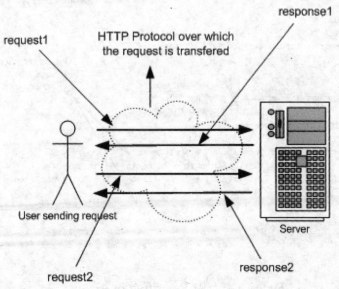

Figure 4.3: HTTP Protocol in action

A protocol is stateless if it can not remember difference between one client request and the other. HTTP is a stateless protocol because each request is executed independently without any knowledge of the requests that came before it.

Above is a pictorial presentation of how a stateless protocol operates. User first sends "request1" and server responds with "response1". When the same user comes back with "request2" server treats this as new user and has no idea that it's the same user who has come with the request. In short every request is a new request for the HTTP protocol so it's called as a stateless protocol.

(B) What are the different ways we can maintain state between requests?

Following are the different ways of maintaining state's between stateless requests:

√   URL rewriting

√   Cookies

√   Hidden fields

√   Sessions

(B) What is URL rewriting?

It's based on the concept of attaching a unique ID (which is generated by the server) in the URL of response from the server. So the server attaches this unique ID in each URL. When the client sends a requests it sends back this ID with the request also which helps the server to identify the client uniquely.

> Note: A sample code for URL rewriting is in the CD in "URLRewriting" folder.

Below is a snippet which is extracted from the code which is provided in the CD.

```java
String strToken = request.getParameter("token");        ◄— 1   Get the current
                                                                token value from
                                                                the querystring

String urlString = null;

PrintWriter objWriter = response.getWriter();
                                                                Get the current token
if (strToken == null)                                           value from the
{                                           Server generates  3  querystring
    Random rand = new Random();      ◄— 2  a unique ID using
                                            the random class
    strToken = Long.toString(rand.nextLong());

    objWriter.println(" Your new token is :- " + strToken);
    urlString = request.getRequestURL().toString() + "?token=" + strToken;
    objWriter.println("<a href='" + urlString + "'> Click here again " + strToken + "</a>");
}
else
{
    urlString = request.getRequestURL().toString() + "?token=" + strToken;
    objWriter.println("<a href='" + urlString + "'> Welcome back your token is " + strToken + "</a>");
}
```

Figure 4.4: URLRewriting in Action

In this sample we have generated a unique ID using the random class of java. This unique ID is then sent in the query string (see step 3 of the above snippet) back to the client. When the client comes back to the server the server first gets the token value from the query string and thus identifying the client uniquely.

(B) What are cookies?

Cookies are piece of data which are stored at the client's browser to track information regarding the user usage and habits. Servlets sends cookies to the browser client using the HTTP response headers. When client gets the cookie information it's stored by the browser in the client's hard disk. Similarly client returns the cookie information using the HTTP request headers.

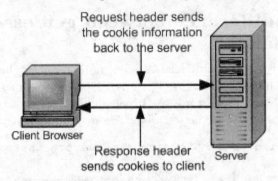

Figure 4.5: Cookies in action

```java
// get the cookies value in string variable
String strfavoritebook =  request.getParameter("BooksPreference");
// create a new cookie with the value passed
Cookie favoritecookiebook =  new Cookie("favoritecookiebook", strfavoritebook);
// Add a simple comment
favoritecookiebook.setComment("User prefers this");           1 Creates a new cookie
// add the cookies to the response object
response.addCookie(favoritecookiebook);           2 Adds the cookie to the response headers
// by default there us nothing selected
String result = "still not selected";
if (request.getCookies() != null)
{
Cookie[] cookies = request.getCookies();           3 Gets all the cookies in the current request
// Loop through all the cookies and get the cookies value
for(int i = 0;i < cookies.length;i++)
{
  if(cookies[i].getName().equals("favoritecookiebook"))
  {
    result = cookies[i].getValue();           4 Get the current cookie value
    break;
  }}}
// Finally using printwriter object to write the cookies back to the browse
PrintWriter out =  response.getWriter();
out.println("" + "");
// and display the out put
out.println("<H2> So your favourite book is " + result  + " </H2>");
out.println("");
```

Figure 4.6: Cookies code walkthrough

Above is a simple snippet which shows how to use cookies. To create a cookie you need to use the "Cookie" class. In the above snippet step1 creates a cookie using the "Cookie" class. In this case "favoritecookiebook" is the name of the cookie. In Step 2 you can see how a cookie has been added to the response. Step 3 code shows how to get all the cookies which has come in the current request header. Step 4 shows the way to get a cookie from a collection in this case we wanted to retrieve "favoritecookiebook" from the cookies collection.

> *Note: You can get the above code in "cookies" folder.*

(B)   What are sessions in Servlets?

(B)   What's the difference between getSession(true) and getSession(false) ?

Session's can be considered as a series of related interactions between client and the server that take place over a period of time. Because HTTP is a stateless protocol these series of interactions are difficult to track. That's where we can use HttpSession object to save in between of these interactions so that server can co-relate between interactions between clients.

```
Step 1 ──► HttpSession presentSession = request.getSession(true);

Step 2 ──► String strName = (String)presentSession.getAttribute("Name");

          PrintWriter objWriter = response.getWriter();

          if (strName == null)
          {
              objWriter.println(" Inserted first time in to session");

              String strobj = new String("Data from Session");

Step 3 ──►    presentSession.setAttribute("Name", strobj);

              strName = strobj;

          }
```

Figure 4.7: Session code walkthrough

Above is the code snippet which displays session data. Step1 returns an HttpSession object from the request object. "true" parameter in the "getsession" function ensures that we get a session object if there is no current session object in request which ensures that we never get a null session object. In Step 2 we are using the "getattribute" function to return the session value. In step 3 we are setting the session value with "Name" key.

> *Note: In source code folder we have a sample project "sessions" which can make your concept clearer.*

(I)   What's the difference between "doPost" and "doGet" methods?

When we invoke a servlet the servlet engine passes information to service () method of the servlet. Service method evaluates whether it's a GET or a POST request type. GET and POST differ from the way data is passed to the server. In GET data is passed as a query string attached to the URL for instance http://www.xyz.com/x.asp?Name=Shiv. So when you pass data through get method you can see the data in your browser URL which can be bad thing for critical data like password. In POST method data is passed through normal input stream. You will not be able to view data like how we get for GET method.

So for POST method below is the HTML code.

    <form name='MyServlet' method='POST' >

For GET method below is the HTML code

    <form name='MyServlet' method='GET'>

(I)   Which are the different ways you can communicate between servlets?

Below are the different ways of communicating between servlets:-

√   Using RequestDispatcher object.

√   Sharing resource using "ServletContext ()" object.

√   Include response of the resource in the response of the servlet.

√   Calling public methods of the resource.

√   Servlet chaining.

(I)   What is functionality of "RequestDispatcher" object?

Above is the code snippet for "requestdispatcher". Code snippet "getServletContext().getRequestDispatcher("/servlet/clsAdd"); "gets the "requestdisptacherobject". In order to call the other servlet class we call the forward method which in turn invokes the service method of the other servlets.

```
public class clsMaths extends HttpServlet
{
    public void service(HttpServletRequest request,
    HttpServletResponse response)
    throws ServletException, IOException
    {
    RequestDispatcher dispatch;
    String strWhattoDo = request.getParameter("Whattodo");

    if (strWhattoDo == "A")
    {
    dispatch = getServletContext().getRequestDispatcher("/servlet/clsAdd");
    }
    else
    {
    dispatch = getServletContext().getRequestDispatcher("/servlet/clsMultiply");
    }
    if (dispatch == null)
    {
    response.sendError(response.SC_NO_CONTENT);
    return;
    }
    HttpSession session = request.getSession();
    dispatch.forward(request, response);
```

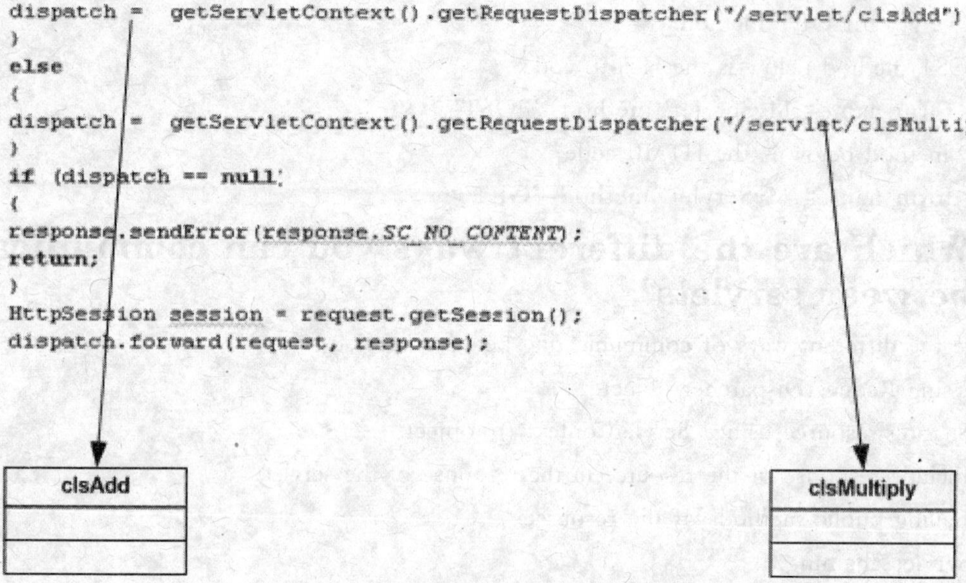

clsAdd

clsMultiply

Figure 4.8: RequestDispatcher in action

> *Note:* There is a sample project "requestdispatcher" which you can open and see. In order to see how the dispatcher will work you can pass the "WhattoDo" as either "A" or "M" as shown in the figure below. Corresponding servlets are called depending on this value.

http://localhost:8080/servlets-examples/servlet/clsMaths?Num1=100&Num2=100&Whattodo=A

Figure 4.9 : - Running the dispatcher project through URL

(I)   How do we share data using "getServletContext ()"?

Using the "getServletContext ()" we can make data available at application level. So servlets which lies in the same application can get the data. Below are important snippets which you will need to add, get and remove data which can be shared across servlets.

```
Step1 ——▶ getServletContext().setAttribute("Customer",Customer.instance());
Step2 ——▶ Customer objCustomer = (Customer)getServletContext().getAttribute("Customer");
Step3 ——▶ getServletContext().removeAttribute("Customer");
```

Figure 4.10: Sharing data using "getServletContext ()"

You can see in Step1 how "getServletContext().setAttribute()" method can be used add new objects to the "getServletContext" collection. Step2 shows how we can get the object back using "getAttribute()" and manipulate the same. Step3 shows how to remove an already shared application object from the collection. "getServletContext()" object is shared across servlets with in a application and thus can be used to share data between servlets.

(B) Explain the concept of SSI?

Server Side Includes (SSI) are commands and directives placed in Web pages that are evaluated by the Web server when the Web page is being served. SSI are not supported by all web servers. So before using SSI read the web server documentation for the support. SSI is useful when you want a small part of the page to be dynamically generated rather than loading the whole page again.

Below is the code for SSI which needs to be inserted in between the HTML tags.

```
<SERVLET CODE=MyServlet CODEBASE=path
initparam1=initvalue1  initparam2=initvalue2>
<PARAM NAME=param1 VALUE=value1>
<PARAM NAME=param2 VALUE=value2>
</SERVLET>
```

Here the CODE attribute specifies the servlet name. The CODEBASE attribute indicates the servlet location. If you are using a servlet deployed in the same Web server, you can omit the CODEBASE attribute. You can pass any request parameters to the servlet using the PARAM tags.

Below is the code how the SSI looks in the HTML

```
<HTML>
<HEAD>
<TITLE>Using SSL</TITLE>
<BODY>
<SERVLET CODE=MyServlet CODEBASE=path
initparam1=initvalue1  initparam2=initvalue2>
<PARAM NAME=param1 VALUE=value1>
<PARAM NAME=param2 VALUE=value2>
</SERVLET>
</BODY>
</HTML>
```

(I) What are filters in JAVA?

Filters are nothing but simple java classes which can manipulate request before it reaches the resource on the web server. Resource can be a HTML file, servlet class, JSP etc. It can also intercept responses sent back to client and thus can manipulate the response before they reach the client browser.

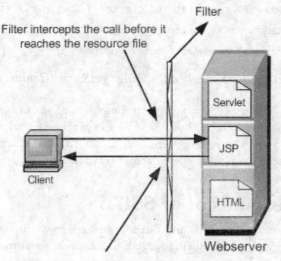

Figure 4.11: Filter in action

(A) Can you explain in short how do you go about implementing filters using Apache Tomcat?

Twist: - Explain step by step of how to implement filters?

```
public class clsTimeFilter implements Filter  ──► Step1
{
    private FilterConfig config = null;

    public void init(FilterConfig config) throws ServletException
    {this.config = config;}

    public void destroy(){config = null;}

    public void doFilter (ServletRequest request,
            ServletResponse response,
            FilterChain chain) throws IOException, ServletException {
    // Log the time in a tremporary variable
    long beforetime = System.currentTimeMillis();
    // call the invoked the servlet
    chain.doFilter(request, response);                              ──► Step 2
    // log the time after the servlet request is finished
    long aftertime = System.currentTimeMillis();
    // Get the URL name of the servlet which was invoked
    String strUrlname = "";
    if (request instanceof HttpServletRequest)
    {
      strUrlname = ((HttpServletRequest)request).getRequestURI();
    }
    // Send the time required to serve the servlets to a LOG file
    config.getServletContext().log(strUrlname + " was accessed for : " + (aftertime - beforetime)

    }
}
```

Step 3 ◄── `chain.doFilter(request, response);`

Step 4 ◄── `config.getServletContext().log(...)`

Figure 4.12: Filter code walkthrough

In order to make a class as a filter we need to inherit from the "Filter" class. You can see the same in the code sample below in Step1.

Above class "clsTimeFilter" logs the time required for resource to load. You can see in the above code in Step2 we have taken beforetime and aftertime values. In between of them we have called the "dofilter" (Which is Step 3). Finally at Step4 we send the difference of the aftertime and beforetime to the log file.

Define the class in web.xml as a filter

```
<filter>
        <filter-name>Mytimer</filter-name>
        <filter-class>clsTimeFilter</filter-class>
</filter>

<filter-mapping>
        <filter-name>Mytimer</filter-name>
        <url-pattern>/*</url-pattern>
</filter-mapping>
```

Define the mapping with URL in web.xml

Figure 4.13: Filter mapped to URL

Once we compile the class file we need to do two important steps one is define the filter and map the filter to the URL. As we are using tomcat we need to define the same in "web.xml" file. Above is a snippet of "web.xml" file with both the entries. The first entry defines the filter name and second maps it to a URL. Currently the URL pattern is "*" that means any servlet requested will invoke the "clsTimeFilter" filter.

Once you have deployed the filter and you request a URL you can see the output sent by the filter to the LOG of tomcat.

```
May 15, 2006 3:10:49 PM org.apache.catalina.core.ApplicationContext log
INFO: /servlets-examples/servlet/HelloworldExample was accessed for : 15Milli Seconds
```

Figure 4.14: Log file entry

Note: You can get the source code for the filter in "Filters" folder.

(I) what's the difference between Authentication and authorization?

Authentication is the process the application identifies that you are who. For example when a user logs into an application with a username and password, application checks that the entered credentials against its user data store and responds with success or failure. Authorization, on the other hand, is when the application checks to see if you're allowed to do something. For instance are you allowed to do delete or modify a resource.

(B) Explain in brief the directory structure of a web application?

Below is the directory structure of a web application:

webapp/

> WEB-INF/web.xml

> WEB-INF/classes

> WEB-INF/lib

√   The webapp directory contains the JSP files, images, and HTML files. The webapp directory can also contain subdirectories such as images or html or can be organized by function, such as public or private.

√   The WEB-INF/web.xml file is called the deployment descriptor for the Web application. This file contains configuration information for the Web application, including the mappings of URLs to servlets and filters. The web.xml file also contains configuration information for security, MIME type mapping, error pages, and locale settings

√   The WEB-INF/classes directory contains the class files for the servlets, JSP files, tag libraries, and any other utility classes that are used in the Web application.

√   The WEB-INF/lib directory contains JAR files for libraries that are used by the Web application. These are generally third-party libraries or classes for any tag libraries used by the Web application.

> *Note: Running JSP is a breeze if the web server supports it. In CD we have provided Tomcat 5.5 installation. Tomcat 5.5 support JSP. You only need to create a folder for your project in webapps folder and put in your JSP files.*

(B) Can you explain JSP page life cycle?

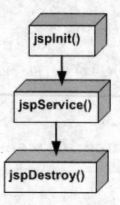

Figure 4.15: JSP page life cycle

When first time a JSP page is request necessary servlet code is generated and loaded in the servlet container. Now until the JSP page is not changed the compiled servlet code serves any request which comes from the browser. When you again change the JSP page the JSP engine again compiles a servlet code for the same.

√ JSP page is first initialized by jspInit() method. This initializes the JSP in much the same way as servlets are initialized, when the first request is intercepted and just after translation.

√ Every time a request comes to the JSP, the container generated _jspService() method is invoked, the request is processed, and response generated.

√ When the JSP is destroyed by the server, the jspDestroy() method is called and this can be used for clean up purposes.

(B) What is EL?

EL stands for expression language. An expression language makes it possible to easily access application data.In the below expression amountofwine variable value will be rendered.

There are ${amountofwine} litres of wine in the bottle.

(I) How does EL search for an attribute?

EL parser searches the attribute in following order:

√ Page

√ Request

√ Session (if it exists)

√ Application

If no match is found for then it displays empty string.

(B) What are the implicit EL objects in JSP?

Following are the implicit EL objects:

PageContext: The context for the JSP page.

Provides access to various objects for instance:

servletContext: The context for the JSP page's servlet and any web components contained in the same application.

session: The session object for the client.

request: The request triggering the execution of the JSP page.

response: The response returned by the JSP page. See Constructing Responses.

In addition, several implicit objects are available that allow easy access to the following objects:

param: Maps a request parameter name to a single value

paramValues: Maps a request parameter name to an array of values

header: Maps a request header name to a single value

headerValues: Maps a request header name to an array of values

cookie: Maps a cookie name to a single cookie

initParam: Maps a context initialization parameter name to a single value

Finally, there are objects that allow access to the various scoped variables described in Using Scope Objects.

pageScope: Maps page-scoped variable names to their values

requestScope: Maps request-scoped variable names to their values

sessionScope: Maps session-scoped variable names to their values

applicationScope: Maps application-scoped variable names to their values

For instance the below snippet will indentify the browser used by the client.

> Browser: ${header["user-agent"]}

(I)   How can we disable EL?

You can disable using isELIgnored attribute of the page directive:

> <%@ page isELIgnored ="true|false" %>

(I)   what is JSTL?

JSTL is also called as JSP tag libraries. They are collection of custom actions which can be accessed as JSP tags.

> *Note: In CD we have Jakarta tag libs jakarta-taglibs-standard-1.1.2.zip which you can use to practice sample tags and see how it works. When you unzip the file there are two files jstl.jar and standard.jar which you need to copy it in to your application's WEB-INF/lib directory.*

(A)   Can you explain in short what are the different types of JSTL tags are?

Tags are classified in to four groups:-

√   Core tags

√   Formatting tags

√   XML tags

√   SQL tags

Core tags

<c:if> for conditional flow

<c:forEach> and <c:forTokens> for iteration

<c:choose>...<c:when>....<c:otherwise> for selective flow between mutually exclusive code

<c:set> and <c:remove> for working with scoped variables

<c:out> for rendering the value of variables and expressions

<c:catch> for working with Java exceptions

<c:url> for creating and working with URLs

Formatting tags

Used to format and display text, the date, the time, and numbers. Below are some frequently used tags:

<fmt:formatNumber>: To render numerical value with specific precision or format

<fmt:formatDate>: To render date and time values in a specific format (and according to international locale-specific conventions)

<fmt:message>: To display an internationalized message (for example, a message in a different language using a different character set)

XML tags

XML tags are meant to process XML data. It supports data-parsing, transforming XML, plus data and flow control based on XPath expressions. These tags are used only when you need to work directly, within the JSP, with XML data.

SQL tags

They are designed to work directly with SQL tags. But most of the time you will see they are used for prototyping and not for final product.

Just before we move ahead with some other questions. Let's understand how to install JSTL so that everything works. Below are three installation steps:

√ Unzip "jakarta-taglibs-standard-1.1.2.zip" and you will see two files jstl.jar and standard.jar in lib directory.

√ Copy both jstl.jar and standard.jar to "\webapps\ROOT\WEB-INF\lib" directory in tomcat.

√ Copy all tld files from the unzipped location to \webapps\ROOT\WEB-INF" directory.

√ Modify the web.xml file to include all TLD files. Below is snippet of some tld's included in web.xml file.

```
<taglib>
        <taglib-uri>http://java.sun.com/jstl/fmt</taglib-uri>
        <taglib-location>/WEB-INF/fmt.tld</taglib-location>
        </taglib>
        <taglib>
        <taglib-uri>http://java.sun.com/jstl/fmt-rt</taglib-uri>
        <taglib-location>/WEB-INF/fmt-rt.tld</taglib-location>
</taglib>

<taglib>
        <taglib-uri>http://java.sun.com/jstl/core</taglib-uri>
        <taglib-location>/WEB-INF/c.tld</taglib-location>
</taglib>

<taglib>
        <taglib-uri>http://java.sun.com/jstl/core-rt</taglib-uri>
        <taglib-location>/WEB-INF/c-rt.tld</taglib-location>
</taglib>
```

```
<taglib>
      <taglib-uri>http://java.sun.com/jstl/sql</taglib-uri>
      <taglib-location>/WEB-INF/sql.tld</taglib-location>
</taglib>

<taglib>
      <taglib-uri>http://java.sun.com/jstl/sql-rt</taglib-uri>
      <taglib-location>/WEB-INF/sql-rt.tld</taglib-location>
</taglib>

<taglib>
      <taglib-uri>http://java.sun.com/jstl/x</taglib-uri>
      <taglib-location>/WEB-INF/x.tld</taglib-location>
</taglib>

<taglib>
      <taglib-uri>http://java.sun.com/jstl/x-rt</taglib-uri>
      <taglib-location>/WEB-INF/x-rt.tld</taglib-location>
</taglib>
```

(I)   How can we use beans in JSP?

JSP provides three tags to work with beans:

√   <jsp:useBean id="bean name" class="bean class" scope = "page | request | session |application "/>

Bean name = the name that refers to the bean.

Bean class = name of the java class that defines the bean.

√   <jsp:setProperty name = "id" property = "someProperty" value = "someValue" />

id = the name of the bean as specified in the useBean tag.

property = name of the property to be passed to the bean.

value = value of that particular property .

√   <jsp:getProperty name = "id" property = "someProperty" />

Here the property is the name of the property whose value is to be obtained from the bean.Below is a code snippet which shows how MyUserClass is used and the values accessed.

```
<jsp:useBean id="user" class="MyUserClass" scope="session"/>
<HTML>
<BODY>
You entered<BR>
Name: <%= user.getUsername() %><BR>
Email: <%= user.getEmail() %><BR>
</BODY>
</HTML>
```

(I)   What is the use of <jsp:include> ?

It includes the output of one JSP in to other JSP file at the location of the tag.

Below is the syntax for the same:

    <jsp:include page="...url.." flush="true or false"/>

page: A URL that is relative to the current JSP page at request time

flush: Determines if the buffer for the output is flushed immediately, before the included page's output.

(I)   What is <jsp:forward> tag for ?

It forwards the current request to another JSP page. Below is the syntax for the same:

    <jsp:forward page="...url..." />

We can also forward parameter to the other page using the param tag

```
<jsp:forward page="..url...">
    <jsp:param ..../>
</jsp:forward>
```

(B)   What are JSP directives?

JSP directives do not produce any output. They are used to set global values like class declaration, content type etc. Directives have scope for entire JSP file. They start with <%@ and ends with %>. There are three main directives that can be used in JSP:

√   page directive

√   include directive

√   taglib directive

(I)   what are Page directives?

Page directive is used to define page attributes the JSP file. Below is a sample of the same:

    <%@ page language="Java" import="java.rmi.*,java.util.*" session="true" buffer="12kb"
    autoFlush="true" errorPage="error.jsp" %>

To summarize some of the important page attributes:

import: Comma separated list of packages or classes, just like import statements in usual Java code.

session: Specifies whether this page can use HTTP session. If set "true" session (which refers to the javax.servlet.http.HttpSession) is available and can be used to access the current/new session for the page. If "false", the page does not participate in a session and the implicit session object is unavailable.

buffer: If a buffer size is specified (such as "50kb") then output is buffered with a buffer size not less than that value.

isThreadSafe: Defines the level of thread safety implemented in the page. If set "true" the JSP engine may send multiple client requests to the page at the same time. If "false" then the JSP engine queues up client requests sent to the page for processing, and processes them one request at a time, in the order they were received. This is the same as implementing the javax.servlet.SingleThreadModel interface in a servlet.

errorPage: Defines a URL to another JSP page, which is invoked if an unchecked runtime exception is thrown. The page implementation catches the instance of the Throwable object and passes it to the error page processing.

(I)   what are include directives?

The include directive informs the JSP engine to include the content of the resource in the current JSP page. Below is the syntax for include statement.

        <%@ include file="Filename" %>

Below is a code snippet which shows include directive in action

```
<html>
<head>
      <title>Directive in action</title>
      </head>
      <%@ include file="/companyname.html" %>
      <body>
      <h1>Directive in action</h1>
</body>
</html>
```

companyname.html contains the following:

        <p>Koirala and Koirala Limited</p>

(I)   Can you explain taglib directives?

Taglib are also termed as JSP tag extensions. They provide a way of encapsulating reusable functionality on JSP pages. One of the biggest drawbacks of scripting environments such as JSP is that it's easy to get carried away without thinking about how it will be maintained and grown in the future. For example, the ability to generate dynamic content by using Java code embedded in the page is a very powerful feature of the JSP specification. Custom tags allow such functionality to be encapsulated into reusable components. You can make write your reusable class in JAVA and call the same using XML tag.

There are four files which play an important role:

√   Main class file which encapsulates the logic.

√   Tag library descriptor file.

√   Web.xml file which has the tag library descriptor file location.

√   Finally the JSP file which calls it.

Below is the image which shows the four files in one go.

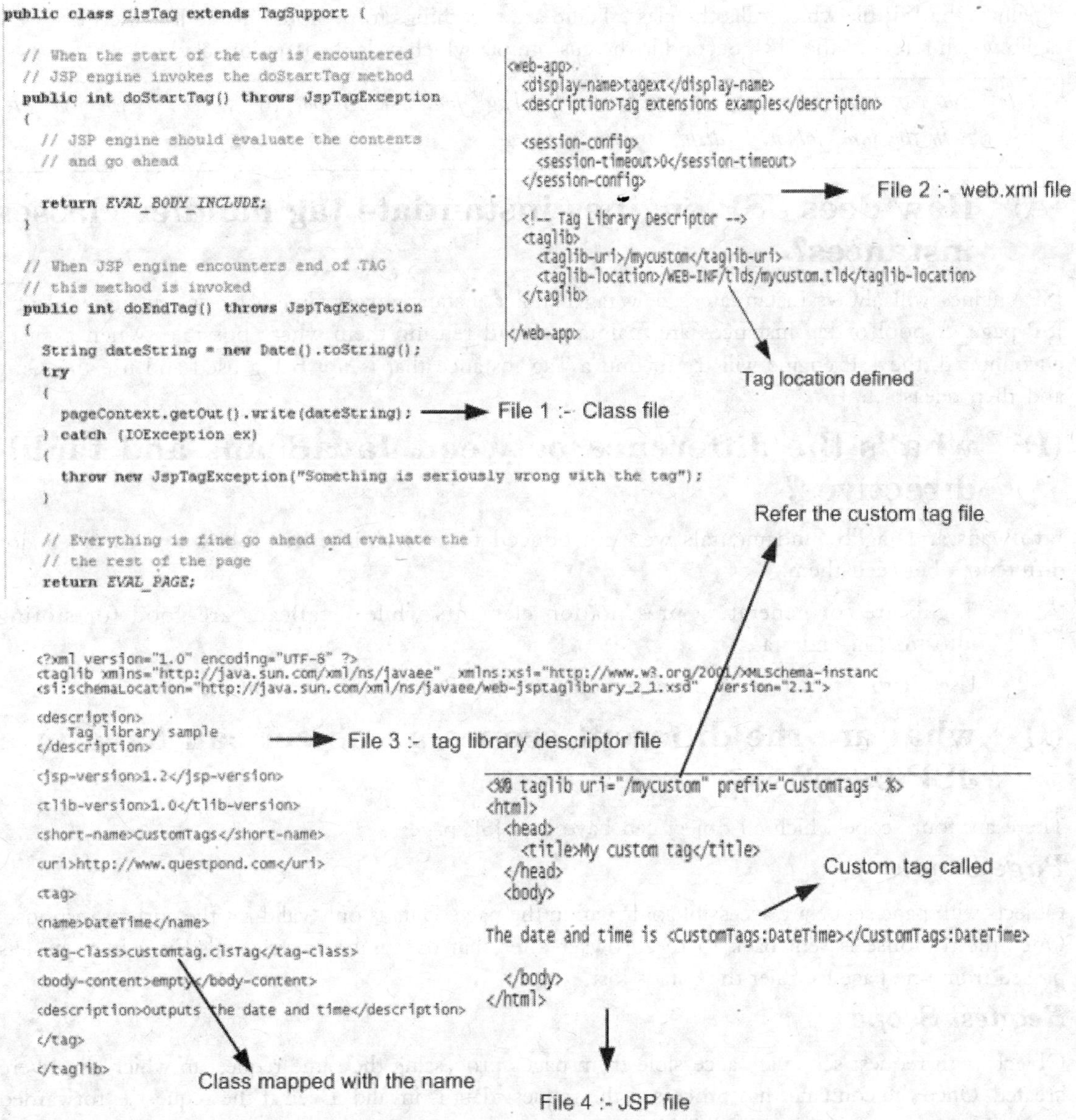

```
public class clsTag extends TagSupport {

    // When the start of the tag is encountered
    // JSP engine invokes the doStartTag method
    public int doStartTag() throws JspTagException
    {
        // JSP engine should evaluate the contents
        // and go ahead

        return EVAL_BODY_INCLUDE;
    }

    // When JSP engine encounters end of TAG
    // this method is invoked
    public int doEndTag() throws JspTagException
    {
        String dateString = new Date().toString();
        try
        {
            pageContext.getOut().write(dateString);       ──────▶  File 1 :- Class file
        } catch (IOException ex)
        {
            throw new JspTagException("Something is seriously wrong with the tag");
        }

        // Everything is fine go ahead and evaluate the
        // the rest of the page
        return EVAL_PAGE;
```

```
<web-app>
    <display-name>tagext</display-name>
    <description>Tag extensions examples</description>

    <session-config>
        <session-timeout>0</session-timeout>
    </session-config>                                  ──────▶  File 2 :- web.xml file

    <!-- Tag Library Descriptor -->
    <taglib>
        <taglib-uri>/mycustom</taglib-uri>
        <taglib-location>/WEB-INF/tlds/mycustom.tld</taglib-location>
    </taglib>

</web-app>
```

Tag location defined

Refer the custom tag file

```
<?xml version="1.0" encoding="UTF-8" ?>
<taglib xmlns="http://java.sun.com/xml/ns/javaee"  xmlns:xsi="http://www.w3.org/2001/XMLSchema-instance"
<si:schemaLocation="http://java.sun.com/xml/ns/javaee/web-jsptaglibrary_2_1.xsd"  version="2.1">

<description>
    Tag library sample          ──────▶  File 3 :- tag library descriptor file
</description>

<jsp-version>1.2</jsp-version>

<tlib-version>1.0</tlib-version>

<short-name>CustomTags</short-name>

<uri>http://www.questpond.com</uri>

<tag>

<name>DateTime</name>

<tag-class>customtag.clsTag</tag-class>

<body-content>empty</body-content>

<description>Outputs the date and time</description>

</tag>

</taglib>
```

Class mapped with the name

```
<%@ taglib uri="/mycustom" prefix="CustomTags" %>
<html>
    <head>
        <title>My custom tag</title>
    </head>
    <body>
```
Custom tag called

```
The date and time is <CustomTags:DateTime></CustomTags:DateTime>

    </body>
</html>
```

File 4 :- JSP file

Figure 4.16: taglib directive in action

The first file is the class file which will have the reusable code which will be called in the JSP file. The above class is also called as tag handler class. One of the important things to note is doStartTag() and doEndTag(). doStartTag is called when the JSP engine encounters an open tag and doEndTag is called when it encounters a closed tag.

The second important file is the tag descriptor file. This file maps the class name with a name which will be used to call this class.

The third file is the web.xml file. We need to define the tag library descriptor file location in web.xml file.

Finally is the JSP file which calls the class. There are two things to be noted in the JSP file first is the taglib which refers to the URI. Second is the custom tag which calls the datetime class.

> *Note: You can find the above code sample in "JspTag" folder. Both the class as well as the JSP file is in the same folder. It displays date and time.*

(A) How does JSP engines instantiate tag handler classes instances?

JSP engines will always instantiate a new tag handler instance every time a tag is encountered in a JSP page. A pool of tag instances are maintained and reusing them where possible. When a tag is encountered, the JSP engine will try to find a Tag instance that is not being used and use the same and then release it.

(I) what's the difference between JavaBeans and taglib directives?

JavaBeans and taglib fundamentals were introduced for reusability. But following are the major differences between them:

√   Taglib are for generating presentation elements while JavaBeans are good for storing information and state.

√   Use custom tags to implement actions and JavaBeans to present information.

(I) what are the different scopes an object can have in a JSP page?

There are four scope which an object can have in a JSP page:

Page Scope

Objects with page scope are accessible only within the page. Data is only valid for the current response. Once the response is sent back to the browser after that data is no more valid. Even if request is passed from one page to other the data is lost.

Request Scope

Objects with request scope are accessible from pages processing the same request in which they were created. Once the container has processed the request data is invalid. Even if the request is forwarded to another page, the data is still available.

Session Scope

Objects with session scope are accessible in same session. Session is the time users spend using the application, which ends when they close their browser or when they go to another Web site. So, for example, when users log in, their username could be stored in the session and displayed on every page they access. This data lasts until they leave the Web site or log out.

Application Scope

Application scope objects are basically global object and accessible to all JSP pages which lie in the same application. This creates a global object that's available to all pages. Application scope variables are typically created and populated when an application starts and then used as read-only for the rest of the application.

(I)   what are different implicit objects of JSP?

pageContext: The PageContext object.

pageScope: A Map of all the objects that have page scope.

requestScope: A Map of all the objects that have request scope.

sessionScope: A Map of all the objects that have session scope.

applicationScope: A Map of all the objects that have application scope.

param: A Map of all the form parameters that were passed to your JSP page (for example, the HTML <input name="ourName" type="text"/> is passed to your JSP page as a form parameter).

paramValues: HTML allows for multiple values for a single form parameter. This is a Map of all the parameters, just like param, but in this object the values are an array containing all of the values for a given parameter in the event that there's more than one.

header: A Map of all the request headers.

headerValues: For the same reasons as paramValues, a headerValues object is provided.

cookie: A Map of all the cookies passed to your JSP. The value returned is a Cookie object.

initParam: A Map that maps context initialization parameter names to their parameter values.

(I)   what are different Authentication Options available in servlets?

There are four ways of authentication:

√   HTTP basic authentication

√   HTTP digest authentication

√   HTTPS client authentication

√   Form-based authentication

Let's try to understand how the above four ways work.

HTTP basic authentication

In HTTP basic authentication the server uses the username and password send by the client. The password is sent using simple base64 encoding but it's not encrypted.

HTTP digest authentication

HTTP digest authentication is same as HTTP basic authentication but the biggest difference is password is encrypted and transmitted using SHA or MD5.

HTTPS client authentication

HTTPS client authentication is based on HTTP over SSL. It requires that the end client should possess a PKC (Public Key Certificate). This verifies the browsers identity.

Form-based authentication

In FORM-based the web container invokes a login page. The invoked login page is used to collect username and password.

We will be seeing how to implement the above four using tomcat.

(A)   Can you explain how do we practically implement security on a resource?

(A)   How do we practically implement form based authentication?

Note: We will answer this question from the perspective of tomcat server.

```xml
<web-app>

        <welcome-file-list>
                <welcome-file>index.html</welcome-file>
        </welcome-file-list>

        <security-constraint>

                <web-resource-collection>
                        <web-resource-name>SecurePages</web-resource-name>
                        <description>Security constraint for resources in the secur
                        <url-pattern>/secure/*</url-pattern>
                        <http-method>POST</http-method>
                        <http-method>GET</http-method>
                </web-resource-collection>

                <auth-constraint>
                        <description>only let the system user login </description>
                        <role-name>admin</role-name>
                </auth-constraint>

                <user-data-constraint>
                        <description>SSL not required</description>
                        <transport-guarantee>NONE</transport-guarantee>
                </user-data-constraint>

        </security-constraint>
        <login-config>
                <auth-method>FORM</auth-method>
                <form-login-config>
                        <form-login-page>/LoginForm.html</form-login-page>
                        <form-error-page>/LoginError.html</form-error-page>
                </form-login-config>
        </login-config>
        <security-role>
                <description>The Secure ROLE</description>
                <role-name>admin</role-name>
        </security-role>

</web-app>


        <tomcat-users>
          <role rolename="tomcat"/>
          <role rolename="role1"/>
          <role rolename="manager"/>
          <role rolename="admin"/>
          <user username="tomcat" password="tomcat" roles="tomcat"/>
          <user username="role1" password="tomcat" roles="role1"/>
          <user username="both" password="tomcat" roles="tomcat,role1"/>
          <user username="interviewer" password="interviewer" roles="admin"/>
          <user username="admin" password="" roles="admin,manager"/>
        </tomcat-users>
```

Figure 4.17: Authentication steps in Web.xml

Below are the five important steps to implement security on a resource.

√   Define the URL pattern on which security will be applied.

√   Define the roles which are allowed to access the resource.

√   Define all the roles in the web application.

√   Define the authentication method.

√   Relate the users with roles.

We will try to understand the above steps in more detail using the figure above. In the above figure you can see the sequence of steps.

Define the URL pattern on which security will be applied

In this step we define the resource which we want to protect. This is defined in the web.xml file as shown in the figure above. In the <url-pattern> we have defined secure as the web application.

Define the roles which are allowed to access the resource

In step 2 we define which roles are allowed to access the resource. You can see in the above figure it's done by using <auth-constraint> tag in web.xml.

Define all the roles in the web application

In step 3 we define roles for the web application. We also need to mention the security role in <security-role>. Just a note the <auth-constraint> element specifies that application users must also be in the role of "Admin", and the <security-role> element defines that role.

Define the authentication method

This is the most important part defining which type of authentication we want to use. It's defined by using the <auth-method> tag. In this scenario we are using FORM authentication. You can also see sub tags <form-login-config> which define the main login page and the error page.

Relate the users with roles

Finally we need to define the actual users which can be attached to the roles. In the above figure you can see we have "interviewer" as user which is attached to admin role. Users can be defined in tomcat-users.xml file.

> *Note: We have a sample application in formlogin folder which demonstrates how to execute the above steps practically. Copy the folder and paste it in webapps folder and execute the same to see how it works.*

(I)   How do we authenticate using JDBC?

(I)   Can you explain JDBCRealm?

A realm is a "database" of usernames, passwords, and user roles. When we say JDBCrealm we mean all these attributes are stored in table. In order to connect to JDBC you need to make a context.xml and save the same in "META-INF "folder of the web application. Below is the context.xml snippet.

```
<Context path="/security" docBase="security" debug="0">
    <Realm className="org.apache.catalina.realm.JDBCRealm" debug="99"
```

```
       driverName="com.mysql.jdbc.Driver"
       connectionURL="jdbc:mysql://localhost:3306/
       security?autoReconnect=true"
       connectionName="MyConn"
       connectionPassword="Password1"
       userTable="tblusers"
       userNameCol="username"
       userCredCol="password"
       userRoleTable="user_roles"
       roleNameCol="role_name" />
</Context>
```

(A)   Can you explain how do you configure JNDIRealm?

Left to the users ? . That's because it's rarely asked but yes it's asked.

(I)   How did you implement caching in JSP?

OSCache is an open-source caching library that's available free of charge from the OpenSymphony organization (for more details visit http://www.opensymphony.com/oscache). OSCache has a set of JSP tags that make it easy to implement page caching in your JSP application.

Following are some Cache techniques it fulfills:

Cache entry

An object that's stored into a page cache is known as a cache entry. In a JSP application, a cache entry is typically the output of a JSP page, a portion of a JSP page, or a servlet.

Cache key

A page cache is like a hash table. When you save a cache entry in a page cache, you must provide a cache key to identify the cache data. You can use keys like URI, other parameters like username, ipaddress to indentify cache data.

Cache duration

This is the period of time that a cache entry will remain in a page cache before it expires. When a cache entry expires, it's removed from the cache and will be regenerated again.

Cache scope

This defines at what scope the data is stored application or session scope.

```
<os:cache time="60">
     <%= new java.util.Date().toString() %></p>
</os:cache>
```

The above tag says that refresh after every 60 seconds the user requests data. So if user1 is requesting the page it will display fresh date and if an other user requests with in 60 seconds it will show same data. If any other user requests the page after 60 second he will again see refreshed date.

(B) What is the difference between Servletcontext and ServletConfig ?

ServletConfig contains configuration data for the servlet in the form of name and value pairs.Using the ServletConfigwe get reference to the ServletContext object. ServletContext gives the servlet access to information about its runtime environment such as web server logging facilities, version info, URL details, web server attributes etc.

(I) How do we prevent browser from caching output of my JSP pages?

You can prevent pages from caching JSP pages output using the below code snippet.

```
<%response.setHeader("Cache-Control","no-cache"); //HTTP 1.1
response.setHeader("Pragma","no-cache"); //HTTP 1.0
response.setDateHeader ("Expires", 0); //prevents caching at the proxy
server
%>
```

(I) Can we explicitly destroy a servlet object?

No we can not destroy a servlet explicitly its all done by the container. Even if you try calling the destroy method container does not respond to it.

5

EJB

(B) What is EJB?

As JAVA became popular and many developers started developing there business logic in JAVA and in order to manage these business components /logic properly they started having there own application servers. Looking at the growth and importance of business components many vendors started floating there own application servers. These application servers dictated there own communication protocol to the business components. Due to which when the business components had to change application server they had to be modified and changed according to new protocol of application server.

EJB is a standard for building server side components in JAVA. It specifies an agreement between components and application servers that enables any component to run in any application server. EJB components are deployable and can be imported in to an application server which hosts these components. EJB are not intended for client side they are server side components. They are specially meant for complex server side operations like executing complex algorithms or high volume business transactions.

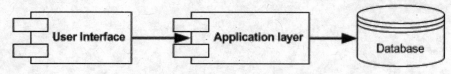

Figure 5.1: Basic three tier architecture

Above is the most popular architecture in software industry. Three tier architecture has many advantages but the most important of them is that you can change any layer with least changes. For instance you can change the business logic with out making changes to UI or the database side. EJB provides the application layer logic. Application layer logic is also called as middle tier. EJB provides a standard specifications-based way to develop and deploy enterprise-class systems. It's like moving towards an actually thought JAVA dream that we can run on any vendor platform. This is in contrast to the vendor-specific way we used to develop where each application server had its own way of doing things and where the developer was tied up to a application server.

(I) What are the different kind of EJB's?

There are three kinds of EJB's:

Session beans

Session beans are construct in EJB. They represent business logic of an application. They represent a group of logical related functionality. For instance you can have a customer session bean which can have functionality like customer interest calculation, customer reporting, customer tax calculation etc. But as these functionalities logically belong to customer they will be included in the customer session bean. In short session bean has business logic.

There are two types of session beans:

Stateless: they do not maintain state across method calls. So every time client makes a call it's like a new object from scratch.

Stateful: These beans can hold client state across method invocations. This is possible with the use of instance variables declared in the class definition. Every time the client calls it they can get there previous states.

Stateless session bean provide greater scalability as EJB container does not have to maintain state across method invocations. Storing state for EJB container is huge activity.

Entity beans

Entity bean represent persistent data in an EJB application. They provide object-oriented abstraction to a relational database. When Session bean needs to access data it calls the entity beans. Entity beans do read, write, update and delete from tables. For instance you have a customer table then you will have customer entity bean which maps to the table and can do the CRUD (Create, Read, Update and Delete) operation to the customer table. From architecture angle you can think entity bean as the data access layer of a system.

Message-driven beans

There are situations in project where you would like to communicate asynchronously with some other systems. This is achieved by using message-driven beans. For instance when user places order you would like to submit it asynchronously to the order system and then move ahead with some other work. You would then later comeback after sometime to see if the order is completely or the order system will notify you about the completion of the order.

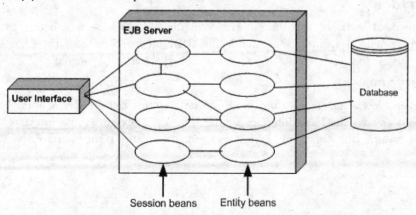

Figure 5.2: Session and Entity beans in action

Above figure will give a complete view of how session and entity beans are placed in architecture. User interface interacts with session beans. Session beans actually contain the business logic. You can see from the above figure session bean can interact with other session beans to fulfill certain business functionality. For instance a customer session bean will interact with an Account session bean to get accounts related to that customer. But session bean never interact with database directly. In order to interact with database they go through the entity beans. Entity beans represent a persistent data in EJB and they are mainly responsible for any interaction with database.

(I) you are designing architecture for a project how do you decide whether you should use session, entity or message driven bean?

In the previous question we have answered this question. But we will just revise the points:-

√   Session beans should only implement business logic and work flow.

√   Entity beans are data objects and represent persistent data. They are only responsible to do database activities like add, update and delete

√   Message-driven beans are used for receiving asynchronous messages from other systems.

As project moves on developers get carried away by putting business logic in to entity beans and some times session beans directly communicating with database. Many a time's programmers tempt to connect UI directly to entity beans which are again a bad practice. With this practice we will be pushing more business logic to the UI. All the above three beans have there roles defined and should be strictly adhered.

(A) Can you explain "EJBHome" and "EJBObject" in EJB?

(I) Can client directly create object of session or entity beans?

No client can not directly create object of session, entity or message driven beans. Ok let's try to get in to depth of how session and entity beans can be accessed by end clients. There are two important interfaces which needs to be used in order that we can create and use session, entity and message driven bean objects:

Bean Interface

Client uses the Bean interface to communicate with the session bean which resides on the EJB application server. The Bean interface extends the EJBObject interface of the javax.ejb package. This interface has all the methods, functions which the final session bean has.

Home Interface

In order the client gets a reference to the Bean interface it must call the Beans home interface. The Home interface extends EJBHome interface of the javax.ejb package. Home Interface of a bean is responsible for creating the object and giving the reference of the Bean interface.

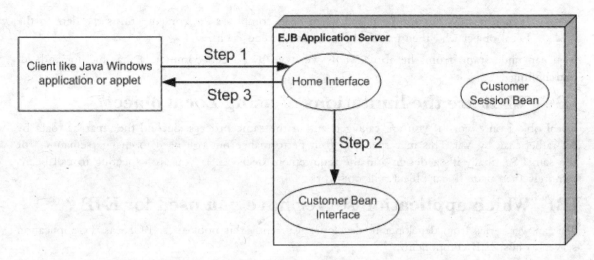

Figure 5.3: Home and Bean Interface in action

Above figure depicts the complete flow of how the Java application or the Java client gets a reference of the customer bean interface. Step1 Java application calls the home interface to get a reference of customer session object. Home interface then creates an object of customer session bean which can be referenced by using customer bean interface. Finally step 3 java clients gets reference of the customer session bean object through customer bean interface.

> *Note:* *During interview when you are explaining the fundamental draw the above diagram on a piece of paper and explain the fundamental to the interviewer. It will surely impress the interviewer.*

(B) Can you explain the concept of local interfaces?

On of the biggest issues of creating objects using home interface is performance. Below are the steps to follow when you call the EJB object:

√   JAVA client calls the local stub.

√   Stub Marshal's the values in to some other form which the network understands and sends it to the skeleton.

√   Skeleton then de-marshals it back to a form which is suitable for JAVA.

√   Skeleton then calls the EJB object and methods.

√   EJB object then does object creation, connection pooling, transaction etc.

√   Once EJB object calls the bean and the bean completes its functionalities. All the above steps must again be repeated to reach back to the JAVA client.

So you can easily guess from the above step that its lot of work. But this has been improved in EJB 2.0 using Local objects. Local objects implement local interface rather than using remote interface. Just to have a comparison below are the steps how the local object works.

√   JAVA client calls the local object.

√   Local object does connection pooling, transactions and security.

√   It then passes calls the bean and when bean completes its work it returns the data to the Local object who then passes the same to the end client.

You can understand from the above steps we have by passed completely marshalling and de-marshalling.

(B)   What are the limitations of using Local object?

Local object only work if you are calling beans in the same process. Second they marshal data by ref rather than by Val. This may speed up your performance but you need to change semantics for the same. So finally it's a design and the requirement decision. If you are expecting to call beans remotely then using local object will not work.

(B)   Which application server have you used for EJB ?

This answer varies from developer to developer. Currently this book uses JBOSS as the application server to host EJB components.

> *Note: Before we move ahead lets make sure that you can run JBOSS properly. Below are the steps to make sure that your JBOSS is running properly.*

√   Unzip "jboss-4.0.4.GA" which is provided in the CD.

√   Set you environment variable JBOSS_HOME to the directory where you have unzipped your JBOSS. You can see in the figure below it's unzipped to "C:\JBOSS\jboss-4.0.4.GA".

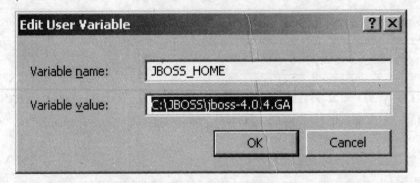

Figure 5.4: Set the environment variable JBOSS_HOME

√   Run the MS-DOS batch file from the "bin" directory. You can see from the figure below "Started" indicates that JBOSS is running successfully. In case you get socket error do make sure that no other web server is running on the PC. If it is then make sure it runs on some other port.

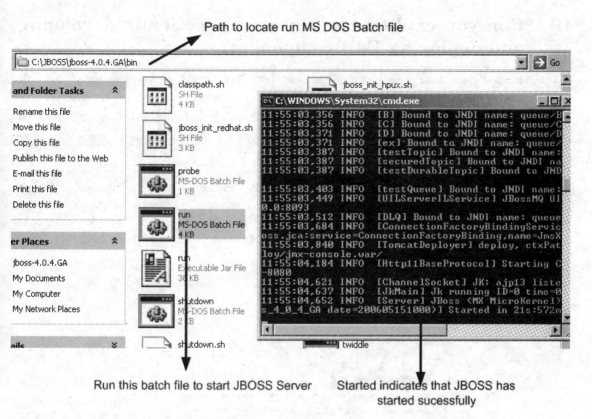

Path to locate run MS DOS Batch file

Run this batch file to start JBOSS Server   Started indicates that JBOSS has
started sucessfully

Figure 5.5: JBOSS running successfully

√   Finally once JBOSS is running you can make sure by running the below URL on browser.

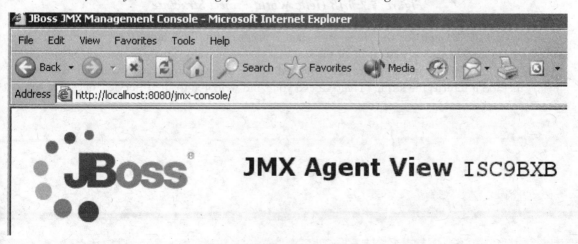

Figure 5.6: The JMX console

(I)   Can you explain step by step practically developing and deploying EJB component?

> Note: *We will take a bit to answer this question. This question will be asked to test if you have really practically worked with EJB. So we will just run through a sample project using JBOSS. During interview you do not really need to explain all the steps but just consolidate the below explanation. Second answers will vary according to the application server you are using in your project.*

We will create a simple component which will have a "hello" method. The "hello" method will display "Hello to Every one and Welcome to Interview Question Series". First step is to create the project with the three objects Bean, Client and Home. Below is the "Hello" project view. You can get the source code from the CD in "Source Code\EJB" directory. Also please note the reference to "jboss-j2ee.jar" file which is needed to compile EJB projects.

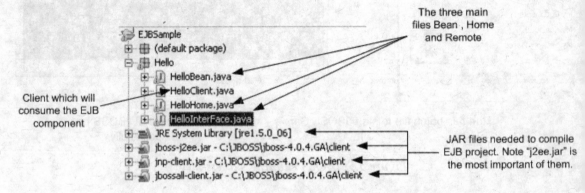

Figure 5.7: EJB Hello World Project Structure

Let's make a walk through for the three important objects Hello, Bean and Home object. Let's start with the bean class. As said previously all the bean classes should implement. "javax.ejb.SessionBean" class. All the "ejb" prefix methods are implemented in the below source code. You can also see the "hello" method it returns the string "Hello to everyone and welcome to the Interview question series".

```
public class HelloBean implements javax.ejb.SessionBean
{
    private SessionContext ctx;

    public void ejbCreate() {
        System.out.println("You are inside ejbCreate()");
    }

    public void ejbRemove() {
        System.out.println("You are inside ejbRemove()");
    }

    public void ejbActivate() {
        System.out.println("You are inside ejbActivate()");
    }

    public void ejbPassivate() {
        System.out.println("You are inside ejbPassivate()");
    }

    public void setSessionContext(javax.ejb.SessionContext ctx) {
        this.ctx = ctx;
    }

    public String hello()
    {
        return "Hello to everyone and welcome to the Interview question series";
    }
}
```

Figure 5.8: HelloBean class

Now that we have our core bean class. We need to define the remote interface and Home interface. Remote interface will be used by the end client to reference the session bean object. Home object will create the object of session bean and give a the reference of the interface.

```
package Hello;
import java.rmi.RemoteException;
public interface HelloInterFace extends javax.ejb.EJBObject
{
    public String hello() throws java.rmi.RemoteException;
}
```
← Remote interface which will be referred by the client

```
package Hello;
import javax.ejb.EJBHome;
import javax.ejb.CreateException;
import java.rmi.RemoteException;

public interface HelloHome extends javax.ejb.EJBHome
{
    Hello.HelloInterFace create() throws
                    java.rmi.RemoteException,
                    javax.ejb.CreateException;
}
```
← EJBHome object which is responsible for creating the objects

Figure 5.9: Remote and Home object

Once our three objects are defined compile them to ensure that there are no errors. In order to deploy an EJB component we need to define the "ejb-jar.xml". Below is the snippet of the file. You can see the entries of the three objects.

```
<!DOCTYPE ejb-jar PUBLIC "-//Sun Microsystems, Inc.//DTD Enterprise JavaBeans 2.0//EN"
"http://java.sun.com/dtd/ejb-jar_2_0.dtd">
<ejb-jar>
    <display-name>Hello</display-name>
    <enterprise-beans>
        <session>
                <display-name>Hello</display-name>
                <ejb-name>Hello</ejb-name>
                <home>Hello.HelloHome</home>
                <remote>Hello.HelloInterFace</remote>
                <ejb-class>Hello.HelloBean</ejb-class>
                <session-type>Stateless</session-type>
                <transaction-type>Container</transaction-type>
        </session>
    </enterprise-beans>
</ejb-jar>
```

Figure 5.10: deployment file ejb-jar.xml

This step is not compulsory and varies depending on application server you are using. In this step we will just define a proper JNDI name for the "Hello" EJB objects. This file should be named as "jboss.xml".

```
<?xml version="1.0" encoding="UTF-8"?>
<jboss>
   <enterprise-beans>
     <session>
       <ejb-name>Hello</ejb-name>
       <jndi-name>hello/Hello</jndi-name>
     </session>
   </enterprise-beans>
</jboss>
```

Figure 5.11: JNDI name definition file jboss.xml

Now that we have all the basic steps defined we need to compile and deploy the project. So below is the ANT script which we can execute. In CD we have "apache-ant-1.6.5-bin.zip" in "CD\Software" which can be used to execute this script.

```
<project name="Deploying a ejb" default="jar" basedir=".">
<target name="init"
    description="Initializes properties that are used by the other targets. ">
        <tstamp/>
        <property name="build" value="/home/stateful" />
</target>
<target name="prepare" depends="init"
    description="Creates META-INF directory" >
        <echo message="Creating META-INF directory ..." />
        <mkdir dir="${build}/build/META-INF" />
</target>
<target name="compile" depends="prepare"
    description="Compiles source code">
        <echo message="Compiling source code ..."/>
        <javac
        srcdir="${build}"
        destdir="${build}/build"
        includes="*.java"/>
</target>
<target name="copy" depends="compile">
        <echo message="Copying ejb-jar.xml file to META-INF directory ..."/>
        <copy
        file="ejb-jar.xml"
        todir="${build}/build/META-INF"
        overwrite="yes"/>
</target>
        <target name="jar" depends="copy">
        <echo message="Creating JAR file "/>
        <jar destfile="C:\JBOSS\jboss-4.0.4.GA\server\default\deploy\Hello.jar"
        basedir="${build}/build"
        excludes="*.properties"/>
</target>
</project>
```

Figure 5.12 : ANT file for compiling and deploying

Now we are all set to deploy start the JBOSS server and run the ANT script. If everything is proper you will see something as shown below.

```
BUILD SUCCESSFUL
Total time: 1 second
C:\ANT\apache-ant-1.6.5\bin>ant.bat
Buildfile: build.xml

init:

prepare:
      [echo] Creating META-INF directory ...

compile:
      [echo] Compiling source code ...

copy:
      [echo] Copying ejb-jar.xml file to META-INF directory ...
      [copy] Copying 1 file to C:\home\stateful\build\META-INF

jar:
      [echo] Creating JAR file
      [jar] Building jar: C:\JBOSS\jboss-4.0.4.GA\server\default\dep
r

BUILD SUCCESSFUL
Total time: 2 seconds
C:\ANT\apache-ant-1.6.5\bin>
```

Figure 5.13 : ANT file showing success deployment

The script creates JAR file of all the classes and copies it to the JBOSS "\Server\Default\Deploy" folder. JBOSS picks up and start deploying the same. So as soon as you run the ANT script you can see the "Hello.jar" is deployed on the JBOSS console.

```
15:50:35,348 INFO  [EjbModule] Undeployed Hello
15:50:35,473 INFO  [EjbModule] Deploying Hello
15:50:35,504 INFO  [ProxyFactory] Bound EJB Home 'Hello' to jndi 'hello/Hello'
15:50:35,504 INFO  [EJBDeployer] Deployed: file:/C:/JBOSS/jboss-4.0.4.GA/server
default/deploy/Hello.jar
```

Figure 5.14 : JBOSS successfully deploying the components

Ok now the component is deployed its time to consume and see the output. So below is the client snippet which consumes the EJB object. Looking at the below figure you can understand what every step does.

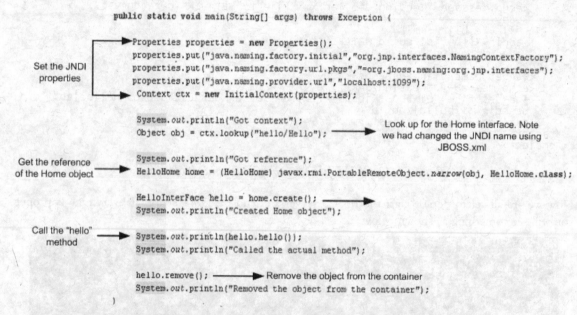

Figure 5.15: Client code consuming EJB objects.

Yeeeeea!!! If everything works then you should see something as shown below.

```
Console ✖
<terminated> HelloClient [Java Application] C:\Program Files\Java\jre1.5.0_06\bin\javaw.exe (Jun 25,
Got context
Got reference
Created Home object
Hello to everyone and welcome to the Interview question series
Called the actual method
Removed the object from the container
```

Figure 5.16: Output of Hello EJB

The above deployment which we have gone through is really a pain. Really do not know how many live projects use ANT for EJB deployment. But the basic reason to show using ANT was two folds first to understand what is ANT and second to know fundamentally how EJB deployment happens. In big size projects it's advisable to use "JBOSS Eclipse IDE". You can get the same in "Software" folder by name "JBossIDE-1.6.0.GA-Bundle-win32.zip". As this is an interview question book we are not going in detail of how to use the IDE. But you can use the same and get hands on the same.

The above steps as said before are just to make your fundamentals clear. The interviewer just wants to hear the following and you probably have a million dollar appointment letter in your hand:-

√   Create Home, Remote and Session objects.

√   Create the deployment XML ejb-jar.xml. (Note JBOSS.XML is something for JBOSS and
         does not apply for other application servers)

√   Start your application server.

√   Deploy the three objects.

√   Create a client to consume the same.

(I)   what is Passivation and Activation in EJB?

When we are dealing with stateful session beans we need to store the client conversation of the bean so that it can be available in client's next request. But when we talk about server it has limited resources. If the conversation of the bean is large then the server can run out of resource. So in order to preserve resources EJB server swaps this conversational data in memory to hard disk thus allowing memory to be reclaimed. This process of saving the memory data to hard disk is called as "Passivation". Now when the client comes back the conversational data is again swapped from the hard disk to the bean. This process is called as "Activation". The container informs the bean that its about to passivate or activate using the "ejbPassivate()" and "ejbActivate()" methods.

(I)   Can beans who are involved in transaction have
"Passivation" process?

No.

(A)   How does the server decide which beans to passivate
and activate?

Most servers use the (LRU) Last Recently Used time as a strategy. Which mean passivate the beans which have been called recently.

(A)   In what format is the conversational data written to the
disk?

Bean conversational data is saved in the disk as serialized object. This is possible because "javax.ejb.EnterpriseBean" implements "java.io.Serializable" interface. So during passivation time it converts the bean conversational data to a bit-blob and during activation it just reverses the process.

(B)   Can you explain in brief Life cycle for Stateless and Stateful beans?

Life cycle for stateless session beans

√   When the application server is not started or just starting there are no instances of beans.

√   EJB Container looks in to the pooling policy and instantiates new beans accordingly. For instance if the pooling policy says to create a pool of 10 object it will create accordingly.

√   Container instantiates the bean using "Class.newInstance("MyBean.class").

√   After the object is created EJB container calls the "setSessionContext()" to set the context object so that bean can make a call back to the container if it ever needs to.

√   Container then calls "ejbCreate()" method and this initializes you bean. Just a note to make when a client makes a new object or destroys an EJB object. It's not necessary that EJB container will do it instantly. It will decide depending on policies that whether it should really destroy this object or move it pool or should not create an object and take one from the pool.

√   Finally container makes calls to the business methods of the bean. All the business methods are called depending on the client makes calls. All the method calls are treated in the same way as session beans are in the same state after the method call. When a request comes in from client1 the container can take bean1 from the pool process the request and bring bean1 to a previous state. Later when again client1 calls container can take bean2 process the request and bring bean2 to the previous state. So the object treats every request as a new request and does not care to save the previous data of the request.

√   Finally when the container is about the remove the object it calls the "ejbRemove()" of the bean.

Life cycle of stateful session beans

Life cycle of the stateful session beans is same as stateless only leaving the below points:

√   First as its stateful there is no pool of objects.

√   Second with every client call there are "ejbPassivate" and "ejbActivate" methods to save and retain the conversational state.

6

Struts

(I) What's MVC pattern?

> *Note: The base of struts is MVC so let's try to understand struts concept first then move on to the actual implementation.*

The main purpose of using MVC pattern is to decouple the GUI from the Data. It also gives the ability to provide multiple views for the same Data. MVC pattern separates objects into three important sections:

Model: This section is specially for maintaining data. It is actually where your business logic, querying database, database connection etc. is actually implemented.

Views: Displaying all or some portion of data, or probably different view of data. View is responsible for look and feel, Sorting, formatting etc.

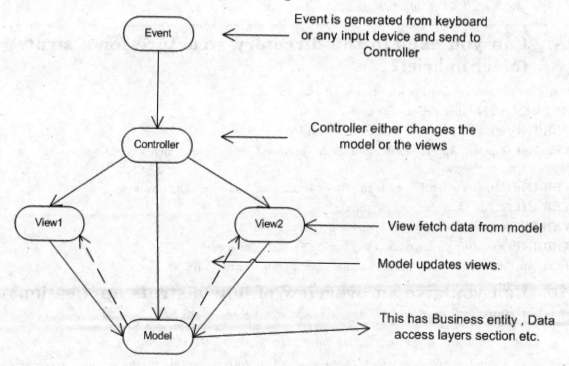

Figure 6.1: MVC Architecture

Controller: They are event handling section which affects either the model or the view. Controller responds to the mouse or keyboard input to command model and view to change. Controllers are associated with views. User interaction triggers the events to change the model, which in turn calls some methods of model to update its state to notify other registered views to refresh their display.

(B)   Define struts?

Struts are an open source framework for developing JAVA web applications. It extends Java Servlets API and helps developers to adopt MVC architecture. MVC pattern is good but developing the same can be real pain. Using struts it's a breeze to implement MVC in projects. Struts provide a standard way of implementing MVC.

Note: In CD we have the struts zip which can be very handy for practicing struts. You can install the apache tomcat provided in this CD and copy "struts-blank.war" from struts unzipped folder to "Tomcat 5.5\webapps\" folder. Just to check if struts is running you can test it by hitting http://localhost:8080/struts-blank/Welcome.do URL. You should get the welcome message "To get started on your own application, copy the struts-blank.war to a new WAR file using the name for your application. Place it in your container's "webapp" folder (or equivalent), and let your container auto-deploy the application. Edit the skeleton configuration files as needed, restart your container and you are on your way! (You can find the application.properties file with this message in the /WEB-INF/src/java/resources folder.)". That means you are all set to practice struts.

(A)   Can you explain the directory structure for a struts folder in brief?

Below are the folders from point of view of root folder.

META-INF: This directory has the Meta information.

WEB-INF/classes: This location has the actual JAVA classes.

WEB-INF/classes/ApplicationResources.properties: Contains text which application can use. For instance error messages.

WEB-INF/lib/struts.jar: Contains the Struts servlet, helper classes, taglib code etc.

WEB-INF/*.tld: The Struts tag libraries.

WEB-INF/struts-config.xml: A Struts configuration file.

WEB-INF/web.xml: Configuration file for the servlet container

Index.jsp: All JSP files come in the root directory as this one Index.jsp.

(I)   Can you give an overview of how a struts application flows?

Twist: What are action and action form classes in Struts?

Let's make a simple application which uses struts and try to get what are the basic things required. During interview you do not need to explain to such greater details but you can summarize the same. This will be a damn simple program which actually converts numbers to words. That means if type 1 we get "One" as the output, for "2" we get "Two" etc. We will restrict only till value "10".

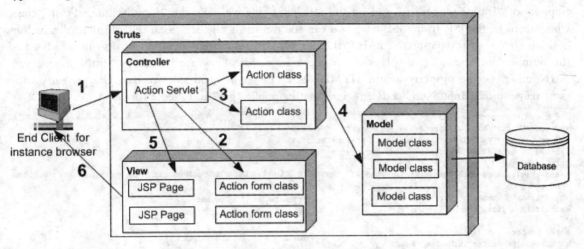

Figure 6.2: Flow of a Struts Application

Before we proceed ahead lets see the basic components which will make a struts application. In the above figure we also have the execution order of the components. You can see the three important sections:

View: This is the view of the application so it has JSP pages and the corresponding action form class pages for the JSP pages. Action form classes are class representation of the JSP page data. When we browse through the sample you will get in to what we are talking, for now just remember that they are class data representation of the JSP pages.

Controller: This is the heart of the struts framework. They form the bridge between model classes and View. Action classes take Action form objects and model class object to perform the required functionality.

Model: Model classes encapsulate the business logic and data access routines.

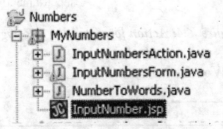

Figure 6.3 : Our Sample Struts project

Above shown is the explorer snap which has all the necessary files which will create our sample struts application. You can find the complete application in "\Source Code\Struts" folder. It has two folders "Numbers" and "myProject". The "Numbers" folder has all the classes which are needed and the "myProject" folder is the complete struts structure folder which you can paste in "webapps" folder of Tomcat. Below is the way MVC mapping is done to the physical files in the struts project.

View ("InputNumber.jsp" and "InputNumbersForm.java").

"InputNumber.jsp" is the page which will collect data from the end user. You can see below code snippets of "InputNumber.jsp" and on the left hand side we have the "InputNumbersForm" class which maps to the JSP. In the JSP page you can see the struts tags for instance "<html:text" which is nothing but "<input type=text>" in HTML. Currently there are only two text boxes one which takes the number and the other displays the number in words. They are named as "intNumber" and "strNumber" in the property of the HTML tag. In the right hand side we have the property with same name in the "InputNumbersForm" class with a public "get" and "set" property.

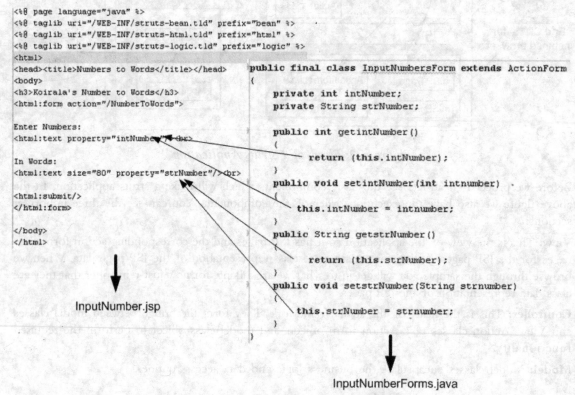

Figure 6.4: Action form and the JSP page

Koirala's Number to Words

Enter Numbers: 7

In Words: Seven

Submit

Figure 6.5: JSP page in action

After we run the JSP page it would look something like above. You can see user had entered "7" and is displayed in words as "Seven".

Model class ("NumberToWords.java")

```
public class NumberToWords{
ArrayList resultList = new ArrayList();
    // Fill all the numbers in to a arraylist with.
    // corresponding word mapping
    public NumberToWords()
    {   resultList.add(new String("Zero"));
        resultList.add(new String("One"));
        resultList.add(new String("Two"));
        resultList.add(new String("Three"));
        resultList.add(new String("Four"));
        resultList.add(new String("Five"));
        resultList.add(new String("Six"));
        resultList.add(new String("Seven"));
        resultList.add(new String("Eight"));
        resultList.add(new String("Nine"));
        resultList.add(new String("Ten"));}
    // Lookup function which return the word
    public String GetWords(int intnumber)
    {   String strRet = "";
        try
        {strRet = resultList.get(intnumber).toString();}
        catch(IndexOutOfBoundsException ex)
        {strRet = "Numbers are only till Ten";}
        return strRet;}}
```

— Array list with data

— Function which returns number string and takes numbers as inputs

Figure 6.6: Model class

Model classes normally have business logic and data access. So "NumbersToWords.java" class will be the model class which will give us number in words when we input actual number values. Basically for simplicity we will keep all the data in "Arraylist" and fill the same in the constructor of the class. It will also have a function "GetWords" which will return the number in full string.

Controller (InputNumbersAction.java)

The controller is the main heart of struts architecture. All Action class will inherit from "Action" as shown above. You can see above "InputNumbersAction" class inherits from "Action". We then need to override the "execute" method which has "ActionForm" as the parameter. Using "ActionForm" object you can get and set any data on the JSP page. So what ever modification you make to the "ActionForm" objects will be reflected on the JSP page. So in the "execute" method we use the "InputNumbersForm" object which takes data that has been filled in the JSP page then use "NumberToWords" class to get the conversion. Also note the "mapping.findForward" which then uses "success" which is defined in the "<forward name" in the "struts-config.xml" file. Below is the modified "struts-config.xml" file.

```
public final class InputNumbersAction
                extends Action
{
     public ActionForward execute(ActionMapping mapping,
              ActionForm form,
              HttpServletRequest request,
              HttpServletResponse response)
       throws Exception
     {
          // Take the action form object which is
          // the representation of the JSP file data
          InputNumbersForm f = (InputNumbersForm) form;
          // Call the form object to get the number entered
          int intNumber = f.getintNumber();
          // Call the model class numbertowords to convert the
          // number to words
          NumberToWords objnumbertoword = new NumberToWords();
          String strNumber = objnumbertoword.GetWords(intNumber);
          // Finally set the string back to the action form object
          f.setstrNumber(strNumber);
          // and redirect the user to the same page.
          //See how the success is mapped in the struts-config file.
          return (mapping.findForward("success"));
     }
```

Figure 6.7: Action class

```
<!-- ================================================= Form Bean Definitions -->
    <form-beans>
        <form-bean name="NumbersForm" type="MyNumbers.InputNumbersForm"/>
    </form-beans>
```
                   Name referred in form beans   **Form class which will have JSP page data**

```
<!-- ================================================= Action Mapping Definitions -->
    <action-mappings>

        <action    path="/NumberToWords"
               type="MyNumbers.InputNumbersAction"  ------>   Action class which will
               name="NumbersForm"                             handle JSP pages request
               input="/InputNumbers.jsp"  ------>  JSP page
               scope="request">
        <forward name="success" path="/InputNumbers.jsp"/>
        <forward name="failure" path="/InputNumbers.jsp"/>
        </action>

    end samples -->
    </action-mappings>
```

Figure 6.8: struts-config.xml file for the sample project

There are two main sections which need to be modified:

√ Action Mapping section

√ Form beans section

"<action>" attribute specifies the action class that will be executed in this case its "MyNumbers.InputNumbersAction" class. "Input" attribute defines what's the input page which will be used to take data inputs. "Scope" sets the scope for the form bean associated with this action. For instance use "request" for request scope or "session" for session scope. Now what links the "MyNumbers.InputNumbersForm" to the "InputNumbers.jsp"?. Hmmm see the "name" attribute and then see the "<form-beans>" section. You can see the "name" attribute links them i.e. "NumbersForm". You can also see the type defined in the "<form-beans>" section is "MyNumbers.InputNumbersForm" class.

You are all set and you can copy the same in your "webapps" folder of your tomcat server run the application to see the number to word conversion.

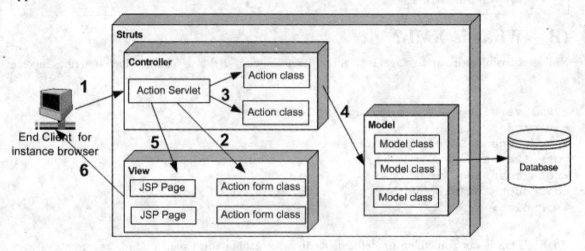

Figure 6.9: Flow of a Struts Application

So just to summarize how the execution flows in the struts application.

√ User makes browser makes a request to the Struts application that is processed by ActionServlet (Controller).

√ ActionServlet (Controller) populates the ActionForm (View) object with HTML / JSP form data method.

√ ActionServlet (Controller) executes the Action object (Controller).

√ Action object uses the model and does the necessary execution and passes the control back to the ActionServlet

√ Action (Controller) forwards control to the JSP pages.

√ JSP pages use model data to generate a response to the browser.

7
XML and Web Services

> Note: In this chapter we will first just skim through basic XML interview questions so that you do
> not get stuck up with simple questions and then move ahead for web services. XML forms the
> base for web services.

(B)   What is XML?

XML (Extensible markup language) is all about describing data. Below is a XML which describes invoice
data.

```
<?xml version="1.0" encoding="ISO-8859-1"?>
<invoice>
<productname>Shoes</productname>
<qty>12</qty>
<totalcost>100</totalcost>
<discount>10</discount>
</invoice>
```

An XML tag is not something predefined but it is something you have to define according to your
needs. For instance in the above example of invoice all tags are defined according to business needs.
The XML document is self explanatory, any one can easily understand looking at the XML data
what exactly it means.

(I)   What is the version information in XML?

"version" tag shows which version of XML is used.

(B)   What is ROOT element in XML?

In our XML sample given previously <invoice></invoice> tag is the root element. Root element
is the top most elements for a XML.

(B)   If XML does not have closing tag will it work?

No, every tag in XML which is opened should have a closing tag. For instance in the top if I
remove </discount> tag that XML will not be understood by lot of application.

(B)   Is XML case sensitive?

Yes, they are case sensitive.

(B)   What is the difference between XML and HTML?

XML describes data while HTML describes how the data should be displayed. So HTML is about displaying information while XML is about describing information.

(B)   Is XML meant to replace HTML?

No, they both go together one is for describing data while other is for displaying data.

(A)   Can you explain why your project needed XML?

> *Note: This is an interview question where the interviewer wants to know why you have chosen XML.*

Remember XML was meant to exchange data between two entities as you can define your user friendly tags with ease. In real world scenarios XML is meant to exchange data. For instance you have two applications who want to exchange information. But because they work in two complete opposite technologies it's difficult to do it technically. For instance one application is made in JAVA and the other in .NET. But both languages understand XML so one of the applications will spit XML file which will be consumed and parsed by other applications

You can give a scenario of two applications which are working separately and how you chose XML as the data transport medium.

(B)   What is DTD (Document Type definition)?

It defines how your XML should structure. For instance in the above XML we want to make it compulsory to provide "qty" and "totalcost", also that these two elements can only contain numeric. So you can define the DTD document and use that DTD document with in that XML.

(B)   What is well formed XML?

If a XML document is confirming to XML rules (all tags started are closed, there is a root element etc) then it's a well formed XML.

(B)   What is a valid XML?

If XML is confirming to DTD rules then it's a valid XML.

(B)   What is CDATA section in XML?

All data is normally parsed in XML but if you want to exclude some elements you will need to put those elements in CDATA.

(B)   What is CSS?

With CSS you can format a XML document.

(B)   What is XSL?

XSL (the eXtensible Stylesheet Language) is used to transform XML document to some other document. So its transformation document which can convert XML to some other document. For instance you can apply XSL to XML and convert it to HTML document or probably CSV files.

(B) What is element and attributes in XML?

In the below example invoice is the element and the invnumber the attribute.

<invoice invnumber=1002></invoice>

(A) What are the standard ways of parsing XML document?

Twist: What is a XML parser?

XML parser sits in between the XML document and the application who want to use the XML document. Parser exposes set of well defined interfaces which can be used by the application for adding, modifying and deleting the XML document contents. Now whatever interfaces XML parser exposes should be standard or else that would lead to different vendors preparing there own custom way of interacting with XML document.

There are two standard specifications which are very common and should be followed by a XML parser:

DOM: Document Object Model.

DOM is a W3C recommended way for treating XML documents. In DOM we load entire XML document into memory and allows us to manipulate the structure and data of XML document.

SAX: Simple API for XML.

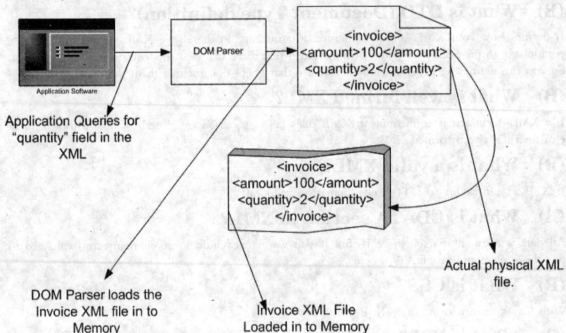

Figure 7.1: DOM Parser loading XML document

SAX is event driven way for processing XML documents. In DOM we load the whole XML document in to memory and then application manipulates the XML document. But this is not always the best way to process large XML documents which have huge data elements. For instance you only want one element from the whole XML document or you only want to see if the XML is proper which means loading the whole XML in memory will be quiet resource intensive. SAX parsers parse the XML document sequentially and emit events like start and end of the document, elements, text content etc. So applications who are interested in processing these events can register implementations of callback interfaces. SAX parser then only sends those event messages which the application has demanded.

Above is a pictorial representation of how DOM parser works. Application queries the DOM Parser for "quantity" field. DOM parser loads the complete XML file in to memory.

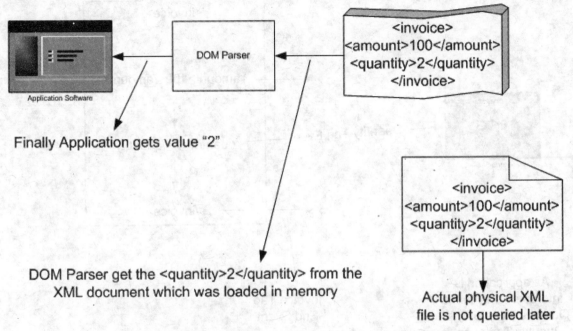

Figure 7.2: Returning the Quantity value back to application

DOM parser then picks up the "quantity" tag from the memory loaded XML file and returns back to the application.

SAX parser does not load the whole DOM in to memory but has event based approach. SAX parser while parsing the XML file emits events. For example in the above figure its has emitted Invoice tag start event, Amount Tag event, Quantity tag event and Invoice end tag event. But our application software is only interested in quantity value. So the application has to register to the SAX parser saying that he is only interested in quantity field and not any other field or element of the XML document. Depending on what interest the application software has SAX parser only sends those events to the application the rest of events is suppressed. For instance in the above figure only quantity tag event is sent to the application software and the rest of the events are suppressed.

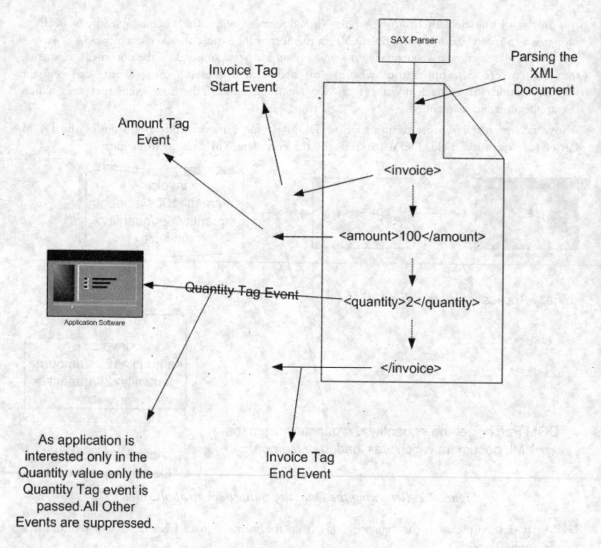

Figure 7.3: SAX parser in action

(A)   In What scenarios will you use a DOM parser and SAX parser?

√   If you do not need all the data from the XML file then SAX approach is much preferred than DOM as DOM can be quiet memory intensive. In short if you need large portion of the XML document its better to have DOM.

√   With SAX parser you have to write more code than DOM.

√   If you want to write the XML in to a file DOM is the efficient way to do it.

√   Some time you only need to validate the XML structure and do not want to retrieve any Data for those instances SAX is the right approach.

(B)   What is XSLT?

XSLT is a rule based language used to transform XML documents in to other file formats. XSLT are nothing but generic transformation rules which can be applied to transform XML document to HTML, CS, Rich text etc.

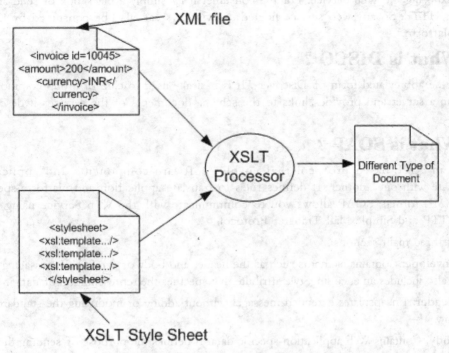

Figure 7.4: XSLT Processor in Actions

You can see in the above figure how the XSLT processor takes the XML file and applies the XSLT transformation to produce a different document.

(I)   Define XPATH?

It is an XML query language to select specific parts of an XML document. Using XPATH you can address or filter elements and text in a XML document. For instance a simple XPATH expression like "Invoice/Amount" states find "Amount" node which are children of "Invoice" node.

(A)   What is the concept of XPOINTER?

XPOINTER is used to locate data within XML document. XPOINTER can point to a particular portion of a XML document, for instance

    address.xml#xpointer(/descendant::streetnumber[@id=9])

So the above XPOINTER points streetnumber=9 in "address.xml".

(B)   What is a Web Service ?

Web Services are business logic components which provide functionality via the Internet using standard protocols such as HTTP.

Web Services uses Simple Object Access Protocol (SOAP) in order to expose the business functionality.SOAP defines a standardized format in XML which can be exchanged between two entities over standard protocols such as HTTP. SOAP is platform independent so the consumer of a Web Service is therefore completely shielded from any implementation details about the platform exposing the Web Service. For the consumer it is simply a black box of send and receive XML over HTTP. So any web service hosted on windows can also be consumed by UNIX and LINUX platform.

(B)   What is DISCO ?

DISCO is the abbreviated form of Discovery. It is basically used to club or group common services together on a server and provides links to the schema documents of the services it describes may require.

(B)   What is SOAP ?

SOAP is an XML-based protocol that enables software components and applications to communicate with one another. It defines rules to translate application and platform-specific data into the XML format. SOAP allows you to communicate with the Web Service using protocols such as HTTP and Simple Mail Transfer Protocol.

SOAP has three main sections:

√   **Envelope:** Contains elements such as the header and body of the SOAP messaging structure. It also includes an encodingStyle attribute that specifies the representation of data in messages.

√   **Header:** Encapsulates extended messages without adding or modifying the standard message flow.

√   **Body:** Contains Web application-specific data. It defines the purpose of sending the message. The body element should be the first element under the envelope element if there is no header element.

Below is a snippet of a sample SOAP header.

```
POST/Inventory HTTP/1.1
Host: localhost
Content-Type: text/xml; charset="utf-8"
Content-Length: <content_length>
SOAPAction: "<URI specified>"
<SOAP-ENV:Envelope  xmlns:SOAP-ENV="http://schemas.xmlsoap.org/soap/
envelope/">
<SOAP-ENV:encodingStyle="http://schemas.xmlsoap.org/soap/encoding/">
<SOAP-ENV:Body>
<m:GetLastName xmlns:m="Test_URI">
<symbol></symbol>
</m:GetLastName>
</SOAP-ENV:Body>
</SOAP-ENV:Envelope>
```

(B) What is WSDL ?

WSDL is an XML-based file that describes a Web service. A WSDL document describes the methods provided by a Web service and the input, output, and connection parameters. Below is a small code snippet for WSDL:-

```
<?xml version="1.0"?>
<definitions name="virtual-library"
targetNamespace="http://soapservice.com/ virtual-library.wsdl"
xmlns:tns="http://soapservice.com/ virtual-library.wsdl"
xmlns:xsd="http://www.w3.org/2000/10/XMLSchema"
xmlns:xsd1="http://soapservice.com/ virtual-library.xsd"
xmlns:soap="http://schemas.xmlsoap.org/wsdl/soap/"
xmlns="http://schemas.xmlsoap.org/wsdl/">
<message name="GetFlowerList">
     <part name="symbol" element="xsd:string"/>
</message>
<message name="GetFlowerList">
     <part name="result" type="xsd:float"/>
</message>
<portType name=" virtual-libraryPortType">
     <operation name="GetLastRecord"-*">
          <input message="tns:GetPriceInput"/>
          <output message="tns:GetStockPriceOutput"/>
     </operation>
</portType>
<binding name="virtual_librarySoapBinding" type=
"tns:virtual_libraryPortType">
     <soap:binding style="rpc"
transport="http://schemas.xmlsoap.org/soap/http"/>
     <operation name="GetLastRecord">
          <soap:operation soapAction="http://soapservice.com/
          GetLastRecord"/>
     <input>
          <soap:body use="encoded" namespace="http://soapservice.com/
          virtual_library"
          encodingStyle="http://schemas.xmlsoap.org/soap/encoding/"/>
     </input>
     <output>
          <soap:body use="encoded" namespace="http://soapservice.com/
          virtual_library"
          encodingStyle="http://schemas.xmlsoap.org/soap/encoding/"/>
     </output>
     </operation>>
</binding>
<service name="virtual_libraryService">
     <documentation>Virtual Library Service</documentation>
          <port name="virtual_libraryPort" binding="tns:
          virtual_librarySoapBinding">
     <soap:address location="http://soapservice.com/virtual_library"/>
```

```
    </port>
</service>
</definitions>
```

(B)   Can you explain UDDI ?

Universal Description, Discovery, and Integration (UDDI) is an industry standard that is used to locate Web services on the Internet. It is an XML-based registry that enables enterprises to list their Web services on the Internet. UDDI enables organizations to perform secure online transactions.

The UDDI company registry contains a comprehensive list of available Web services and provides links to discovery documents of Web services. These discovery documents, called DISCO files, contain links to WSDL documents.

(B)   Can you explain JAXP ?

JAXP is like an abstraction layer which sits on top of DOM and SAX API's that process XML documents. It allows us to switch between SAX and DOM parsers effortlesly. JAXP can convert documents to other formats such as HTML using XML style sheets.

(B)   What is a XML registry?

An XML registry is an infrastructure that enables the building, deployment, and discovery of Web services. It is a neutral third party that facilitates dynamic and loosely coupled business-to-business (B2B) interactions. A registry is available to organizations as a shared resource, often in the form of a Web-based service.

(B)   What is JAXR?

JAXR is a standard API used to access XML registries from the JAVA platform. An XML registry is a listing of services available on the Web. JAXR provides APIs for the client applications to query the registries, or publish their own information in them using the registry standards.

It acts as a pluggable layer that allows access to registries implemented on different standards, such as Universal Description Discovery and Integration (UDDI) and Electronic Business using eXtensible Markup Language (ebXML). You can see from the figure below how JAXR API interacts with the respective provider to get data.

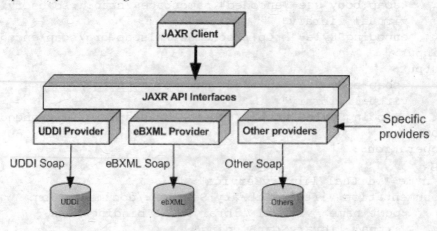

Figure 7.5: JAXR architecture

(I)   What is JAXM?

JAXM allows the exchange of business documents in the form of SOAP messages by conforming to SOAP Attachment specifications.

(I)   Can you explain how JAXM messaging model works?

JAXM has two types of messaging models one in synchronous and the other asynchronous. In the first model the client directly sends and receives messages and in second it uses a messaging provider as an intermediate.

In the first model you can see from the figure below it directly interacts with the source. This is synchronous processing that means the client sends a request and wait for the response.

In the second model client send message to the messaging provider and returns back. Messaging provider then performs the routing of message to the end source. If unable to send messages the provider keeps on trying until the message is sent.

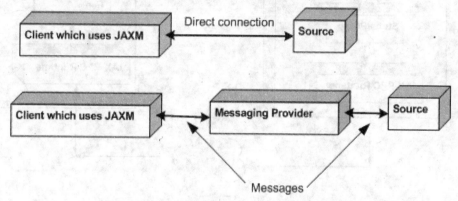

Figure 7.6: JAXM messaging models

The JAXM client decides to use the message provider or not.

(I)   Can you explain JAX-RPC?

First let's understand what's RPC and the rest will follow. RPC enables client to work with remote procedures that reside on different machines in a network. So in short the client calls the server, server does something useful and returns back the results to the client. RMI and CORBA are good examples of RPC.SOAP define the XML-based protocol for exchange of information in a distributed environment, specifying the envelope structure, encoding rules, and a convention for representing remote procedure call and responses. JAX-RPC uses SOAP to call remote procudres.JAX-RPC enables JAX-RPC clients to invoke Web services developed across heterogeneous platforms.

> *Note: In CD we have setups for tomcat50-jwsdp (container) and jwsdp-2_0-windows-i586 (Java web services developer pack). Feel free to use them and to see how web services work. Following are the installation steps:*
>   √   *Unzip tomcat container and run startup.bat.*
>   √   *Run setup of JWSDP and provide the path of tomcat container.*
>   √   *Set the environment variable JWSDP_HOME to your JWSDP installation directory.*

As said first JAX-RPC is a remote procedure call-based programming model. Its main aim is to provide an API for JAVA application to communicate with each other using SOAP protocol. Let's do a walkthrough of how the whole JAX-RPC architecture stands. Below is the figure which shows how different components interact to make JAX-RPC architecture work.

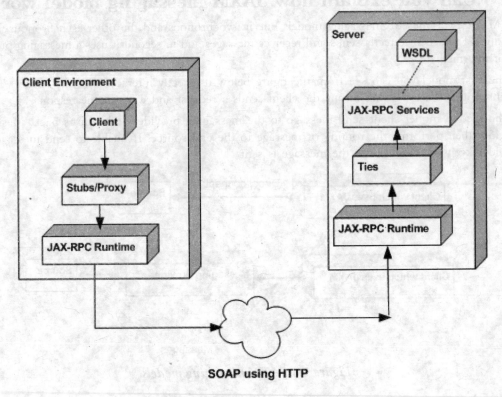

Figure 7.7: JAX-RPC architecture

We have two main entities the client and the server. Client is the one who will consume the web service and server is the one who will fulfill the request. On the client side we have the stub which has the same interface as the server. Client uses this stub and passes the information to the runtime. At the server side we have the tie component which is also called as the skeleton. Service Definition interface also called as WSDL defines the common communication between stub and ties. The communication between stub and ties happens using HTTP and SOAP protocol.

(A) How do you practically implement Web Services?

Below are the basic steps you need for creating a web service:-

√   Create an interface.

√   Write implementation for the interface.

√   Generate SOAP

√   Deploy the same on the web server.

The above are the basic steps needed for any web service. We will be using tomcat and JWSDP to demonstrate the same. With CD we have shipped TOMCAT container and the JWSDP setup.

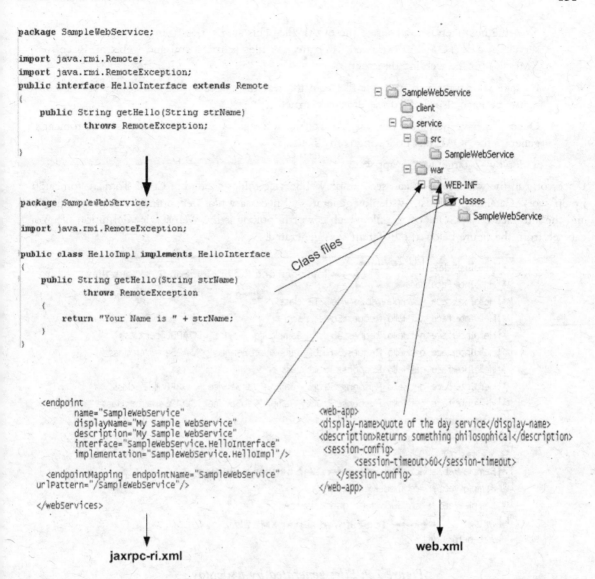

Figure 7.8: Web Service in action

√   The first step is to create the interface class which will be used by the client to communicate with the web service. In the above figure we have the HelloInterface with the getHello method.

√   Second step is to define implementation for the same. You can see in the above figure a HelloImpl class which implements the HelloInterface interface. Now put the compiled class files in to the directory structure defined.

Note: You will always need to follow the directory structure strictly. Again the directory structure varies from server to server.

√   Now the next step is to generate the SOAP file. This step varies from the web server to web server. In case TOMCAT we need to create two files jaxrpc-ri.xml and web.xml. Place these XML files in the web-inf directory.

√   Package your project in to a war file. Run the war from with in the war folder. In the above figure we have also defined the directory structure.

√   Once you have prepared the war file use the wsdeploy utility which comes with tomcat to generate the SOAP file. Following is the syntax :

     wsdeploy −o target.war myapp.war

Once you run the wsdeploy you can see SampleWebService folder created in C:\MyTomcat\tomcat50-jwsdp\work\Catalina\localhost. Wsdeploy generates all necessary files depending on the two xml files and the interface classes. One of the file which is worth looking is the Web service definition file. You can see from the figure below the different files generated.

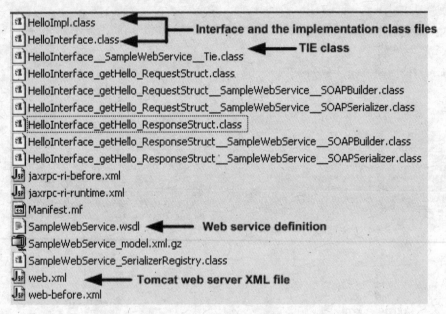

Figure 7.9: Files generated by wsdeploy

In the JAXRPC\bin folder you can see the wscompile and wsdeploy exe. Wscompile can be used to generate the WSDL file. Wsdeploy does a two fold job it generates all the necessary files and also deploys the same on the web server. You can view the WSDL in browser by appending? WSDL after your URL. See the below figure how the WSDL XML looks in the browser.

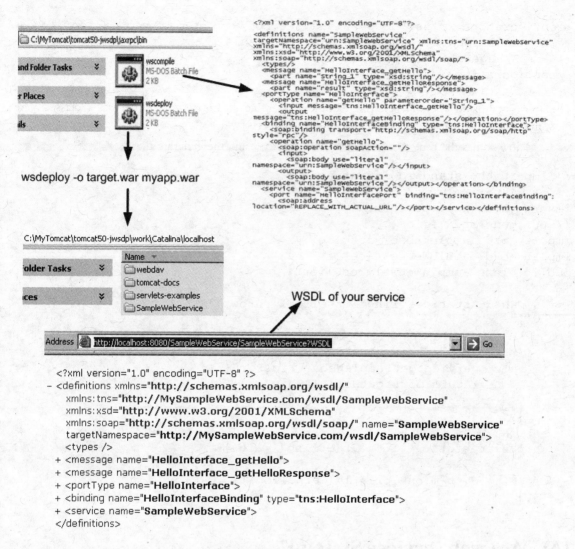

Figure 7.10: WSDL output

(B)   How do we consume a web service?

There are three ways to consume a client.

√   Client uses stub to consume the web service.

√   Client uses DLL to consume the web service.

√   Client uses dynamic proxies.

This book will cover only using stub,

Below are the steps to consume a web service using stub:

√   Generate the client stub   using wscompile command line wscompile -gen:client -keep -d .
         clientconfig.xml

         where clientconfig.xml has the wsdl file name. Below is the code snippet for clientconfig.xml

```
<configuration xmlns="http://java.sun.com/xml/ns/jax-rpc/ri/config">
     <wsdl location="SampleWebService.wsdl"
     packageName="SampleWebService" />
</configuration>
```

The above command line will generate SampleWebService directory with all necessary classes. The most important file from client perspective is the _impl class.

√   Now comes the time to consume the webservice using the generate files

```
// Import the standard libraries
import javax.xml.rpc.Service;
import javax.xml.rpc.Stub;
// our generated files
import qotd.SampleWebservice_Impl;
import qotd.SampleWebservicePortType;
public class SampleWebserviceClient
{
      public static String GetHello() throws Exception
      {
            SampleWebservice_Impl service = new SampleWebservice_Impl();
            SampleWebservicePortType port =
            service.getSampleWebservicePort();
            return port.getHello("Shiv");

      }

      public static void main(String[] args)
      {
            System.out.println(GetHello());
      }
}
```

(A)   Are web services Stateful?

Web services are not stateful by itself. But they can be made stateful by using ServletEndpointContext. In the init method of the web service you can get reference to the context. In the below code snippet Yourvariable is the variable which stores the context value.

```
public void init(Object context) throws ServiceException
{
      Yourvariable = (ServletEndpointContext) context;
}
```

Later when ever we need data from the context using the session object as shown in the below code snippet. We have used the YourVariable to get the session object and then use the getAttribute function to get the session value.

HttpSession session = Yourvariable .getHttpSession();

Integer val = (Integer) session.getAttribute("HitCount");

8

Internationalization

(A) Can you explain i18n and l10n?

(B) Can you explain internationalization and localization?

i18n stands for internationalization (there are 18 characters between the beginning i and the final n). Hmmm looks like the word was made for lazy people like me. The act of getting ready internationally is called internationalization.

l10n stands for localization (10 characters between the first l and the final n). Localization is the means by which i18n applications can be used for local regions.

(B) What is Locale?

A Locale is a relatively simple object. It identifies a specific language and a geographic region. It represents the language and cultural preferences of a geographic area. A Locale's language is specified by the ISO 639 standard, which describes valid language codes that can be used to construct a Locale object.

The Locale class has the following important constructors:

Locale(String language, String country)

Locale(String language, String country, String variant)

Language represents the language code en English, fr French, zh Chinese, ja Japanese etc.

Country represents country code US United States, FR France, CA Canada etc.

Variant can be used to create a more specific Locale than what's possible with just language and country codes.

(I) How do we display numbers, currency and Dates according to proper Locale format?

When we say 1,456 is one thousand and four hundred and fifty six in USA but its one and four fifty six in France. That can be easily achieved by java.text.NumberFormat. To instantiate a NumberFormat object, use the factory method getInstance, which returns a NumberFormat object suitable for your default locale. You can, of course, ask for an object with a specific locale in mind. To specify a locale other than your default, use getInstance (Locale locale).

Same holds true for currency. Each locale has its own preferences for currency symbols, negative amount format, leading zeros, group separators, decimal point symbol, and currency symbol position. Currency and numbers have a lot in common. Although you still use NumberFormat, you call a different factory method to get a currency format object, getCurrencyInstance. This method will return a currency format object for the default locale. You can use this factory method just like you used the number factory method; call getCurrencyInstance(Locale locale) to specify a specific locale. Again, use the format method to produce a user visible String object. The currency formatter will handle all the details of selecting the correct currency symbol, placing that symbol in the string, and applying grouping rules.

The java.text.DateFormat class provides the getDateInstance method that creates a formatter for your default locale. The format method works in the same way as the other format methods covered so far, and applies the specific format rules for your chosen locale.

(I)   what are resource bundles?

Resource bundles are used to provide a map from string keys to values that depend on the desired locale. Resource bundles are usually read in from properties files that look like this:

        HelloEnglish=Hello

        HelloHindi=Namaste

Assuming the above file backs the resource bundle, a call to bundle.getObject("HelloHindi ") would return the string "Namaste".

(I)   How do we load a resource bundle file?

        bundle = ResourceBundle.getBundle("Myresource.hindi");

(I)   How can we do inheritance in resource bundles?

Left for reader as home work.

9

JNI

(B) What is Native Interface in JAVA?

JNI is a mechanism by which you can invoke method written in native language like C and C++. Native languages allow you to use a platform specific feature which is not in control of java language. For instance if you want java to interact directly with some specific type of hardware it will be extremely difficult to achieve it. So you can write a C code and declare its native methods and call the same in Java.

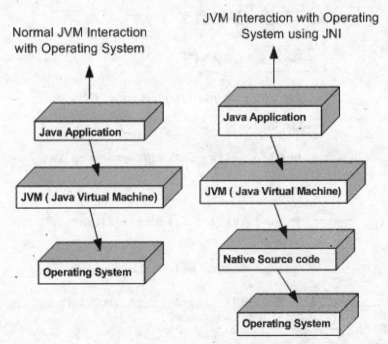

Figure 9.1: JNI in action

The above figure indicates how JVM interacts with JNI and with out. With JNI it has the extra layer of C or C++ DLL i.e. native source code or native methods which interacts with the operating system.

(I) Can you say in brief steps required to implement Native interfaces in Java?

There are basically five steps which are needed to implement JNI in Java as shown in below figure.

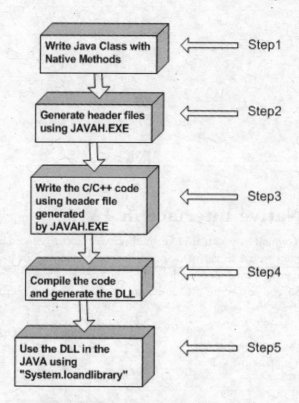

Figure 9.2: Steps in implementing JNI.

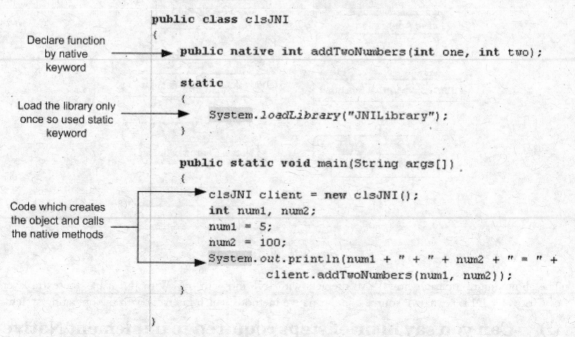

```
public class clsJNI
{
    public native int addTwoNumbers(int one, int two);

    static
    {
        System.loadLibrary("JNILibrary");
    }

    public static void main(String args[])
    {
        clsJNI client = new clsJNI();
        int num1, num2;
        num1 = 5;
        num2 = 100;
        System.out.println(num1 + " + " + num2 + " = " +
                client.addTwoNumbers(num1, num2));
    }
}
```

Declare function by native keyword

Load the library only once so used static keyword

Code which creates the object and calls the native methods

Figure 9.3: Step1 Write java class with native methods

To understand "JNI" we will make a small sample project which will add two numbers. Ok, let's start with step1 in which we have to write the main java file which has the native method "addTwoNumbers" defined. You can also see "System.loanLibrary ('JNILibrary')" which loads the C++ DLL. This code is defined using "static" which means this sentence will be called only once. In the main method we create the object , add the two numbers and display the results of the same.

Now that we have defined the "native" method its time to generate the header file which can be used in C++ code to create our addition dll "JNILibrary". So go to "bin" folder using dos prompt and use the "javah.exe" with the class name "clsJNI" to generate the header file. You can see in the same folder "clsJNI.H" is created.

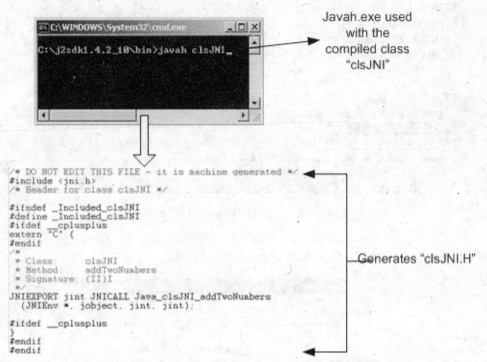

Figure 9.4: Step2 JAVAH.EXE generates "clsJNI.H"

Now that we have the header file which can be used to create the C++ class lets create a sample project using VC++. My whole point of using VC++ editor is that I am having windows installed but you can take other editors also. Open the VC++ editor and select "win32 DLL" project as shown below.

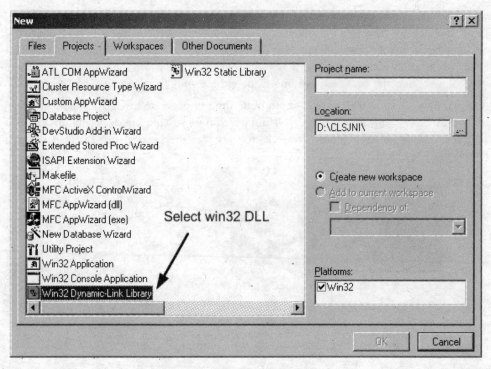

Figure 9.5: Select Win32 DLL project

Copy the header file generated in the same location in which VC++ has created the project file i.e. ".dsw" file. You can see "clsJNI.h" copied to that location.

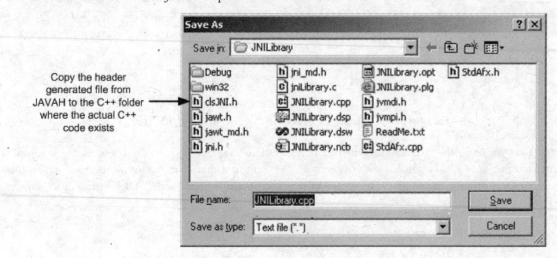

Figure 9.6: Copy clsJNI.H file to the C++ folder

Now the most important step, writing the C++ dll library which is step3. You can see the "clsJNI.H" included as a header file in the top of the C++ code. Second is the actual method which has the implementation and corresponds to the native method which was defined in step1. Please note this method has "JNIEnv" type of pointer defined in the input parameter. "JNIEnv" pointer is used by the native program to communicate to java objects. In java we had define the native method as "addTwoNumbers" in C++ it is "Java_clsJNI_addTwoNumbers" which is of convention "Java_CLASSNAME_METHODNAME".

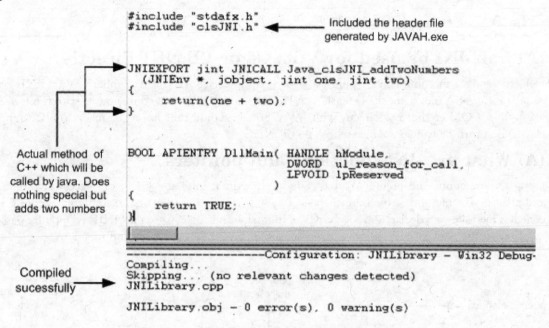

```
#include "stdafx.h"
#include "clsJNI.h"          ◄──── Included the header file
                                     generated by JAVAH.exe


JNIEXPORT jint JNICALL Java_clsJNI_addTwoNumbers
    (JNIEnv *, jobject, jint one, jint two)
{
    return(one + two);
}


BOOL APIENTRY DllMain( HANDLE hModule,
                       DWORD  ul_reason_for_call,
                       LPVOID lpReserved
                     )
{
    return TRUE;
}
```

Actual method of C++ which will be called by java. Does nothing special but adds two numbers

```
---------------------------Configuration: JNILibrary - Win32 Debug-
Compiling...
Skipping... (no relevant changes detected)
JNILibrary.cpp

JNILibrary.obj - 0 error(s), 0 warning(s)
```

Compiled sucessfully

Figure 9.7: Step3 and Step4 C++ code and compilation

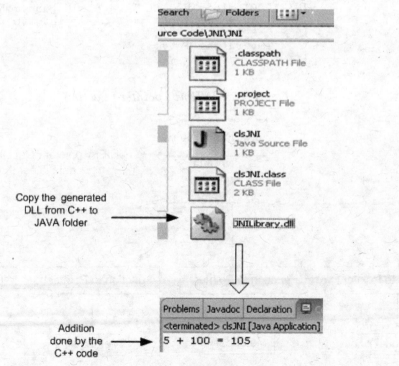

Copy the generated DLL from C++ to JAVA folder

Addition done by the C++ code

```
Problems  Javadoc  Declaration
<terminated> clsJNI [Java Application]
5 + 100 = 105
```

Figure 9.8: Step5 JNI in Action

Finally Step4 we compile the program to get out "JNILibrary" dll. Copy the generated dll in the java folder where the java class will use this dll. Hurray below is the output and you are ready to tackle any kind if JNI interview question.

> *Note: You can get the above source in "JNI" directory in the CD.*

(A) Can JNI be used for VB6, C# or VB.NET directly?

JNI enables java to communicate only via C or C++ interface. If you remember JAVAH.EXE only generates C header files with ".h" extensions. VB6, C# and VB.NET can communicate with C interfaces via interop, COM etc but not directly with JAVA. So all method calls has to be made to a C wrapper class and in turn he will communicate to VB6 or .NET.

(A) What are JNI functions and pointers?

Using JNI functions and pointers native code (code written in C and C++) can access java objects and also invoke methods which are in Java. If you remember in the first example when the C++ code has the following declaration for "addTwoNumbers" and you can see the "JNIEnv" pointer passed to it so that the native C++ code can communicate or invoke java methods and functions.

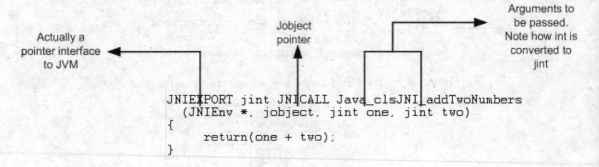

Figure 9.9: "JNIEnv" pointer in action

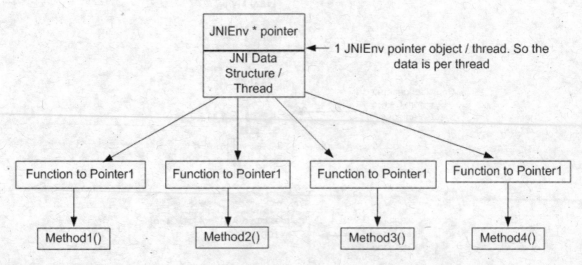

Figure 9.10: "JNIEnv" pointer in depth

Some people really like to go in to depth of what exactly is "JNIEnv" pointer made of. So let's have a look in to real depth of what exactly is "JNIEnv" pointer made of who know it can cost a job to you. It's basically table of function pointers. It contains more than 250 function pointers and in the coming new version there can be much more than that.

The above image depicts how "JNIEnv" pointer looks like. There is one main pointer which points to other pointer which is a function pointer. So the native language can get reference to any of the pointer and invoke the method written in Java. Below are some sample snippets in which C and C++ can access them

```
//In C you can refer the function in the following way
(*env)->FunctionName(env, ...)
// In C++ it's much simpler
env->FunctionName(...)
```

(A) How does the garbage collector know JNI objects are no more used?

Twist: What are the different types of references JNI supports?

One of the important issues when manipulating java objects from native code is garbage collection of these objects once native code does not have any references to them. So how does the garbage collector determine that Java objects are no more used in the native code. In order to make the garbage collector mechanism simpler it provides three different types of references:

√ Local references

√ Global references

√ Weak global references

Local References

```
#include <windows.h>
#include <string.h>
#include "Myprogram.h"

BOOL WINAPI DllMain(HANDLE hHandle, DWORD dwReason,
                    LPVOID lpReserved)
{
    return TRUE;
}

JNIEXPORT jstring JNICALL Java_Myprogram_DisplaySomething(JNIEnv * env,
                    jclass, jstring strString)
{
    char *lpBuff = (char*)env->GetStringUTFChars(strString, 0);
    _strupr(lpBuff);
    jstring jstr = env->NewStringUTF(lpBuff);
    env->ReleaseStringUTFChars(strString, lpBuff);
    return jstr;
}
```

lpBuff is a local variable and will be destroyed as soon as the subroutine is executed

All the local variables are destroyed as soon as the function is returned.

Figure 9.11: Local references in JNI

Local references are the most commonly used when using JNI. Life time of the local referenced objects is destroyed once they go out of scope. So when any native functions return after the call all object references are out of scope after that and they can be garbage collected. It's the most preferred way as you do not have to explicitly destroy object in the native language (C or C++).

You can see from the figure above the local variables will be out if scope as soon as "DisplaySomething" method will be executed and thus garbage collector can easily know that the java objects used in this can removed from heap. Also note the way "JNIEnv" is used to call the "NewString" method.

In order to ensure that we use local reference you can use the "DeleteLocalRef" method which deletes object allocation from heap. Consider the below snippet where there is a huge loop in the native code. Now even though all the variables are declared locally java garbage collector can only know that objects are out of reference after the for loop is executed. In such type of scenarios you can use the "DeleteLocalRef" to remove the object from memory immediately after we display the string or else the garbage collector will act only after the function returns.

```c
#include <stdio.h>
#include <jni.h>
#include "MyLocalReferences.h"
JNIEXPORT jint JNICALL Java_MyLocalReferences_StringLoop(JNIEnv *env,
                                                         jobject obj,
                                                         jstring str)
{
    char buffer [500];
    int intcount;

    for(intcount=0; intcount<5000; intcount++)
    {
        const char *mynewStr;
        printf("\nPlease enter the string : ");
        scanf("%s", buffer);
        mynewStr = (*env)->NewStringUTF(env,buffer);
        printf("Output %s", mynewStr);

        // delete the reference as soon as the string is displayed
        //*******************************************************
        (*env)->DeleteLocalRef(env, mynewStr);
        //*******************************************************
    }
    return 0;
}
```

Huge for loop which will not make object eligible for garbage collections

Delete the local reference as soon as the string is displayed

Figure 9.12: "DeleteLocalRef" in action

Global References

Global referenced objects can be accessed across multiple invocations of a native method. They can be used across multiple threads and will exist until the programmer does not free them. As compared to local reference they will not be garbage collected unless the programmer wants it.

```
#include <stdio.h>
#include <jni.h>
#include "MyGlobalReferences.h"

JNIEXPORT jstring JNICALL Java_MyGlobalReferences_MyString(JNIEnv *env,
                                                           jobject obj,
                                                           jstring str)
{
    static jclass mystrCls = NULL;
    if (mystrCls == NULL)
    {
        // get the reference to the local object which you want to create
        // globally
        jclass localRefCls = (*env)->FindClass(env,"java/lang/String");

        // just to ensure that the program does not crash further
        if (localRefCls == NULL)
        {
            return NULL;
        }

        // Create the global object
        mystrCls =(*env)->NewGlobalRef(env,localRefCls);

        // delete the local object which was used to create the global object

        (*env)->DeleteLocalRef(env,localRefCls);

        if (mystrCls == NULL)
        {
            return NULL;
        }
    }
    return (*env)->NewStringUTF(env, str);
}
```

Load the type of object which needs to be global →

Create the global object using "NewGlobalRef" →

Pass the local object type whose global object has to be created.

Delete the local object after use.

Figure 9.13: Global references in action

Above snippet shows how global reference objects are created. You can see in the above first by using "findclass" we get the class type reference. The same class type is used to create global objects using "NewGlobalRef" keyword. One of the points to be noticed is that object created by "NewGlobalRef" is further stored in a static datatype. So these kinds of objects will never be garbage collected.

Twist: How to do you delete global objects?

Using "DeleteGlobalRef" function we can delete global objects in JNI.

Weak Global References

Weak Global reference objects are like global reference described previously. But the only difference is that it allows underlying objects to be garbage collected which are referred by weak references. A weak reference is one that does not prevent the referenced object from being garbage collected. A weak reference is a reference that does not keep the object it refers to alive in other words the class will never use it. A local or global reference keeps the referenced object from being garbage collected. A weak global reference, on the other hand, allows the referenced object to be garbage collected if they are pointed by weak references. Once the underlying objects which have weak references are garbage collected the main weak global object is also cleared.

You can create or delete a weak global reference object using "jweak NewWeakGlobalRef(JNIEnv *env, jobject obj)" or "void DeleteWeakGlobalRef(JNIEnv *env, jweak obj)" respectively.

C or C++ native code can test whether a weak global reference is cleared by using IsSameObject to compare the reference against NULL. If you have local, global or weak global object use the "IsSameObject" function as shown in the snippet below for comparison.

　　　　(*env)->IsSameObject(env, obj1, obj2)

This returns JNI_TRUE (or 1) if obj1 and obj2 refer to the same object or else returns JNI_FALSE (or 0).

A NULL reference in JNI refers to the null object in the Java virtual machine. If obj is a local or a global reference, you may use "(*env)->IsSameObject(env, obj, NULL)" or "obj == NULL".

(I)　how does the native language C or C++ understand data types in JAVA?

Native languages like C and C++ definitely have a different data structure and type than JAVA. So there should be some kind of mechanism which can help the native language to map the same. If you noticed in the previous C++ code there were many references to jint, jobject etc which are nothing but JNI data types corresponding to JAVA data types. Below is the mapping table which describes in detail how data types in JAVA maps to C and C++ using JNI data types.

Java	C/C++	JNI	Bytes
boolean	unsigned char	jboolean	1
byte	signed char	jbyte	1
char	unsigned short	jchar	2
double	double	jdouble	8
float	float	jfloat	4
int	int32	jint	4
long	int64	jlong	8
short	int16	jshort	2

Figure 9.14: Java Datatype mapping with C++

(A)　Can you explain exception handling in JNI?

JNI does not have an error trapping mechanism as such which can help us propagate the error to the caller. So error trapping has to be done by the native code itself. There are two ways in which native code can implement error handling mechanism:-

√　　　The native method returns immediately and leaves how the error has to be handled to the caller.

Below is the code snippet which just exits when there are errors. In this case we are trying to load the "localRefCls" object. If the object is NULL just return to the caller returning a null object.

```
JNIEXPORT jstring JNICALL Java_MyGlobalReferences_MyString(JNIEnv *env,
                                                           jobject obj,
                                                           jstring str)
{
    static jclass mystrCls = NULL;
    if (mystrCls == NULL)
    {
        // get the reference to the local object which you want to create
        // globally
        jclass localRefCls = (*env)->FindClass(env,"java/lang/String");

        // just to ensure that the program does not crash further
        if (localRefCls == NULL)
        {
            return NULL;  ←————  If there is not class as such just exit
        }                        to the main caller and let him handle
    }                            the same.
}
```

Figure 9.15: Just exit to the caller if there are exceptions

√   Clear the exception and choose how to handle the exception by itself.

Below is code snippet in which the native code handles the exception. There are four important steps first get the exception in "jthrowable" type, check if the object has errors, get the exception class and throw it back to the calling java code. In order to follow my explanation you can follow the arrow in the below code snippet.

```
// Get exception occurred in jthrowable type object
jthrowable  throwExcep = (*env)->ExceptionOccured(env);  ←————  Get the exception
/*if exception found*/

if (throwExcep)  ←————         Check if there is a exception
{

    // declare the new class object which will refer the exception class
    jclass newExcepClass;

    // invoke ExceptionDescribe for description
    (*env)->ExceptionDescribe(env);
                                                              Get the exception
    // clear the exception so that the C++ native code does not behave    class type
    // unexpectedly
    (*env)->ExceptionClear(env);

    // Get the exception class and assign it declared object
    // of datatype jclass
    newExcepClass = (*env)->FindClass(env, "java/lang/IllegalArgumentException");

    // Finally throw the exception to the caller

    (*env)->ThrowNew(env, newExcepClass, "Illegal exception thrown from the Native code");
```

Finally throw the exception to the caller

Figure 9.16: Throwing the exception to the caller

(A) What are limitations for "JNIEnv" pointer in multi-threading scenarios?

"JNIEnv" pointer and its data are allocated per thread. So this pointer can not be shared across threads. "JNIEnv" pointer is accessible only with its own thread. If you want to ever pass data between threads it's only through global references.

(I) What are the advantages and disadvantages of using "JNI"?

Advantages of using JNI:

√ Because you can use C or C++ there can be a huge performance boost.

√ Inaccessible features of an OS or a platform can be done which was very much impossible with Java. For instance accessing some hardware features.

Disadvantages of using JNI:

√ Less portable as we are using native languages.

√ Cumbersome and harder to debug code which can cost huge for maintenance.

10

Architecture

(B)   What are design patterns ?

Design patterns are recurring solution to recurring problems in software architecture.

(A)   Can you list down all patterns and their classification?

There are three basic classification of patterns Creational, Structural and Behavioral patterns.

Creational Patterns

√   **Abstract Factory:** Creates an instance of several families of classes

√   **Builder :** Separates object construction from its representation

√   **Factory Method:** Creates an instance of several derived classes

√   **Prototype:** A fully initialized instance to be copied or cloned

√   **Singleton:** A class in which only a single instance can exist

Note: The best way to remember Creational pattern is by ABFPS (Abraham Became First President of States).

Structural Patterns

√   **Adapter:** Match interfaces of different classes.

√   **Bridge:** Separates an object's interface from its implementation.

√   **Composite:** A tree structure of simple and composite objects.

√   **Decorator :** Add responsibilities to objects dynamically.

√   **Façade:** A single class that represents an entire subsystem.

√   **Flyweight:** A fine-grained instance used for efficient sharing.

√   **Proxy:** An object representing another object.

Note: To remember structural pattern best is (ABCDFFP)

Behavioral Patterns

√   **Mediator:** Defines simplified communication between classes.

√   **Memento:** Capture and restore an object's internal state.

√   **Interpreter:** A way to include language elements in a program.

√   **Iterator:** Sequentially access the elements of a collection.

√   **Chain of Resp:** A way of passing a request between a chain of objects.

√   **Command:** Encapsulate a command request as an object.

√   **State:** Alter an object's behavior when its state changes.

√   **Strategy:** Encapsulates an algorithm inside a class.

√   **Observer:** A way of notifying change to a number of classes.

√   **Template Method:** Defer the exact steps of an algorithm to a subclass.

√   **Visitor:** Defines a new operation to a class without change.

> *Note:*   *Just remember Music....... 2 MICS On TV (MMIICCSSOTV).*

> *Note:*   *No source code is provided for architecture section as much of the things can be clear from good UML diagrams.*

(A) What is the difference between Factory and Abstract Factory Patterns?

> *Note:*   *This is quiet a confusing architect question especially in design pattern section. Interviewer can take you for a nice ride. So get the difference in your heart.*

First read the definition provided in the first question about both these patterns. The common thing they have is that they belong to creational patterns. In short they hide the complexity of creating objects.

The main difference between factory and Abstract factory is factory method uses inheritance to decide which object has to be instantiated while abstract factory uses delegation to decide instantiation of object. We can say Abstract factory uses factory method to complete the architecture. Abstract Factory is one level higher in abstraction over Factory.

The two class diagrams below will provide overview of what is the actual difference. First figure shows a sample implementation of Factory Patterns. In this figure there are two basic sections:

√   The actual product section i.e. Class "Product" it inherits from an abstract class "AbstractProduct".

√   The creational aspect section i.e. "ConcreteCreator" class which inherits from class "Creator".

√   Now there are some rules the client will have to follow who will need the "Product" object. He will never refer directly to the actual "Product" object he will refer the "Product" object using "AbstractProduct".

√   Second client will never use "New" keyword to create the "Product" object but will use the "Creator" class which in turn will use the "ConcreteCreator" class to create the actual "Product" object.

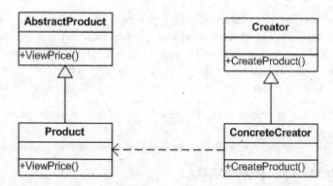

Figure: - 10.1 Class diagram of a factory Pattern

So what are the benefits from this architecture? All creational and initializing aspects are now detached from the actual client. As your creational aspect is now been handled in "ConcreteCreator" and the client has reference to only "Creator", so any implementation change in "CreateProduct" will not affect the client code. In short now your creational aspect of object is completely encapsulated from the client's logic.

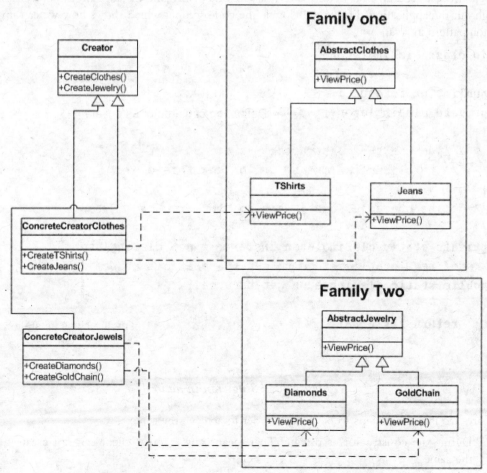

Figure: 10.2 Class Diagram of Abstract Factory

Now let's look at the second class diagram which provides an overview of what actually "Abstract factory" pattern is. It creates objects for families of classes. In short it describes collection of factor methods from various different families. In short it groups related factory methods. Example in this the class "Creator" is implemented using the "Abstract" factory pattern. It now creates objects from multiple families rather one product.

> *Note:* *Just stick up to this definition that Abstract factory classifies factory methods or groups logically related factory method together.*

(I)   What is MVC pattern?

Twist: How can you implement MVC pattern in Servlets and JSP?

This question is answered in struts section in a more detail fashion.

(A)   How can we implement singleton pattern in JAVA?

There are many instances in a project where you will need only one instance to be running. This one instance can be shared across objects. For instance you will only want one instance of database connection object running. Singleton pattern assures that only one instance of the object is running through out the applications life time. Below is the code snippet which shows how we can implement singleton pattern in java.

```
public class clsSingleton
{
    public int intcount;
    private clsSingleton()      <------- Define the constructor as private
    {
        // define the constructor private so that
        // no client can create the object this class
    }
    // define the object as static so that only one instance of the object
    // is created
    private static clsSingleton instance = new clsSingleton();
    // define a static method to get the static instance
    public static clsSingleton getInstance()
    {
        return instance;                    Define the class as static
    }
}
```

Figure 10.3: Singleton in action

There are two important steps to be done in order to achieve the same:

√   Define the constructor as private. That means any external client can not create object of the same.

√   Second define the object as static which needs to be exposed by the singleton pattern so that only one instance of the object is running.

> *Note: You can get the above source code from SingletonPattern folder in the CD.*

(A) How do you implement prototype pattern in JAVA?

    Twist: How to implement cloning in JAVA? What is shallow copy and deep copy ?

Prototype means making a clone of an object. There are scenarios in project where you need to create a clone of the complete object. For such kind of scenarios prototype pattern comes to rescue.

> *Note: Look for Shallow and deep cloning in the OOP's and Core Java chapter.*

(A) Can you give a practical implementation of FAÇADE patterns?

Façade pattern sits on the top of lot of subsystems and makes access easy to interfaces of these subsystems. Basic purpose of Façade is to make interfacing between many modules and classes manageable.

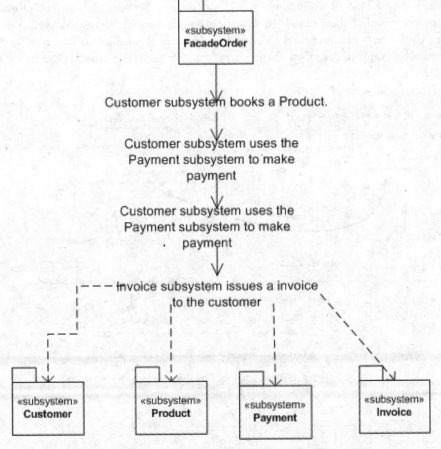

Figure: 10.4 Façade in action

Above is a simple live application of a Façade class. In this we have four subsystems:

√   Customer

√   Product

√   Payment

√   Invoicing

All the four modules when built at initial stage where built completely independent. The main interaction between all these subsystems is customer placing order. This functionality can be attained by using all these subsystems, which involves complex interaction between them.

That is where FAÇADE comes in to action. We have built a FAÇADE called as "FACADEORDER" which sits on the top of all these subsystem and fulfill our functionality.

Facade provides a simplified interface for a subsystem so that it can be used by its clients. One of the good gains of using Facade is it leads to a loose coupling between subsystems.

(I)   How can we implement observer pattern in JAVA?

There are scenarios in project where one object is interested in events happening in other objects. For instance you have stock ticker object definitely an agent object will be interested in stocks data. So whenever stock ticker object changes agent object would like to know what changes has happened. So there should be some kind of communication model defined between the objects. Observer patterns suggest a publisher-subscriber model. In this model there should be an observer and a subject or observable. The observer is interested changes happening in the subject or observable. So when the subject or the observable undergoes a change it will be notified to the observer. So how do we achieve this in JAVA?

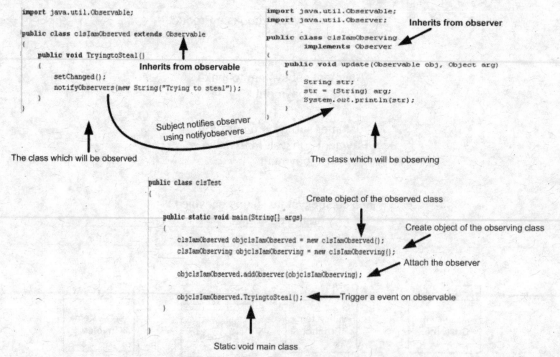

Figure 10.5: Observer pattern in action

In JAVA we have the Observable class and the Observer interface. So the objects which have to be observed should be inherited from the observable class. The object which is interested should implement the Observer interface.

Let's try to understand this fundamental by doing a simple project. Let's define two classes ClsIamObserving and ClsIamObserved. Whenever ClsIamObserving will try to steal the ClsIamObserved should be notified about the same. Below figure defines both the classes.

You can see from the above figure the class to be observed is inherited from Observable. In the same class we have method call as TryingtoSteal. Whenever this method is called it notifies its changes to object which are registered and interested about the changes. On the right hand side you can see the observer class which has Observer interface implemented. We need to implement the Update method of the observer interface. So when we try to call the Tryingtosteal of the subject it's notified to the observer.

You also need to register the observer with observable which is done using the addobserver method in the static void main.

> *Note: You can get the above code sample in CD in observerpattern folder.*

(B)   What is three tier architecture?

The three tier software architecture emerged in the 1990s to overcome the limitations of the two tier architecture.

There are three layers when we talk about three tier architecture:

User Interface (Client): This is mostly the windows user interface or the Web interface but this has only the UI part.

Mid layer: Middle tier provides process management where business logic and rules are executed and can accommodate hundreds of users (as compared to only 100 users with the two tier architecture) by providing functions such as queuing, application execution, and database staging.

Data Access Layer: This is also called by the famous acronym "DAL" component. It has mainly the SQL statement which do the database operation part of the job.

The three tier architecture is used when an effective distributed client/server design is needed that provides (when compared to the two tier) increased performance, flexibility, maintainability, reusability, and scalability, while hiding the complexity of distributed processing from the user.

(A)   What is Service Oriented architecture?

"Services" are components which expose well defined interfaces and these interfaces communicate through XML messages. Using SOA you can build workflow, which uses interfaces of these components. SOA is typically useful when you are crossing heterogeneous technical boundaries, organizations, domain etc.

In JAVA SOA technically uses Web services to communicate with each service which is crossing boundaries. You can look SOA which sits on top of web services and provides a workflow.

SOA uses service components which operate in their own domain boundary. Let us note some points of service:

√   They are independent components and operate in their own boundary and own technology.

√   They have well defined interfaces which use XML and WSDL to describe themselves.

√   Services have URL where anyone can find them and clients can bind to these URL to avail for the service.

√   Services have very loosely coupled architecture. In order to communicate to service you only have to know the WSDL. Your client can then generate proxy from the WSDL of the service.

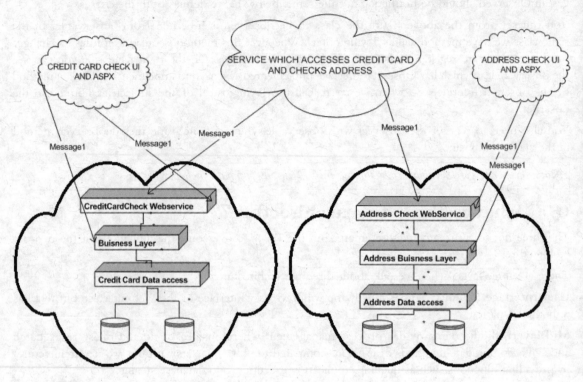

Figure: 10.6 SOA basic architecture

Above figure describes a broader picture of what service oriented architecture will look like. The basic fundamental of SOA is a web service. In above diagram you can see there are two services available. One is the "Credit Card" service and other is "Address Check" web service. Both these services are provided by different company. Now we want to build a functionality which needs to validate a credit card and also check that addresses are proper. In short we will need functionalities of both the "CreditCard" and "AddressCheck" service. Also note the "CreditCard" service has its own business layer and DAL components, which can be in a proprietary language. It's very much possible that the whole Credit card service is made in .NET and the Address check is SAP implementation or JAVA implementation. But because both the systems provide there functionality using Web services which is nothing but basically XML message communication. So we have made new service which sits like a FAÇADE on top of both the web service and performs both functionalities in one common service. You will see I have made a third service which sits on top of both the webservice and consumes them. Also you can see that the UI part of the systems have access to Business layer and Web service of there system. But the service which does both these check has only access to the Web service.

> Note: *It's beyond the scope of this book to discuss about SOA. But just to keep you safe during interview this book has tried to clear some basics of SOA.*

(A) What is aspect oriented programming?

> Note: *This is something which is catching up the market so interviewer can ask you to see how you are in touch with the market. So probably this explanation can be quiet long but bear with me it is worth of it*

I will try and make it as short as possible as this book is not a reference book. Just to save you from interviewer I will give a short description of aspect oriented programming in JAVA.

First let us try and define it which can probably save you during interview

Aspect-oriented software development is a new technology for separation of concerns (SOC) in software development. The techniques of AOSD make it possible to modularize crosscutting aspects of a system.

Ok that statement can save you for the first stage let us get down actually what is it. Let's revisit back how software development cycle evolved.

When we look back at times of COBOL where we used to break the modules in small functionalities and use reusability to its maximum.

Then came the time when we talked in terms of Objects where things were clearer as software was modeled in terms of real life examples. It worked fine and till today is the most accepted way of implementing and organizing project. So why AOP ??

Aspect oriented programming does not oppose OOP's but rather supports it and make's it more maintainable. So remove the logic from head the AOP is replacement of OOP. No its brother of OOP helping him to be better.

When we talk in terms of objects it is an entity which maps to real world domain. Object has attributes which represent the state of object and also define its behavior. By rule of object oriented programming object should be stand alone and communicate with other objects using messages or defined interface.

One object should not communicate with other object directly rather communicate through defined interfaces. Every object satisfies some "Concern" in relation to the system.

> Twist: *What is Concern in AOP?*

"A concern is a particular goal, concept, or area of interest"

There are mainly two types of concern from an object perspective:

√   Core / Main concerns which it should satisfy and is his work.

√   System concerns which are not related to business functionalities but software related concerns example audit trail, Error handling, Security etc.

Ok let us try to understand this principle by some example.

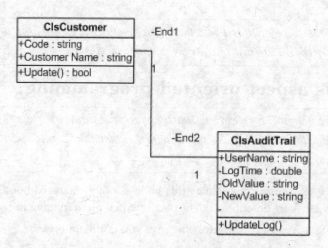

Figure: 10.7 Customer and Audit trail relationships

Above is a class diagram which shows relationshipbetween two classes "ClsCustomer" and "ClsAuditTrail". "ClsCustomer" class does inserting of new customers in to database and "ClsAuditTrail" does the auditing of what is changed in the customer class.

Now there are two concerns in this project:

√   Customer code should not exceed than 10 lengths (Business level concern) greater

√   All customer data which is updated should be audited. (System level concern)

If you see the ClsCustomer the update method is called in Audit trail implementation. If you really look from object oriented point of view we are doing something in customer class which is supposed to be not his implementation: - Audit Trail logging. Thus we have also broken down the rule of encapsulation. In short the class not only handles his work but also some other work which is not his concern.

Ok now let us define crosscutting which is one of important aspects of AOP.

    Twist: What is cross cutting in AOP ?

When one or many concerns span across module it is called as cross cutting. Example in our audit trail example we will probably need to audit trail for customer as well as supplier. So Audit trail can span across other objects also that is termed as cross cutting.

> *Note: In CD we have provided aspectj-1.5.2.jar which you can use for practicing. Before we can use aspectj properly two important things:*
>
>   √   *You need to copy C:\aspectj1.5\lib\aspectjrt.jar to jdk1.x/jre/lib/ext directory.*
>   √   *Then you need to set the class path to C:\aspectj1.5\lib\aspectjrt.jar.*

(A) How can you implement AOP practically in JAVA?

> *Note: We will be using Aspectj for demonstrating AOP in JAVA.*

We will try to demonstrate AOP using a simple helloword program. In the below figure you can see two classes one is Test.java and TestAspect.java. We will try to weave both these classes together.

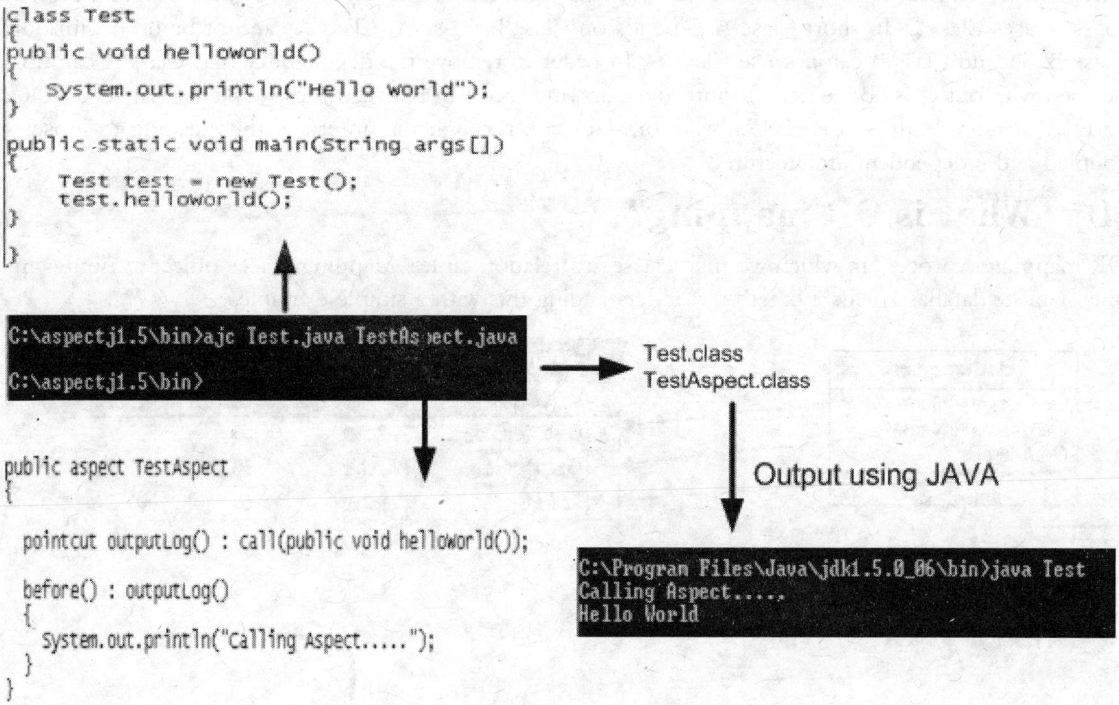

```
class Test
{
public void helloworld()
{
    System.out.println("Hello world");
}

public static void main(String args[])
{
    Test test = new Test();
    test.helloworld();
}
}
```

```
C:\aspectj1.5\bin>ajc Test.java TestAspect.java
C:\aspectj1.5\bin>
```

Test.class
TestAspect.class

```
public aspect TestAspect
{

    pointcut outputLog() : call(public void helloworld());

    before() : outputLog()
    {
        System.out.println("Calling Aspect.....");
    }
}
```

Output using JAVA

```
C:\Program Files\Java\jdk1.5.0_06\bin>java Test
Calling Aspect.....
Hello World
```

Figure 10.8: Output of AspectJ

Test.java is simple class which calls the Helloword. But TestAspect is a bit complicated. So lets go step by step how its flows. We have defines a pointcut called as outputLog.

pointcut outputLog() : call(public void helloWorld());

This pointcut will be executed before calling the helloworld method. Below is the snippet code of the method. You can see the before key word.

```
before() : outputLog()
{
        System.out.println("Calling Aspect.....");
}
```

In order to weave these two classes together we need to use ajc.exe. You can see in the above figure we have given two file inputs to the compiler. It generates Test.class and TestAspect.class. Now we copy these two classes in the bin directory and run the Test.class using javac. You can see in the output the aspect method is first run and then the helloworld method.

Note: You can get the above sample in AOP folder.

(A) What is Inversion of control?

Inversion of control is also termed as Dependency Inversion Principle. Let's say we have class A. Class A uses Class B. In short Class A depends on Class B. In short Class A can not be used with out Class B. Second Class B can not use Class A. In order to remove the dependency that Class A can not be used with out Class B we need to introduce an Interface I in between them. This is termed as IOC or DIP. So now both of the classes will communicate through this interface thus leading to loosely coupled and independent architecture.

(I) What is OR mapping?

OR mapping is process in which we map classes to relation tables. Mapping places object attributes in one or more database fields. Ok let's try understanding this with a simple example.

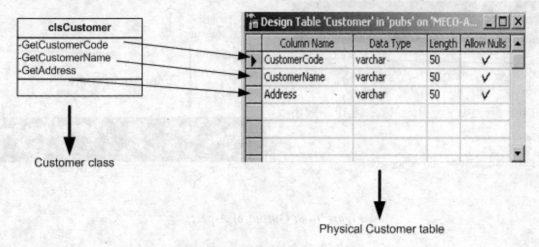

Figure 10.9: OR mapper in action

In the above figure you can see· on the right hand side we have physical customer table with three attributes Customer Code , CustomerName and Address. All these three attributes map the customer class defined in the right hand side. If the table has one to many relation ship similar mapping will be done on the class side also. Due the above mapping you can now handle save and retrieve more effectively. There are many OR mapping tools available in market which read your schema and create classes accordingly. It generates full persistence objects due to which you can minimize your code to a lot greater extent.

> *Note: Architecture is everybody's favorite and the wide combination is difficult to be covered in this book. Many of the things can only come by live experience.*

11

UML

(B) What is UML?

The Unified Modeling Language (UML) is a graphical language for visualizing, specifying, constructing, and documenting the artifacts of a software-intensive system.UML provides blue prints for business process, System function, programming language statements, database schemas and reusable components.

(I) How many types of diagrams are there in UML ?

Twist: Explain in short all types of diagrams in UML ?

There are nine types of diagrams in UML:

Use case diagram

They describe "WHAT" of a system rather than "HOW" the system does it.They are used to identify the primary elements and processes that form the system. The primary elements are termed as "actors" and the processes are called "use cases". Use Case diagrams shows "actors" and there "roles".

Class diagram

From the use case diagram we can now go to detail design of system, for which the primary step is class diagram. The best way to identify classes is to consider all "NOUNS" in use cases as classes, "VERBS" as methods of classes, relation between actors can then be used to define relation between classes. The relationship or association between the classes can be either an "is-a" or "has-a" relationship which can easily be identified from use cases.

Object diagram

An object is an instance of a class. Object diagram captures the state of classes in the system and their relationships or associations at a specific point of time.

State diagram

A state diagram, as the name suggests, represents the different states that objects in the system undergo during their life cycle. Object change in response to certain simulation so this simulation effect is captured in state diagram. So basically it has a initial state and final state and events that happen in between them. Whenever you think that some simulations are complicated you can go for this diagram.

Sequence diagram

Sequence diagrams can be used to explore the logic of a complex operation, function, or procedure. They are called sequence diagrams because sequential nature is shown via ordering of messages. First message starts at the top and the last message ends at bottom. The important aspect of a sequence diagram is that it is time-ordered. This means that the exact sequence of the interactions between the objects is represented step by step. Different objects in the sequence diagram interact with each other by passing "messages".

Collaboration diagram

A collaboration diagram groups together the interactions between different objects to fulfill a common purpose.

Activity diagram

Activity diagram is typically used for business process modeling, for modeling the logic captured by a single use case, or for visualizing the detailed logic of a business rule.Complicated process flows in the system are captured in the activity diagram. Similar to a state diagram, an activity diagram also consists of activities, actions, transitions, initial and final states, and guard conditions. But difference is state diagrams are in context of simulation while activity gives detail view of business logic.

Deployment diagram

Deployment diagrams show the hardware for your system, the software that is installed on that hardware, and the middleware used to connect the disparate machines to one another. It shows how the hardware and software work together to run a system. In one line its shows the deployment view of the system.

Component diagram

The component diagram represents the high-level parts that make up the system. From .NET angle point of view they form the "NAMESPACES". From Java point of view thet form "PACKAGES". This diagram depicts, at a high level, what components form part of the system and how they are interrelated. Its shows the logical grouping of classes or group of other components.

Note: The best way to remember all the blocks of UML is "Serve cool SOUP during church ceremony" that covers State chart, Class diagrams, Sequence diagram, Object diagram, Use Case diagram, Package diagram, Deployment diagram, Collaboration diagram, Component diagram.

(B)   What are advantages of using UML?

Twist: What is Modeling and why UML ?

As the name suggest UNIFIED MODELING LANGUAGE. Modelling has been around for years, not only in software field but also in other trades like civil, mechanical etc. Example in civil engineering drawing the main architecture built of diagram is a model by itself. Modelling makes complex and huge system to break up in to simple and discrete pieces that can be individually understood. Example simple flowchart drawing is modeling.

There are two main advantages of modeling:

√   **Readability:** Representing your whole architecture in flowchart, class diagrams, ER diagrams etc makes your project more readable. Especially when programmer's change jobs handover becomes easier. More the project is not readable more the dependencies.

√   **Reusability:** After the system is more readable and broken down to pieces, it becomes easier to identify redundant and similar modules. Thus increasing reusability.

So why UML? Well different languages have different ways of coding and syntaxes. In order to bring all languages in one roof UML is in to picture. As the term comes in UNIFIED, it unifies all disparate languages in one roof so that can be understood by people who are working on some other platforms.

(A)   What is the sequence of UML diagrams in project?

Twist: How did you implement UML in your project?

First let me say some fact about this question, you can not implement all the nine diagrams given by UML in one project; you can but can be very rare scenario. The way UML is implemented in project varies from project to project and company to company.

Second very important point to remember is normally all diagrams are not implemented in project, but some basic diagrams are important to have in order that project is readable. When we talk about projects every project have phases example (Requirements phase, design phase, coding phase etc). As every phase of the software cycle proceeds these diagrams come in picture. Some diagrams span across multiple phases.

> *Note: If you want to have a detail about software life cycle look out for chapter "Project Management".*

Normally following are different basic phases:

Requirement phase (Use Case Diagrams, Activity diagrams)

Requirement phase is the phase where you normally gather requirement and Use Cases are the best things to make explanation of the system. In requirement phase you can further make complicated Use Cases more simple and easy to understand by using activity diagrams, but I do not see it as must in every project. If the Use cases are really complicated go for a Activity diagram. Example CRUD (creates, read, update and delete) operation use cases have no significance for making activity diagrams. So in short the outcome UML documents from requirement phase will be Use Case and Activity diagram documents (Activity diagram documents will only be there if there are complicated Use Cases to be simplified).

Just a small Twist: Do I need all UML diagrams in a project?

> *Note: This question is specially asked to know have you actually used UML. I have seen many guys trying to give some jack of all answers saying "YES". Beware it is a trap.*

Not all diagrams are needed in project example: - Activity diagrams will only be needed when you want some simplified look of a complicated use case.

Design phase (Class diagrams, object diagrams, Component diagrams, Collaboration diagrams, Deployment diagrams, Sequence diagrams)

Design phase is the phase where you design your technical architecture of your project. Now again in this you do not use all UML documents of a project.

But the next document after the Use Case document will be the Component diagram. Component diagrams form a high level classification of the system. So after "Use Cases" just try to come out with a high level classification / grouping of related functionalities. This should be compulsory diagram as outcome of this document will form "NAMESPACES" structure of .NET project and "PACKAGES" structure jn JAVA projects.

Ok now once your high level grouping is done you can go ahead with class diagrams. Especially from Use Case you get the "NOUNS" and "VERBS" which can form the class name and the method name respectively. From my point of view class diagrams should be compulsory in projects.

Object diagrams are not compulsory it depends on how complicated your project. Object diagrams shows the relation between instances of class at runtime. In short it captures the state and relation of classes at any given moment of time. Example you have class which creates objects of different classes, its like a factory. In class diagram you will only show that it as a simple class with a method called as "CreateObject". But in object diagrams actually you will show the types of instances create from that object.

Collaboration diagrams mainly depict interaction between object to depict some purpose. I find this diagram to be more useful than Object diagrams as they are addressed for some purpose example "Login Process" which will use "Login object", "User Object" etc to fulfill the login purpose. So if you find the process very complicated go for this diagram. I see as a thumb rule if there is an activity diagram which show some serious complicated scenarios. I will like to go for this diagram in order to simplify the explanation.

State chart diagram is again created if your project requires it. If your project has some complicated start and end states to show then this diagram is most useful. Recently I was making a call center project where the agent phone pickup and hang state has to be depicted. So my first state was when agent picks up the phone and the final stage was when agent hangs the phone, in between process was very complicated, which can only be shown by using state chart diagrams.

Sequence diagrams are needed if some sequence is complicated. Do not confuse sequence diagrams with Activity diagram, Activity diagrams map to a Use Case while sequence diagrams show object interaction in sequence.

Deployment diagrams are again not a compulsory requirement. It will show the hardware and software deployment of your system. If you really have leisure in your project go for it or if you want to make the client smile seeing some diagrams.

Implementation phase / Coding phase (Class diagrams for reverse engineering, Other diagrams for validity check)

In this phase mostly class diagrams are re-engineered with the source code. But other diagrams are also present for validity check example state chart diagrams will be used in case to check that the both activity between those states follow the proper logic. If some things have to be changed then again there is iteration backward to the Requirement phase.

Testing phase

This phase mostly goes for the testing department. I am not talking about preparing UTP plans but SITP plans. Where the testing department will look at all diagrams to prepare a test plan and execute it. Example it will see the Use Case document to see the business rules, it will see the activity diagram and sequence diagrams to see the proper flow of modules. If some things are not proper there is iteration back to the Design phase.

Roll out and close over phases.

All document just to re-check that things are proper, example all modules deployed according to the deployment diagrams, are all business rules in Use Cases satisfied.

Let us revise the following points:

√   Not all diagrams are compulsory.

√   The minimum diagrams according to software life cycle phases are:

Requirement phase: Use Case Diagrams

Design Phase: Component diagrams, Class diagrams

Implementation phase: All diagrams derived from pervious phases specially class diagram for reverse engineering.

Testing phase: All diagrams derived from requirement and design phases for verification and preparing test plans.

Roll out and close over phase: All document derived from Design phase and requirement phases.

Below is a sample figure which shows all the documents in relevant phases.

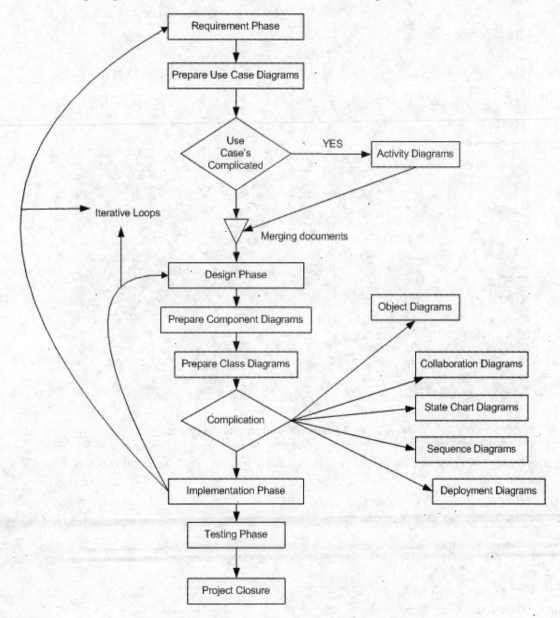

Figure: 11.1 Phase mapping with UML documents

Note: *This book will now attempt to describe every element of a UML diagram. But it is advisable that you should install any decent UML tool and do a small practice of one or two diagrams which will make you comfortable during interview.*

(A) Give a small brief explanation of all Elements in activity diagrams?

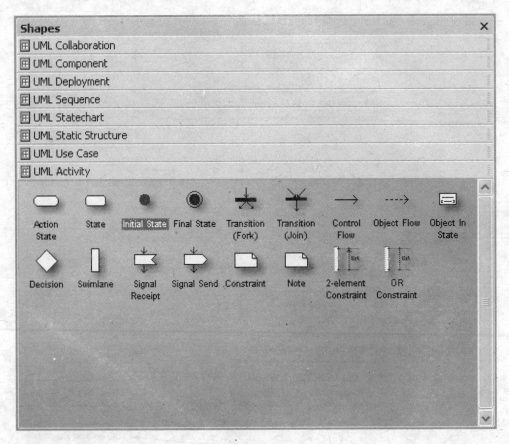

Figure: 11.2 Elements of Activity Diagram

Action State: It is a type of state that has an internal action and one outgoing event that would complete the internal action.

State: It is a condition when following events occur:

√ Object satisfies a condition.

√ Or performs a action.

√ Or wait for a event to happen.

Initial State: It represents a state before any event occurs.

Final State: Represents completion of an activity.

Transition Fork: Denotes beginning of parallel path activities.

Transition Join: Denotes merging of parallel path activities.

Control Flow: Represents relationship between two states and actions. In short it indicates that an object in one state is entering some other state.

Object Flow: Connects an object flow state to control flow or action state.

Object in State: Indicate the object's state after manipulation by multiple activities.

Decisions: Defines if there are any condition's in the path.

Swim Lanes: Assigns responsibility to action states.

Signal receipt Shape: Used to replace an event label on a transition.

Signal Send Shape: Used to replace an event label on a transition.

Constraint: Conditions that must be maintained true in order the system is valid.

2-Element Constraint: It show a constraint on two classes or associations.

OR constraint: It show an OR constraint on two classes or associations.

(A) Explain Different elements of a collaboration diagram?

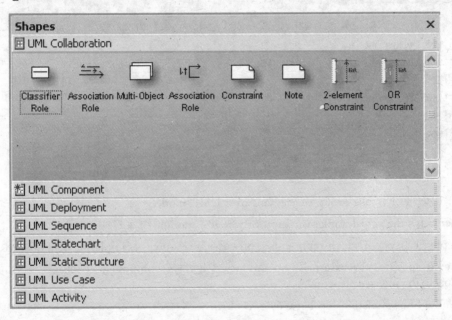

Figure: 11.3 Elements of Collaboration Diagrams

Classifier Role: It classifies a role.

Association Role: It shows the relation between two classifier roles.

Multi-Object: It used to show operation related to entire set of objects rather than on a single object.

Constraint: Conditions which must be maintained as true in order that system is valid.

2-Element Constraint: It shows a constraint on two classes or associations.

OR constraint: It shows an OR constraint on two classes or associations.

(A)   Explain Component diagrams ?

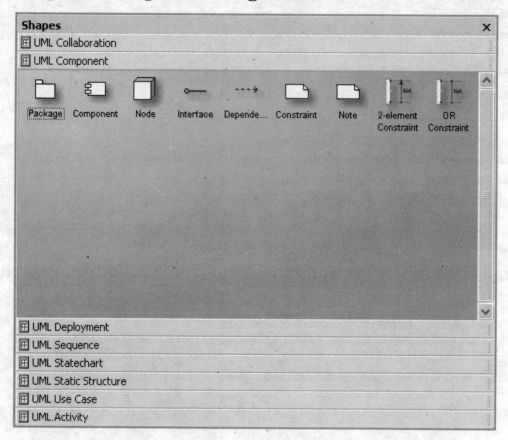

Figure: 11.4 Elements of component diagrams

Package: It logically make group of element of a UML model.

Component: It's the actual implementation or physical module of a UML system.

Node: A physical system which represents a processing resource, example PC or a host machine.

InterFace: It specifies the externally operations of a class, component, package, or other element without specifying internal structure.

Dependency: Shows relationship between two elements.

2-Element Constraint: It shows a constraint on two classes or associations.

OR constraint: It shows an OR constraint on two classes or associations.

(A) Explain all parts of a deployment diagram?

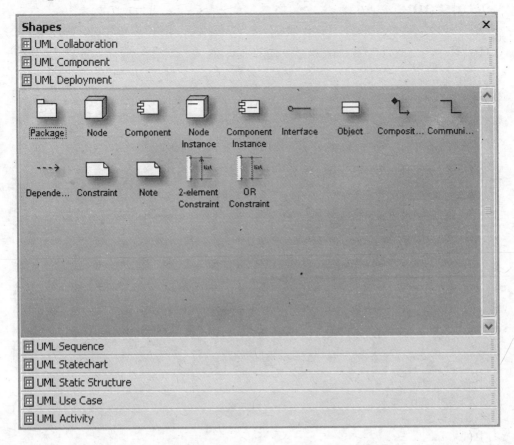

Figure: 11.5 Elements of Deployment Diagram

Package: It logically groups element of a UML model.

Node: A physical system which represents a processing resource, example PC or a host machine.

Component: It's the actual implementation or physical module of a UML system.

Node instance: It's a runtime physical instance of a processing resource.

Component Instance: It represents an implementation unit that has identity at run time and can contain objects. A component could be contained within a node instance.

InterFace: It specifies the external operations of a class, component, package, or other element without specifying internal structure.

Object: Instance of a class.

Composition shape: It is a form of aggregation that indicates that a part may belong to only one element or life time of the element.

Communication: How an actor Dependency: - Shows relationship between two elements.

2-Element Constraint: It shows a constraint on two classes or associations.

OR constraint: It shows an OR constraint on two classes or associations.

(A) Describe the various components in sequence diagrams?

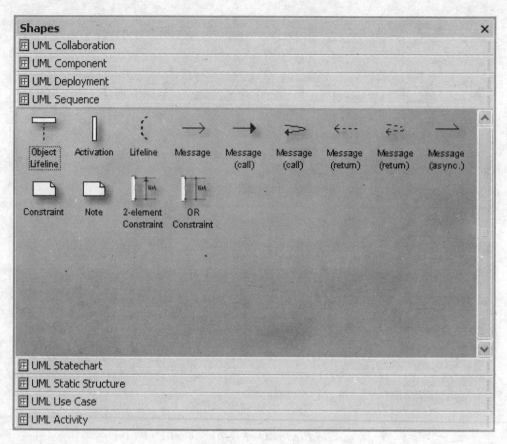

Figure: 11.6 Elements of Sequence diagrams

Object lifeline: It represents the lifetime of an object creation and its destruction. If the object is created or destroyed during the time period the diagram represents, then the lifeline stops or starts at the appropriate point. An object's destruction is marked with a large X.

Activation: It's time period during which actor is performing a action.

Lifeline: This says that there exists some condition on the object lifetime.

Message: It shows communication between objects that conveys information and results in an action.

Message (call): It's same like message but also conveys some information and results in action.

All messages have same definition as the Message (Call) given above.

2-Element Constraint: It shows a constraint on two classes or associations.

OR constraint: It shows an OR constraint on two classes or associations.

(A) What are the element in State Chart diagrams ?

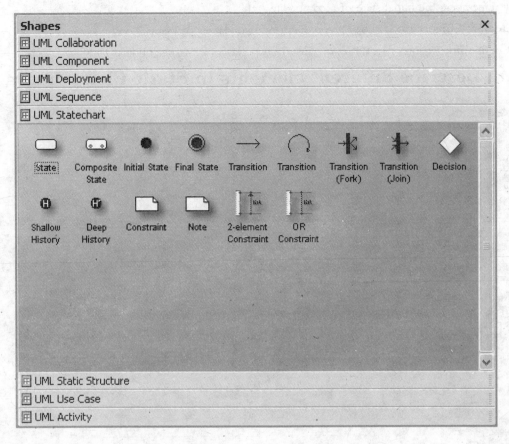

Figure: 11.7 Elements of State Chart Diagrams

State: It's a condition when following events occur:-

√ Object satisfies a condition.

√ Or performs a action.

√ Or waits for a event to happen.

Composite State: It has one or more sub states.

Initial State: It represents a state before any event occurs.

Final State: Represents completion of an activity.

Transition: Shows the change of one state to other.

Transition Fork: Denotes beginning of parallel path activities.

Transition Join: Denotes merging of parallel path activities.

Decision: Indicates condition to move to different states.

Shallow History: Represents the state last visited. When a transition to the indicator fires, an object resumes the state it last had at the same level as the history indicator.

Deep history: A deep history allows you to return from whatever sub-state, whereas a shallow one only remembers the initial state of a composite state.

2-Element Constraint: It shows a constraint on two classes or associations.

OR constraint: It shows an OR constraint on two classes or associations.

(A)   Describe different elements in Static Chart diagrams?

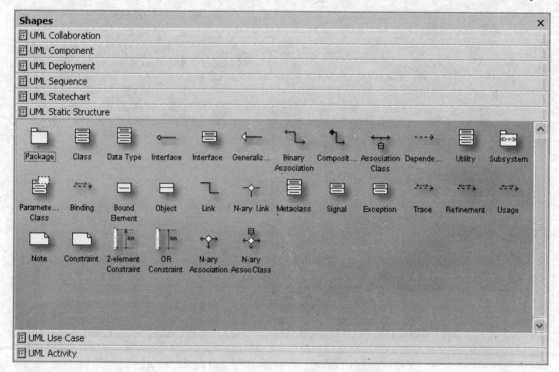

Figure: 11.8 Elements of Static diagrams

Package: It logically groups element of a UML model.

Class: They describe set of objects with similar structure, behavior, and relationships.

Data Type: A data type is an instance of the DataType metaclass defined in the UML metamodel. A data type declares a type of class attribute. This type is available as a string, you can include it when you define attributes for other elements in a model.

Interface: It specifies the externally operations of a class, component, package, or other element without specifying internal structure.

Generalization: It is a relationship between a specific element and a general element, such that the specific element is fully consistent with the general element and includes additional information (such as attributes and associations). For example, the classes Car, Bike, Cycle can all be specific elements of a more general abstract class element named vehicle.

Binary Association: It's a relationship between two classes.

Composition: A composition is a form of aggregation that indicates that a part may belong to only one whole and that the lifetime of the whole determines the lifetime of the part.

Dependency: Shows relationship between two elements.

Utility: Whatever Attributes and operations you define for a utility become global variables and procedures.

Subsystem: It is a package that contains the contents of the entire system or an entire model within the system.

Parameterized class: It is a template that describes a class with one or more unbound formal parameters.

Binding: It is a kind of dependency that indicates a binding of parameterized class or template, parameters to actual values to create a bound, or no parameterized, element.

Bound element: Parameters of the parameterized class are bound to actual values.

Object: Represents instance of a class.

Link: Represents Links between objects.

N-ary Link: Represents link between an objects.

Meta-Class: Whose instances are classes.

Signal: Specifies stimulus between classes for which there is no reply. It is an element which can be generalized and is defined independently of the classes handling the signal.

Exception: Signal raised because of bad execution.

Trace: Indicates historical relationship between two elements.

Refinement: Refinement is a kind of dependency that indicates a historical or derivation relationship between two elements with a mapping between them.

Usage: Usage is a kind of dependency that indicates that one element requires the presence of another element for its correct implementation or functioning.

2-Element Constraint: It shows a constraint on two classes or associations.

OR constraint: It shows an OR constraint on two classes or associations.

(A) Explain the different elements of a Use Case ?

Package: It logically groups element of a UML model.

Use Case: It represents a set of events.

Actor: Role played by an outside object.

Interface: It specifies the externally operations of a class, component, package, or other element without specifying internal structure.

Communication: How an actor Dependency shows relationship between two elements.

Extends: Indicates that the elements come in parent child relationship where one element inherits other elements behavior.

Uses: Here one element uses the other elements behavior. The main difference between Extends and Uses is a "Is a" and "Has a" relationship. "Is a" relationship defines a child parent relationship. Example "XYZ" is a child of "PQR". "Has a" relationship defines an aggregation relationship that "XYZ" has a "BLUE SHIRT".

System boundary: Indicates the system boundary of a Use case.

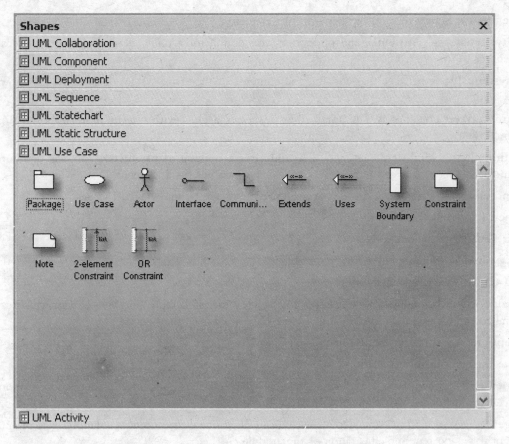

Figure: 11.9 Different Elements of Use Case

2-Element Constraint: It shows a constraint on two classes or associations.

OR constraint: It shows an OR constraint on two classes or associations.

Twist: What is the difference between Activity and sequence diagrams?(I leave this to the readers)

12

Project Management

Note: *This topic is meant specially for JAVA programmers who are looking for better position rather than simple programmer jobs. Project management is not everybody's cup of tea. I have seen 10 year good decent technical guys do not get this position easily. But street smart programmers with average technical guys do really well. How much ever I try to cover this topic in this book......it has so many variations that it's really difficult to predict every scenario of project management interview. But definitely I will try to cover the basics by which you can at least get a feel of what is asked.*

(B) What is project management?

Applying knowledge, skills, tools, techniques in project and deliver project deliverables is a short definition of project management.It's basically managing project time, cost and scope.

(A) Is spending in IT projects constant through out the project?

Note: *It's a tricky question, to know how much depth you have regarding costing of projects.*

Normally in initial stage of projects (requirement and design phase) the cost is very less (as you need maximum business analyst and architecture), but as the project proceeds cost factor starts increasing. The cost is maximum in coding phase (this is where you require programmers, project leads and project manager). Later when the project is in testing and acceptance phase cost is less as we will need only one or two programmers for removing bugs, than the whole team.

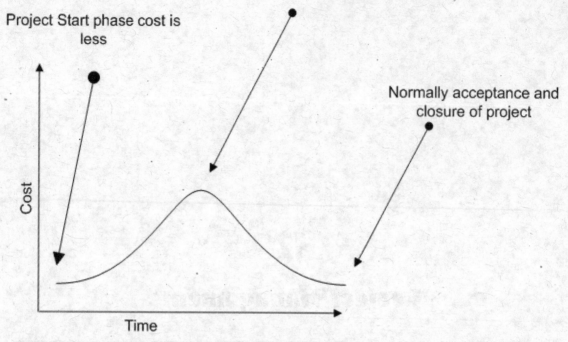

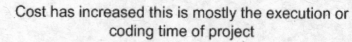

Figure: 12.1 Graph showing cost variation in project.

(B) Who is a stakeholder ?

A stakeholder is anyone who has something to gain or lose as a result of the completion or failure of this project or phase

> Note: *It's not only the end customer the stakeholder. Project managers, Project Lead, even programmers, testing department etc. are stake holders of project. So during project management interview whenever you refer stake holders be clear about the terminology.*

(B) Can you explain project life cycle ?

Twist: How many phases are there in software project ?

There are five stages of any project initiating, planning, executing, controlling, and closeout. These are general phases and change according to domain. Example when writing a book I will have following mappings initiating(contacting publishers,getting copy right etc), planning(Table of contents of book, Number of chapters , tool to use, chapter wise deadlines etc), executing(Actually writing the book), controlling(proof reading, language checks, page alignments etc), and closeout(Finally printing and on the shelf for sale). So this classification is at very broader level , for software development the above figure shows the mapping.

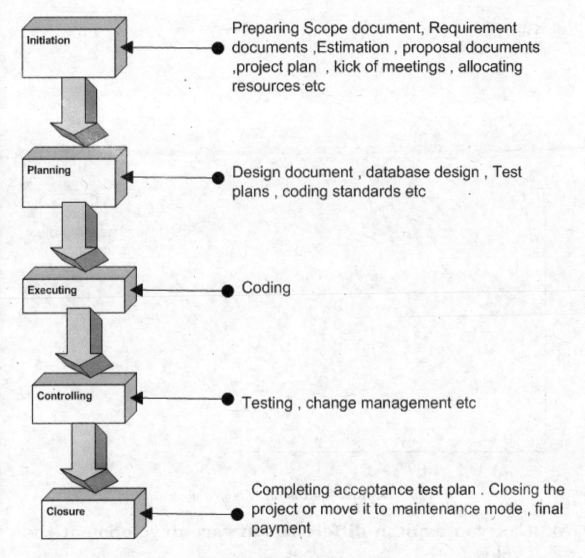

Figure: 12.2 Life cycle of a project

During Software project management interview expected answer is requirement phase, design phase, coding phase, testing phase and project closure. But you can just impress the answer by giving a general answer and then showing the mapping.

(B) Are risk constant through out the project ?

* Never say that risk is high through out the project.

Risk is high at the start of projects, but by proper POC (Proof of concept) risk is brought in control.Good project managers always have proper risk mitigation plan at the start of project. As the project continues one by one risk is eliminated thus bringing down the risk.

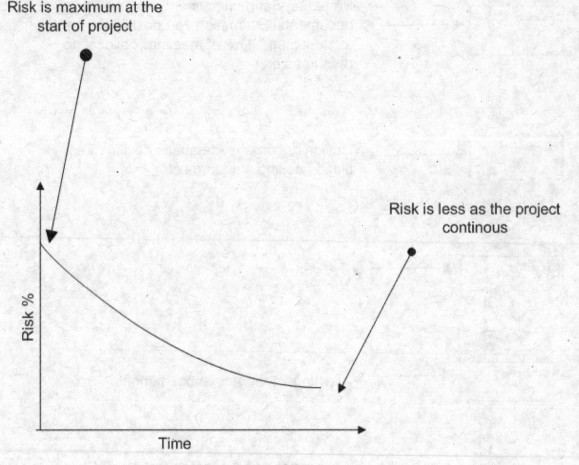

Figure: 12.3 Risk % according to project phases

(A)   Can you explain different software development life cycles ?

Note: This questions is asked to test that as a project manager do you have a know how of all the project life cycles.In PMP (Project management plan) you have to specify saying which software development model you will follow. Definitely depending on client and project scenarios it's the project manager's responsibility to choose a development cycle.

SDLC (System Development Life Cycle) is overall process of developing information systems through multi stage process systems from investigation of initial requirements through analysis, design, implementation and maintenance. The days are gone when one COBOL programmer used to analyze, test and implement software systems. Systems have become complex, huge team members are involved, architects, analyst, programmers, testers, users etc. To manage this number of SDLC models have been created.

Following are popular models which are listed:

√   Waterfall Model.

√   Spiral Model.

√   Build and Fix model.

√   Rapid prototyping Model.

√   Incremental Model.

This section we will go into depth of different SDLC models.

Water Fall Model

This is the oldest model. It has sequence of stages; output of one stage becomes input of other.

Following are stages in Waterfall model:

√   **System Requirement:** This is initial stage of the project where end user requirements are gathered and documented.

√   **System Design:** In this stage detail requirements, screen layout, business rules, process diagram, pseudo code and other documentations are prepared. This is first step in technical phase.

√   **Implementation:** Depending on the design document actual code is written here.

√   **Integration and Testing:** All pieces are brought together and tested. Bugs are removed in this phase.

√   **Acceptance, Installation and Deployment:** This is final stage where software is put in production and runs actual business.

√   **Maintenance:** This is least glamorous phase which runs forever. Code Changes, correction, addition etc are done in this phase.

Waterfall is suited for low risk in areas of User Interface and performance requirements, but high risk in budget and schedule predictability and control. Waterfall assumes that all requirements can be specified in advance. But unfortunately requirement grows and changes through various stages, so it needs feedback from one stage to other.

Spiral Model

Spiral Model removes the drawback of waterfall model, by providing emphasis to go back and reiterate earlier stages a number of times as project progresses. On broader level it's a series of short waterfall cycles, each producing an early prototype representing a part of entire project. It also helps demonstrate a Proof of Concept at early software life cycle.

Build and Fix Model

This is the way free-lancers work Write some code and keep modifying it until the customer is happy. This approach can be quite dangerous and risky.

Rapid Prototyping Model

This model is also called as Rapid Application Development. The initial emphasis is on creating prototype that look and acts like the desired product. Prototype can be created by using tools which is different from those used for final product. Once the prototype is approved, its discarded and real software development is started from scratch. The problem with this model is that sometimes the prototype moves ahead to become the final live product which can be bad from design point of view. It's a effective model but can have higher costing than other models as you require programmers during the initial phase of the software cycle.

Incremental Model

In this model we divide products into builds, where section of product are created and tested separately. Here errors are found in requirement phase itself, user feedback is taken for each stage and code is tested after it is written.

(B) What is triple constraint triangle in project management ?

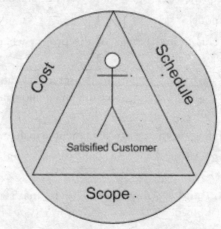

Figure: 12.4 Project Management Triangle

Project Management triangle is depicted as Cost, Schedule and scope.These three aspects form the sides of triangle and the customer is the center point.As customer is always concerned about Cost,Scope and Schedule, so in order to get customer satisfaction project manager should deliver all scope in propose schedule and cost.

If we want to disturb any one of the legs then the other two legs get affected. Example if customer increases the scope then other two sides of the triangle also get affected a lot.

> *Note:* *During project management interviews it's rare that you will be asked directly about constraint triangle. But when you are asked about what are the main factors that affect customer satisfaction you can refer this triangle.*

(B) What is a project baselines ?

It defines a logical closure of any deliverable or cycle. Example you have completed the requirement phase with sign off from the client on the requirement document.So you put a baseline and say that further any changes to this document are change request. Versioning of source code is one type of baseline.

(B) What is effort variance?

Effort Variance = (Actual effort – Estimated Effort) / Estimated Effort.

(B) How is normally a project management plan document organized ?

PMP document forms the bible of a project. It has normally these sections:

√ Project summary

√ Project organization hierarchy

√ WBS / Activity list to be performed with schedule.

√ Work product identification (In short who will do what)

√ Project schedule(GANNT chart or PERT chart).

√ Estimated Cost and completion.

√ Project requirements.

√ Risk identification.

√ Configuration management section.

√ Quality section.

√ Action Item status.

(I) How do you estimate a project?

There are many techniques available for estimating a project:

√ Function points

√ Use Case points

√ WBS etc etc.

(B) What is CAR (Causal Analysis and Resolution)?

The basic purpose of CAR is to analyze all defects, problems and good practices/positive triggers in projects, perform a root cause analysis of the same, identify respective corrective and preventive actions and track these to closure. The advantage of CAR is that root causes are scientifically identified and their corrective and preventive actions are carried out. CAR needs to be performed at project initiation, all phase and project ends and on a monthly basis. Fishbone diagram is one of the ways you can do CAR.

(B) What is DAR (Decision Analysis and Resolution) ?

Decision Analysis and Resolution is to analyze possible decisions using a formal evaluation process that identifies alternatives against established criteria.

Example in a project you are said to use third party tools so you will not depend on only one tool but evaluate three to four more tools so that in case of problems you have alternatives. This is called as DAR

(B) What is a fish bone diagram ?

Twist: What is Ishikawa diagram ?

Dr. Kaoru Ishikawa, invented the fishbone diagram. Therefore, it can be also referred as Ishikawa diagram.

Fishbone diagram is an analysis diagram which provides a systematic way of looking at effects and the causes that create or contribute to those effects. Because of the function of the fishbone diagram, it may be referred to as a cause-and-effect diagram. The design of the diagram looks much like the skeleton of a fish. Therefore, it is often referred to as the fishbone diagram.

Fishbone diagram helps in categorizing potential causes of problems or issues in an orderly way and in identifying root causes.

Below is a sample fish bone diagram which shows why a project dead line was not met. The middle arrow is the main problem "Deadline not met". Then we start analyzing other problems which has led to this problem.Example There is client problem -- as he is always changing the requirement -- this is caused because the company did not sign the SRS --- and this happened as proper project management procedures where not at place. So to solve this problem we either appoint a project manager or give training on project management to senior team members.

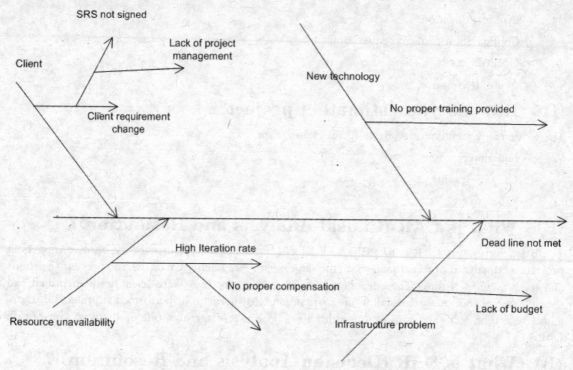

Figure: 12.5 Sample fish bone diagram

(B)   What is pareto principle ?

Twist: What is 80/20 principle ?

Pareto principle also paraphrased as 80/20 principle is simple effective problem tackling way in management. It says that 20% of your problems lead to other 80 % of problems. So rather than concentrating on the 80% of problem if you concentrate on 20% of problems you can save lot of trouble. So in pareto you analyze the problems and only concentrate on 20% of your vital problems. In projects the first 10% and the last 10% of project form the vital part of project.

(B) How do you handle change request?

Normally change request are handled by preparing an Impact analysis document and then doing re-estimation. Example you have an on going project, which has a customer table. Now customer want to also have addresses assigned to it. So you normally raise a change request and then do an impact analysis of the same. Depending on the impact you estimate and let know the client about the financial aspect of the project. Once client sign off or the upper management agrees to the change request you move ahead with implementation.

(I) What is internal change request?

Internal change request are not normally billable change request, it has no financial gains from the client. Example your architecture division of your company has said in mid of the project that the architecture has to be modified. Definitely this has nothing to do with the client, but you make changes to it this is called as Internal change request.

(B) What is difference between SITP and UTP in testing ?

UTP (Unit Test Plan) are done at smallest unit level or stand alone mode. Example you have Customer and invoicing module. So you will do test on Customer and Invoice module independently. But later when we want test both customer and invoice in one set we integrate them and test it. So that's is SITP (System Integration Test Plan)

UTP can be done using NUNIT. Unit testing is done normally by developers and System testing is done normally by testing department in integration mode.

(B) What is the software you have used for project management?

Many companies have there own software defined. There are many project management software available at this moment in market but this can vary from company to company , worst it can very from project to project. But Microsoft project is the most used software at this moment.So just brush your skills on Microsoft project , its used heavily across industry.

(I) What are the metrics followed in project management?

Twist: What metrics will you look at in order to see the project is moving successfully?

Most metric sets deal with a variation of these attributes and are chosen to help project managers gain insight into their product (size, software quality, rework), process (rework, software quality) and project (effort, schedule).

But below is a broader classification:

Project Management Metrics

milestone metrics

√   number of milestones

√   number of proved requirements per milestone

√   controlling level metrics

risk metrics

√   probability of resources availability

√   probability of the requirements validity

√   risk indicators (long schedules, inadequate cost estimating, excessive paperwork, error-prone modules, canceled projects, excessive schedule pressure, low quality, cost overruns, creeping user requirements, excessive time to market, unused or unusable software, unanticipated acceptance criteria, hidden errors)

√   application risk metrics

workflow metrics

√   walkthrough metrics

√   traceability metrics

√   variance metrics

controlling metrics

√   size of control elements

√   structure of control elements

√   documentation level

√   tool application level

management database metrics

√   data quality metrics

√   management data complexity

√   data handling level (performance metrics)

√   visualization level

√   safety and security metrics

Quality Management Metrics

customer satisfaction metrics

√   characteristics size metrics

√   characteristics structure metrics

√   empirical evaluation metrics

√   data presentation metrics

review metrics

√   number of reviews in the process

√   ·   review level metrics

√   review dependence metrics

√   review structure metrics

√   review resources metrics

productivity metrics

√   actual vs. planned metrics

√   performance metrics

√   productivity vs. quality metrics

efficiency metrics

√   time behavior metrics

√   resources behavior metrics

√   actual vs. Planned metrics

quality assurance metrics

√   quality evaluation metrics

√   error prevention metrics

√   measurement level

√   data analysis metrics

Configuration Management Metrics

change control metrics

√   size of change

√   dependencies of changes

√   change interval metrics

√   revisions metrics

version control metrics

√   number of versions

√   number of versions per customer

√   version differences metrics

√   releases metrics (version architecture)

√   data handling level

Note: Following are some questions who do not have a specific answer and vary from person to person or are out of the scope of book. This book will list down the questions just go through them.

(B) You have people in your team who do not meet there deadlines or do not perform what are the actions you will take ?

Twist: Two of your resources have conflicts between them how would you sort it out ?

In such kind of question they want to see your delegation skills. The best answer to this question is a job of a project manager is managing projects and not problems of people, so I will delegate this work to HR or upper authority.... Thanks to my Project Manager for this beautiful answer.

(B) What is black box testing and White box testing?

Black box testing is also termed as functional testing. It ignores how the internal functionality of a system works and depends only what are the outputs on specified inputs. Source code availability is not an important in back box testing. Black box testing is mostly to ensure that it meets the user functionality.

According to IEEE standards following are characteristics of Black box testing:

√   "Testing that ignores the internal mechanism of a system or component and focuses solely on the outputs generated in response to selected inputs and execution conditions;"

√   "Testing conducted to evaluate the compliance of a system or component with specified functional requirements."

One of the ways of black box testing is Manual testing what the tester performs. For instance you can install the application on a machine and tester starts testing is a type of black box testing. In this case the tester is completely unaware of the how the program logic flows and how its coded etc.

White box testing is opposite to Black box it requires internal know how of how the logic flows. As this testing needs know how of the internal structure it can only be done programmers. Unit testing is one of the ways of doing White box testing in which programmers use NUNIT or JNUIT to test each class individually. White box testing can be done by programmer by either stepping through the code or testing the classes and components in isolation.

(B)   What's the difference between Unit testing, Assembly testing and Regression testing?

Unit testing is also called as Component testing. Unit testing ensures that reliable program unit meets their requirements. Unit testing is normally conducted by programmer under the supervision of the project lead or the team Lead. Main objective of this testing is to test each unit in isolation and individually. This is done by knowing what are the inputs to the unit and what the expected outputs for the same. Unit testing is a white box activity. Unit test normally comes in the implementation phase of the project.

For instance in the below figure we are trying to do unit testing on the customer class. So we create the object of Customer class assign "CustomerCode" and "Age" property and check for the response. For instance in this condition we tried to pass a non-numeric value to the "Age" property and the class threw an error saying "Age should be numeric". So here the basic unit testing entity is your class.

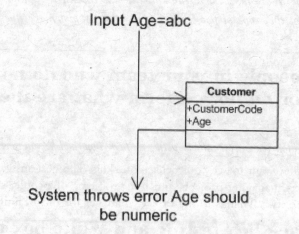

Figure 12.6: Unit testing for sample Customer class

But unit testing is not limited to a component, object or function. So definition of a unit testing will depend on the approach. Below are some examples of unit testing:

√   Check points in UI like tab orders, error messages, look and feel etc.

√   Class, object, component level testing as said previously.

√   In case of functional programming can be a simple method or function.

√   Logic testing for algorithms. Some projects can have some critical algorithm for instance some kind of custom sorting, security implementation etc. So that logic can be tested independently.

But the general thumb rule of what is Unit in Unit testing is that the module self contained and by itself.

Assembly testing goes one step ahead than unit testing. It demonstrates that can the modules interact in a correct, stable and proper manner as defined by the functional specifications provided by the client. Assembly testing is Black box testing style and also called as Integration testing. For instance in the above unit test of the "Customer" class, testing was done in isolation. But in actually the "Customer" class is not going to be stand alone rather it will be used more in conjunction with the "Product" class and also will have UI to do the same. So in short the "Customer" class will work with two more entity one is the "UI" and the other is the "Product" class. So normally assembly testing is done through UI but not necessarily.

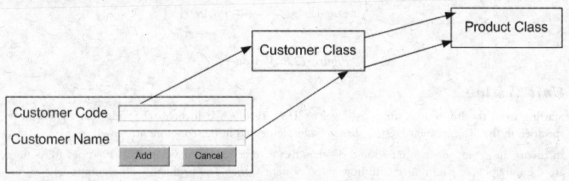

Figure 12.7: Integration Testing

The above figure defines a simple scenario for integration testing. The same "Customer" class is now tested with the "UI" and "Product" to see if the interaction between them matches according to functional specifications.

Regression testing ensures that application function properly even if there are changes or enhancements to system.For instance you change the "Product" class still you will run all the test cases for "Product" , "Customer" and "UI" just to make sure that any changes in "Product" class does not affect interaction with other entities. So you will see when testers do a regression testing they run all the scripts to ensure that nothing has been affected.

(I)   What is V model in testing?

V model map's the type of test to the stage of development in a project.

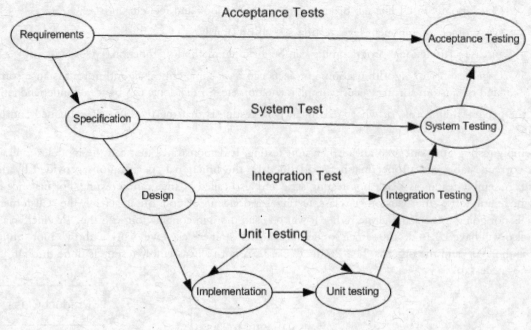

Figure 12.8: V Model

Unit Testing

Starting from the bottom the first test level is "Unit Testing". It involves checking that each feature specified in the "Component Design" has been implemented in the component.

In theory an independent tester should do this, but in practice the developer usually does it, as they are the only people who understand how a component works. The problem with a component is that it performs only a small part of the functionality of a system, and it relies on co-operating with other parts of the system, which may not have been built yet. To overcome this, the developer either builds, or uses special software to trick the component into believe it is working in a fully functional system.

Integration Testing

As the components are constructed and tested they are then linked together to check if they work with each other. It is a fact that two components that have passed all their tests, when connected to each other produce one new component full of faults. These tests can be done by specialists, or by the developers.

Integration Testing is not focused on what the components are doing but on how they communicate with each other, as specified in the "System Design". The "System Design" defines relationships between components.

The tests are organized to check all the interfaces, until all the components have been built and interfaced to each other producing the whole system.

System Testing

Once the entire system has been built then it has to be tested against the "System Specification" to check if it delivers the features required. It is still developer focused, although specialist developers known as systems testers are normally employed to do it.

In essence System Testing is not about checking the individual parts of the design, but about checking the system as a whole. In fact it is one giant component.

System testing can involve a number of specialist types of test to see if all the functional and non-functional requirements have been met. In addition to functional requirements these may include the following types of testing for the non-functional requirements:

√   **Performance:** Are the performance criteria met?

√   **Volume:** Can large volumes of information be handled?

√   **Stress:** Can peak volumes of information be handled?

√   **Documentation:** Is the documentation usable for the system?

√   **Robustness:** Does the system remain stable under adverse circumstances?

There are many others, the need for which is dictated by how the system is supposed to perform.

Acceptance Testing

Acceptance Testing checks the system against the "Requirements". It is similar to systems testing in that the whole system is checked but the important difference is the change in focus:

Systems testing checks that the system that was specified has been delivered. Acceptance Testing checks that the system will deliver what was requested.

The customer should always do acceptance testing and not the developer . The customer knows what is required from the system to achieve value in the business and is the only person qualified to make that judgment. This testing is more of getting the answer for whether is the software delivered as defined by the customer. It's like getting a green flag from the customer that the software is up to the expectation and ready to be used.

(B)   How do you start a project?

Left to the readers

(B)   How did you do resource allocations?

Left to the readers

(I)   How will you do code reviews ?

The way in which code reviews are done change from person to person and also company to company. But the normally when a project is started project people define their architecture, coding standards etc in their design document. So before starting the code review you will have go through the standards defined in the project.

(A)   What is CMMI?

It is a collection of instructions an organization can follow with the purpose to gain better control over its software development process.

(A)   What are the five levels in CMMI?

There are five levels of the CMM. According to the SEI,

Level 1 – Initial

At maturity level 1, processes are usually ad hoc and the organization usually does not provide a stable environment. Success in these organizations depends on the competence and heroics of people in the organization and not on the use of proven processes. In spite of this ad hoc, chaotic environment, maturity level 1 organizations often produce products and services that work; however, they frequently exceed the budget and schedule of their projects.

Maturity level 1 organizations are characterized by a tendency to over commit, abandon processes in the time of crisis, and not be able to repeat their past successes again.

Level 2 – Repeatable

At maturity level 2, software development successes are repeatable. The organization may use some basic project management to track cost and schedule.

Process discipline helps to ensure that existing practices are retained during times of stress. When these practices are in place, projects are performed and managed according to their documented plans.

Project status and the delivery of services are visible to management at defined points (for example, at major milestones and at the completion of major tasks).

Basic project management processes are established to track cost, schedule, and functionality. The necessary process discipline is in place to repeat earlier successes on projects with similar applications.

Level 3 – Defined

At maturity level 3, processes are well characterized and understood, and are described in standards, procedures, tools, and methods.

The organization's set of standard processes, which is the basis for level 3, is established and improved over time. These standard processes are used to establish consistency across the organization. Projects establish their defined processes by the organization's set of standard processes according to tailoring guidelines.

The organization's management establishes process objectives based on the organization's set of standard processes and ensures that these objectives are appropriately addressed.

A critical distinction between level 2 and level 3 is the scope of standards, process descriptions, and procedures. At level 2, the standards, process descriptions, and procedures may be quite different in each specific instance of the process (for example, on a particular project). At level 3, the standards, process descriptions, and procedures for a project are tailored from the organization's set of standard processes to suit a particular project or organizational unit.

Level 4 – Managed

Using precise measurements, management can effectively control the software development effort. In particular, management can identify ways to adjust and adapt the process to particular projects without measurable losses of quality or deviations from specifications.

Sub processes are selected that significantly contribute to overall process performance. These selected sub processes are controlled using statistical and other quantitative techniques.

A critical distinction between maturity level 3 and maturity level 4 is the predictability of process performance. At maturity level 4, the performance of processes is controlled using statistical and other quantitative techniques, and is quantitatively predictable. At maturity level 3, processes are only qualitatively predictable.

Level 5 – Optimizing

Maturity level 5 focuses on persistently improving process performance through both incremental and innovative technological improvements. Quantitative process-improvement objectives for the organization are established, continually revised to reflect changing business objectives, and used as criteria in managing process improvement. The effects of deployed process improvements are measured and evaluated against the quantitative process-improvement objectives. Both the defined processes and the organization set of standard processes are targets of measurable improvement activities.

Process improvements to address common causes of process variation and measurably improve the organization's processes are identified, evaluated, and deployed.

Optimizing processes that are nimble, adaptable and innovative depends on the participation of an empowered workforce aligned with the business values and objectives of the organization. The organization's ability to rapidly respond to changes and opportunities is enhanced by finding ways to accelerate and share learning.

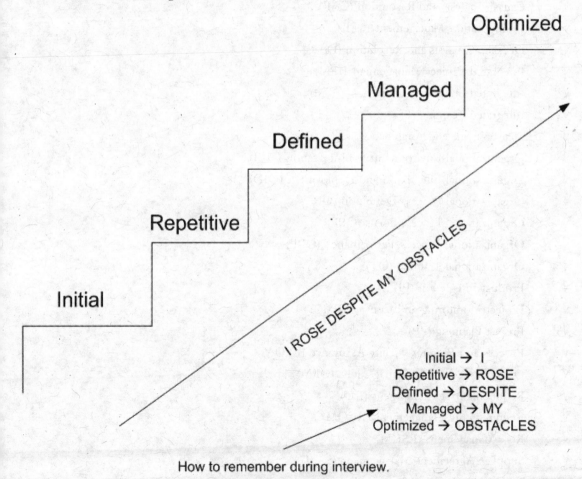

Initial → I
Repetitive → ROSE
Defined → DESPITE
Managed → MY
Optimized → OBSTACLES

How to remember during interview.

Figure 12.9 : - CMMI Levels

A critical distinction between maturity level 4 and maturity level 5 is the type of process variation addressed. At maturity level 4, processes are concerned with addressing special causes of process variation and providing statistical predictability of the results. Though processes may produce predictable results, the results may be insufficient to achieve the established objectives. At maturity level 5, processes are concerned with addressing common causes of process variation and changing the process (that is, shifting the mean of the process performance) to improve process performance (while maintaining statistical probability) to achieve the established quantitative process-improvement objectives.

> *Note: I am sure during interview specially the SQA guys expect all the different levels of CMMI to be in mind. So below is the figure which will help you remembering the same.*

(A) What is continuous and staged representation?

CMMI contains 25 key process areas which organization can follow to adapt CMMI.

√   Causal Analysis and Resolution (CAR)

√   Configuration Management (CM)

√   Decision Analysis and Resolution (DAR)

√   Integrated Project Management (IPM)

√   Integrated Supplier Management (ISM)

√   Integrated Teaming (IT)

√   Measurement and Analysis (MA)

√   Organizational Environment for Integration (OEI)

√   Organizational Innovation and Deployment (OID)

√   Organizational Process Definition (OPD)

√   Organizational Process Focus (OPF)

√   Organizational Process Performance (OPP)

√   Organizational Training (OT)

√   Product Integration (PI)

√   Project Monitoring and Control (PMC)

√   Project Planning (PP)

√   Process and Product Quality Assurance (PPQA)

√   Quantitative Project Management (QPM)

√   Requirements Development (RD)

√   Requirements Management (REQM)

√   Risk Management (RSKM)

√   Supplier Agreement Management (SAM)

√   Technical Solution (TS)

√   Validation (VAL)

√   Verification (VER)

The method by which company wants to adapt to CMMI is called a representation. So either organization can adapt for staged or continuous representation.

In the continuous representation process areas are organized by functional area. For example, a company interested to improve its Project Management capability would focus on IPM, ISM, IT, PMC, PP, QPM, RSKM and SAM.

Process Management

OID - Organizational Innovation and Deployment

OPD - Organizational Process Definition

OPF - Organizational Process Focus

OPP - Organizational Process Performance

OT - Organizational Training

Project Management

IPM - Integrated Project Management

ISM - Integrated Supplier Management

IT - Integrated Teaming

PMC - Project Monitoring and Control

PP - Project Planning

QPM - Quantitative Project Management

RSKM - Risk Management

SAM - Supplier Management Agreement

Engineering

PI - Product Integration

REQM - Requirements Management

RD - Requirements Development

TS - Technical Solution

VAL - Validation

VER - Verification

Support

CAR - Casual Analysis and Resolution

CM - Configuration Management

DAR - Decision Analysis and Resolution

MA - Measurement and Analysis

OEI - Organizational Environment for Integration

PPQA - Process and Product Quality Assurance

Staged representation

While in staged representation the concept of levels comes in to picture. In the staged representation process areas are organized by organizational maturity level. For example, a company interested to obtain a Maturity Level 2 rating would require company processes covering all of the Maturity Level 2 process areas.

Maturity Levels 2

CM - Configuration Management

MA - Measurement and Analysis

PMC - Project Monitoring and Control

PP - Project Planning

PPQA - Process and Product Quality Assurance

REQM - Requirements Management

SAM - Supplier Management Agreement

Maturity Level 3

DAR - Decision Analysis and Resolution

IPM - Integrated Project Management

ISM - Integrated Supplier Management

IT - Integrated Teaming

OEI - Organizational Environment for Integration

OPD - Organizational Process Definition

OPF - Organizational Process Focus

OT - Organizational Training

PI - Product Integration

RD - Requirements Development

RSKM - Risk Management

TS - Technical Solution

VAL - Validation

VER - Verification

Maturity Level 4

QPM - Quantitative Project Management

OPP - Organizational Process Performance

Maturity Level 5

CAR - Casual Analysis and Resolution

OID - Organizational Innovation and Deployment

(A)   Can you explain the process areas?

> *Note:* *No one is going to ask such a question. But they would like to know at least the purpose of each KPA. Second they would like to know what you did to attain compatibility to these process areas. For instance you say that you did Organizational Process Definition. They would like to know how you did it. For instance you can justify it by saying that you made standard documents for coding standards which was then followed at the organization level for reference. Normally every one follows process it's only that they do not know. So try to map the KPA to the process what you follow. The only purpose to paste all the KPA is if in case you are looking for some higher positions in bug companies they really expect you to speak in term of KPA rather than generic term. This whole stuff can be like a quick reference for you before entering the interview room.*

Each process area is defined by a set of goals and practices. There are two categories of goals and practices: generic and specific. Generic goals and practices are a part of every process area. Specific goals and practices are specific to a given process area. A process area is satisfied when company processes cover all of the generic and specific goals and practices for that process area.

Generic goals and practices

Generic goals and practices are a part of every process area.

GG 1 Achieve Specific Goals

GP 1.1 Perform Base Practices

GG 2 Institutionalize a Managed Process

GP 2.1 Establish an Organizational Policy

GP 2.2 Plan the Process

GP 2.3 Provide Resources

GP 2.4 Assign Responsibility

GP 2.5 Train People

GP 2.6 Manage Configurations

GP 2.7 Identify and Involve Relevant Stakeholders

GP 2.8 Monitor and Control the Process

GP 2.9 Objectively Evaluate Adherence

GP 2.10 Review Status with Higher Level Management

GG 3 Institutionalize a Defined Process

GP 3.1 Establish a Defined Process

GP 3.2 Collect Improvement Information

GG 4 Institutionalize a Quantitatively Managed Process

GP 4.1 Establish Quantitative Objectives for the Process

GP 4.2 Stablize Subprocess Performance

GG 5 Institutionalize an Optimizing Process

GP 5.1 Ensure Continuous Process Improvement

GP 5.2 Correct Root Causes of Problems

Process areas

The CMMI contains 25 key process areas indicating the aspects of product development that are to be covered by company processes.

Causal Analysis and Resolution (CAR)

A Support process area at Maturity Level 5

Purpose

The purpose of Causal Analysis and Resolution (CAR) is to identify causes of defects and other problems and take action to prevent them from occurring in the future.

Specific Practices by Goal

SG 1 Determine Causes of Defects

SP 1.1-1 Select Defect Data for Analysis

SP 1.2-1 Analyze Causes

SG 2 Address Causes of Defects

SP 2.1-1 Implement the Action Proposals

SP 2.2-1 Evaluate the Effect of Changes

SP 2.3-1 Record Data

Configuration Management (CM)

A Support process area at Maturity Level 2

Purpose

The purpose of Configuration Management (CM) is to establish and maintain the integrity of work products using configuration identification, configuration control, configuration status accounting, and configuration audits.

Specific Practices by Goal

SG 1 Establish Baselines

SP 1.1-1 Identify Configuration Items

SP 1.2-1 Establish a Configuration Management System

SP 1.3-1 Create or Release Baselines

SG 2 Track and Control Changes

SP 2.1-1 Track Change Requests

SP 2.2-1 Control Configuration Items

SG 3 Establish Integrity

SP 3.1-1 Establish Configuration Management Records

SP 3.2-1 Perform Configuration Audits

Decision Analysis and Resolution (DAR)

A Support process area at Maturity Level 3

Purpose

The purpose of Decision Analysis and Resolution (DAR) is to analyze possible decisions using a formal evaluation process that evaluates identified alternatives against established criteria.

Specific Practices by Goal

SG 1 Evaluate Alternatives

SP 1.1-1 Establish Guidelines for Decision Analysis

SP 1.2-1 Establish Evaluation Criteria

SP 1.3-1 Identify Alternative Solutions

SP 1.4-1 Select Evaluation Methods

SP 1.5-1 Evaluate Alternatives

SP 1.6-1 Select Solutions

Integrated Project Management (IPM)

A Project Management process area at Maturity Level 3

Purpose

The purpose of Integrated Project Management (IPM) is to establish and manage the project and the involvement of the relevant stakeholders according to an integrated and defined process that is tailored from the organization's set of standard processes.

Specific Practices by Goal

SG 1 Use the Project's Defined Process

SP 1.1-1 Establish the Project's Defined Process

SP 1.2-1 Use Organizational Process Assets for Planning Project Activities

SP 1.3-1 Integrate Plans

SP 1.4-1 Manage the Project Using the Integrated Plans

SP 1.5-1 Contribute to the Organizational Process Assets

SG 2 Coordinate and Collaborate with Relevant Stakeholders

SP 2.1-1 Manage Stakeholder Involvement

SP 2.2-1 Manage Dependencies

SP 2.3-1 Resolve Coordination Issues

SG 3 Use the Project's Shared Vision for IPPD

SP 3.1-1 Define Project's Shared Vision for IPPD

SP 3.2-1 Establish the Project's Shared Vision

SG 4 Organize Integrated Teams for IPPD

SP 4.1-1 Determine Integrated Team Structure for the Project

SP 4.2-1 Develop a Preliminary Distribution of Requirements to Integrated Teams

SP 4.3-1 Establish Integrated Teams

Integrated Supplier Management (ISM)

A Project Management process area at Maturity Level 3

Purpose

The purpose of Integrated Supplier Management (ISM) is to proactively identify sources of products that may be used to satisfy the project's requirements and to manage selected suppliers while maintaining a cooperative project-supplier relationship.

Specific Practices by Goal

SG 1 Analyze and Select Sources of Products

SP 1.1-1 Analyze Potential Sources of Products

SP 1.2-1 Evaluate and Determine Sources of Products

SG 2 Coordinate Work with Suppliers

SP 2.1-1 Monitor Selected Supplier Processes

SP 2.2-1 Evaluate Selected Supplier Work Products

SP 2.3-1 Revise the Supplier Agreement or Relationship

Integrated Teaming (IT)

A Project Management process area at Maturity Level 3

Purpose

The purpose of Integrated Teaming (IT) is to form and sustain an integrated team for the development of work products.

Specific Practices by Goal

SG 1 Establish Team Composition

SP 1.1-1 Identify Team Tasks

SP 1.2-1 Identify Needed Knowledge and Skills

SP 1.3-1 Assign Appropriate Team Members

SG 2 Govern Team Operation

SP 2.1-1 Establish a Shared Vision

SP 2.2-1 Establish a Team Charter

SP 2.3-1 Define Roles and Responsibilities

SP 2.4-1 Establish Operating Procedures

SP 2.5-1 Collaborate among Interfacing Teams

Measurement and Analysis (MA)

A Support process area at Maturity Level 2

Purpose

The purpose of Measurement and Analysis (MA) is to develop and sustain a measurement capability that is used to support management information needs.

Specific Practices by Goal

SG 1 Align Measurement and Analysis Activities

SP 1.1-1 Establish Measurement Objectives

SP 1.2-1 Specify Measures

SP 1.3-1 Specify Data Collection and Storage Procedures

SP 1.4-1 Specify Analysis Procedures

SG 2 Provide Measurement Results

SP 2.1-1 Collect Measurement Data

SP 2.2-1 Analyze Measurement Data

SP 2.3-1 Store Data and Results

SP 2.4-1 Communicate Results

Organizational Environment for Integration (OEI)

A Support process area at Maturity Level 3

Purpose

The purpose of Organizational Environment for Integration (OEI) is to provide an Integrated Product and Process Development (IPPD) infrastructure and manage people for integration.

Specific Practices by Goal

SG 1 Provide IPPD Infrastructure

SP 1.1-1 Establish the Organization's Shared Vision

SP 1.2-1 Establish an Integrated Work Environment

SP 1.3-1 Identify IPPD-Unique Skill Requirements

SG 2 Manage People for Integration

SP 2.1-1 Establish Leadership Mechanisms

SP 2.2-1 Establish Incentives for Integration

SP 2.3-1 Establish Mechanisms to Balance Team and Home Organization Responsibilities

Organizational Innovation and Deployment (OID)

A Process Management process area at Maturity Level 5

Purpose

The purpose of Organizational Innovation and Deployment (OID) is to select and deploy incremental and innovative improvements that measurably improve the organization's processes and technologies. The improvements support the organization's quality and process-performance objectives as derived from the organization's business objectives.

Specific Practices by Goal

SG 1 Select Improvements

SP 1.1-1 Collect and Analyze Improvement Proposals

SP 1.2-1 Identify and Analyze Innovations

SP 1.3-1 Pilot Improvements

SP 1.4-1 Select Improvements for Deployment

SG 2 Deploy Improvements

SP 2.1-1 Plan the Deployment areas

SP 2.2-1 Manage the Deployment

SP 2.3-1 Measure Improvement Effects

Organizational Process Definition (OPD)

A Process Management process area at Maturity Level 3

Purpose

The purpose of Organizational Process Definition (OPD) is to establish and maintain a usable set of organizational process assets.

Specific Practices by Goal

SG 1 Establish Organizational Process Assets

SP 1.1-1 Establish Standard Processes

SP 1.2-1 Establish Life-Cycle Model Descriptions

SP 1.3-1 Establish Tailoring Criteria and Guidelines

SP 1.4-1 Establish the Organization's Measurement Repository

SP 1.5-1 Establish the Organization's Process Asset Library

Organizational Process Focus (OPF)

A Process Management process area at Maturity Level 3

Purpose

The purpose of Organizational Process Focus (OPF) is to plan and implement organizational process improvement based on a thorough understanding of the current strengths and weaknesses of the organization's processes and process assets.

Specific Practices by Goal

SG 1 Determine Process Improvement Opportunities

SP 1.1-1 Establish Organizational Process Needs

SP 1.2-1 Appraise the Organization's Processes

SP 1.3-1 Identify the Organization's Process Improvements

SG 2 Plan and Implement Process Improvement Activities

SP 2.1-1 Establish Process Action Plans

SP 2.2-1 Implement Process Action Plans

SP 2.3-1 Deploy Organizational Process Assets

SP 2.4-1 Incorporate Process-Related Experiences into the Organizational Process Assets

Organizational Process Performance (OPP)

A Process Management process area at Maturity Level 4

Purpose

The purpose of Organizational Process Performance (OPP) is to establish and maintain a quantitative understanding of the performance of the organization's set of standard processes in support of quality and process-performance objectives, and to provide the process performance data, baselines, and models to quantitatively manage the organization's projects.

Specific Practices by Goal

SG 1 Establish Performance Baselines and Models

SP 1.1-1 Select Processes

SP 1.2-1 Establish Process Performance Measures

SP 1.3-1 Establish Quality and Process Performance Objectives

SP 1.4-1 Establish Process Performance Baselines

SP 1.5-1 Establish Process Performance Models

Organizational Training (OT)

A Process Management process area at Maturity Level 3

Purpose

The purpose of Organizational Training (OT) is to develop the skills and knowledge of people so that they can perform their roles effectively and efficiently.

Specific Practices by Goal

SG 1 Establish an Organizational Training Capability

SP 1.1-1 Establish the Strategic Training Needs

SP 1.2-1 Determine Which Training Needs Are the Responsibility of the Organization

SP 1.3-1 Establish an Organizational Training Tactical Plan

SP 1.4-1 Establish Training Capability

SG 2 Provide Necessary Training

SP 2.1-1 Deliver Training

SP 2.2-1 Establish Training Records

SP 2.3-1 Assess Training Effectiveness

Product Integration (PI)

An Engineering process area at Maturity Level 3

Purpose

The purpose of Product Integration (PI) is to assemble the product from the product components, ensure that the product, as integrated, functions properly and deliver the product.

Specific Practices by Goal

SG 1 Prepare for Product Integration

SP 1.1-1 Determine Integration Sequence

SP 1.2-1 Establish the Product Integration Environment

SP 1.3-1 Establish Product Integration Procedures and Criteria

SG 2 Ensure Interface Compatibility

SP 2.1-1 Review Interface Descriptions for Completeness

SP 2.2-1 Manage Interfaces

SG 3 Assemble Product Components and Deliver the Product

SP 3.1-1 Confirm Readiness of Product Components for Integration

SP 3.2-1 Assemble Product Components

SP 3.3-1 Evaluate Assembled Product Components

SP 3.4-1 Package and Deliver the Product or Product Component

Project Monitoring and Control (PMC)

A Project Management process area at Maturity Level 2

Purpose

The purpose of Project Monitoring and Control (PMC) is to provide an understanding of the project's progress so that appropriate corrective actions can be taken when the project's performance deviates significantly from the plan.

Specific Practices by Goal

sSG 1 Monitor Project Against Plan

SP 1.1-1 Monitor Project Planning Parameters

SP 1.2-1 Monitor Commitments

SP 1.3-1 Monitor Project Risks

SP 1.4-1 Monitor Data Management

SP 1.5-1 Monitor Stakeholder Involvement

SP 1.6-1 Conduct Progress Reviews

SP 1.7-1 Conduct Milestone Reviews

SG 2 Manage Corrective Action to Closure

SP 2.1-1 Analyze Issues

SP 2.2-1 Take Corrective Action

SP 2.3-1 Manage Corrective Action

Project Planning (PP)

A Project Management process area at Maturity Level 2

Purpose

The purpose of Project Planning (PP) is to establish and maintain plans that define project activities.

Specific Practices by Goal

SG 1 Establish Estimates

SP 1.1-1 Estimate the Scope of the Project

SP 1.2-1 Establish Estimates of Work Product and Task Attributes

SP 1.3-1 Define Project Life Cycle

SP 1.4-1 Determine Estimates of Effort and Cost

SG 2 Develop a Project Plan

SP 2.1-1 Establish the Budget and Schedule

SP 2.2-1 Identify Project Risks

SP 2.3-1 Plan for Data Management

SP 2.4-1 Plan for Project Resources

SP 2.5-1 Plan for Needed Knowledge and Skills

SP 2.6-1 Plan Stakeholder Involvement

SP 2.7-1 Establish the Project Plan

SG 3 Obtain Commitment to the Plan

SP 3.1-1 Review Plans that Affect the Project

SP 3.2-1 Reconcile Work and Resource Levels

SP 3.3-1 Obtain Plan Commitment

Process and Product Quality Assurance (PPQA)

A Support process area at Maturity Level 2

Purpose

The purpose of Process and Product Quality Assurance (PPQA) is to provide staff and management with objective insight into processes and associated work products.

Specific Practices by Goal

SG 1 Objectively Evaluate Processes and Work Products

SP 1.1-1 Objectively Evaluate Processes

SP 1.2-1 Objectively Evaluate Work Products and Services

SG 2 Provide Objective Insight

SP 2.1-1 Communicate and Ensure Resolution of Noncompliance Issues

SP 2.2-1 Establish Records

Quantitative Project Management (QPM)

A Project Management process area at Maturity Level 4

Purpose

The purpose of the Quantitative Project Management (QPM) process area is to quantitatively manage the project's defined process to achieve the project's established quality and process-performance objectives.

Specific Practices by Goal

SG 1 Quantitatively Manage the Project

SP 1.1-1 Establish the Project's Objectives

SP 1.2-1 Compose the Defined Processes

SP 1.3-1 Select the Subprocesses that Will Be Statistically Managed

SP 1.4-1 Manage Project Performance

SG 2 Statistically Manage Subprocess Performance

SP 2.1-1 Select Measures and Analytic Techniques

SP 2.2-1 Apply Statistical Methods to Understand Variation

SP 2.3-1 Monitor Performance of the Selected Subprocesses

SP 2.4-1 Record Statistical Management Data

Requirements Development (RD)

An Engineering process area at Maturity Level 3

Purpose

The purpose of Requirements Development (RD) is to produce and analyze customer, product, and product-component requirements.

Specific Practices by Goal

SG 1 Develop Customer Requirements

SP 1.1-1 Collect Stakeholder Needs

SP 1.1-2 Elicit Needs

SP 1.2-1 Develop the Customer Requirements

SG 2 Develop Product Requirements

SP 2.1-1 Establish Product and Product-Component Requirements

SP 2.2-1 Allocate Product-Component Requirements

SP 2.3-1 Identify Interface Requirements

SG 3 Analyze and Validate Requirements

SP 3.1-1 Establish Operational Concepts and Scenarios

SP 3.2-1 Establish a Definition of Required Functionality

SP 3.3-1 Analyze Requirements

SP 3.4-3 Analyze Requirements to Achieve Balance

SP 3.5-1 Validate Requirements

SP 3.5-2 Validate Requirements with Comprehensive Methods

Requirements Management (REQM)

An Engineering process area at Maturity Level 2

Purpose

The purpose of Requirements Management (REQM) is to manage the requirements of the project's products and product components and to identify inconsistencies between those requirements and the project's plans and work products.

Specific Practices by Goal

SG 1 Manage Requirements

SP 1.1-1 Obtain an Understanding of Requirements

SP 1.2-2 Obtain Commitment to Requirements

SP 1.3-1 Manage Requirements Changes

SP 1.4-2 Maintain Bidirectional Traceability of Requirements

SP 1.5-1 Identify Inconsistencies between Project Work and Requirements

Risk Management (RSKM)

A Project Management process area at Maturity Level 3

Purpose

The purpose of Risk Management (RSKM) is to identify potential problems before they occur so that risk-handling activities can be planned and invoked as needed across the life of the product or project to mitigate adverse impacts on achieving objectives.

Specific Practices by Goal

SG 1 Prepare for Risk Management

SP 1.1-1 Determine Risk Sources and Categories

SP 1.2-1 Define Risk Parameters

SP 1.3-1 Establish a Risk Management Strategy

SG 2 Identify and Analyze Risks

SP 2.1-1 Identify Risks

SP 2.2-1 Evaluate, Categorize, and Prioritize Risks

SG 3 Mitigate Risks

SP 3.1-1 Develop Risk Mitigation Plans

SP 3.2-1 Implement Risk Mitigation Plans

Supplier Agreement Management (SAM)

A Project Management process area at Maturity Level 2

Purpose

The purpose of Supplier Agreement Management (SAM) is to manage the acquisition of products from suppliers for which there exists a formal agreement.

Specific Practices by Goal

SG 1 Establish Supplier Agreements

SP 1.1-1 Determine Acquisition Type

SP 1.2-1 Select Suppliers

SP 1.3-1 Establish Supplier Agreements

SG 2 Satisfy Supplier Agreements

SP 2.1-1 Review COTS Products

SP 2.2-1 Execute the Supplier Agreement

SP 2.3-1 Accept the Acquired Product

SP 2.4-1 Transition Products

Technical Solution (TS)

An Engineering process area at Maturity Level 3

Purpose

The purpose of Technical Solution (TS) is to design, develop, and implement solutions to requirements. Solutions, designs, and implementations encompass products, product components, and product-related life-cycle processes either alone or in appropriate combination.

Specific Practices by Goal

SG 1 Select Product-Component Solutions

SP 1.1-1 Develop Alternative Solutions and Selection Criteria

SP 1.1-2 Develop Detailed Alternative Solutions and Selection Criteria

SP 1.2-2 Evolve Operational Concepts and Scenarios

SP 1.3-1 Select Product-Component Solutions

SG 2 Develop the Design

SP 2.1-1 Design the Product or Product Component

SP 2.2-3 Establish a Technical Data Package

SP 2.3-1 Establish Interface Descriptions

SP 2.3-3 Design Interfaces Using Criteria

SP 2.4-3 Perform Make, Buy, or Reuse Analyses

SG 3 Implement the Product Design

SP 3.1-1 Implement the Design

SP 3.2-1 Develop Product Support Documentation

Validation (VAL)

An Engineering process area at Maturity Level 3

Purpose

The purpose of Validation (VAL) is to demonstrate that a product or product component fulfills its intended use when placed in its intended environment.

Specific Practices by Goal

SG 1 Prepare for Validation

SP 1.1-1 Select Products for Validation

SP 1.2-2 Establish the Validation Environment

SP 1.3-3 Establish Validation Procedures and Criteria

SG 2 Validate Product or Product Components

SP 2.1-1 Perform Validation

SP 2.2-1 Analyze Validation Results

Verification (VER)

An Engineering process area at Maturity Level 3

Purpose

The purpose of Verification (VER) is to ensure that selected work products meets their specified requirements.

Specific Practices by Goal

SG 1 Prepare for Verification

SP 1.1-1 Select Work Products for Verification

SP 1.2-2 Establish the Verification Environment

SP 1.3-3 Establish Verification Procedures and Criteria

SG 2 Perform Peer Reviews

SP 2.1-1 Prepare for Peer Reviews

SP 2.2-1 Conduct Peer Reviews

SP 2.3-2 Analyze Peer Review Data

SG 3 Verify Selected Work Products

SP 3.1-1 Perform Verification

SP 3.2-2 Analyze Verification Results and Identify Corrective Action

(A)   What is SIX sigma?

Sigma means deviation in Greek language. Deviation means how much variations exist in a set of data. For instance let's say in a software maintenance project out of 100 defects 68 defects are rectified to the mark and remaining bounce back that means your bug fixing process is on "2 Sigma" level. I had described only from bug fixing perspective. But this can be applicable to any process organization.

SIGMA LEVEL	DEFECTS PER MILLION OPPORTUNITIES
1	690,000
2	308,537
3	66,807
4	6,210
5	233
6	3.4

Figure 12.10: SIX Sigma Values

So I should only have 3.4 defects in a million defects then I can say I am six sigma.

(A)   What is DMAIC and DMADV ?

Six Sigma has two key methodologies DMAIC and DMADV. DMAIC is used to improve an existing business process. DMADV is used to create new product designs or process designs in such a way that it results in a more predictable, mature and defect free performance.

DMAIC

Basic methodology consists of the following five phases:

√   Define - formally define the process improvement goals that are consistent with customer demands and enterprise strategy.

√   Measure - to define baseline measurements on current process for future comparison. Map and measure process in question and collect required process data.

√   Analyze - to verify relationship and causality of factors. What is the relationship? Are there other factors that have not been considered?

√   Improve - to optimize the process based upon the analysis using techniques like Design of experiments.

√   Control - setup pilot runs to establish process capability, transition to production and thereafter continuously measure the process and institute control mechanisms to ensure that variances are corrected before they result in defects.

DMADV

Basic methodology consists of the following five phases:

√   Define - formally define the goals of the design activity that are consistent with customer demands and enterprise strategy.

√   Measures - to identify CTQs, product capabilities, production process capability, risk assessment, etc.

√   Analyze - to develop and design alternatives, create high-level design and evaluate design capability to select the best design.

√   Design - to develop detail design, optimize design, and plan for design verification. This phase may require simulations.

√   Verify-to design, setup pilot runs, implement production process and handover to process owners. This phase may also require simulations.

(A) What are the various roles in Six Sigma implementation?

Attaining Six Sigma is team effort and can not be attained individually. Driving Six Sigma itself in an organization is huge project as it involves lot of mentoring and change of attitude of the current workers. So when an organization wants to drive the Six Sigma way they appoint persons with certain roles as defined below.

Executive Leadership includes CEO and other key top management team members. They are responsible for setting up a vision for Six Sigma implementation. They also empower the other role holders with the freedom and resources to explore new ideas for breakthrough improvements.

Champions are responsible for the Six Sigma implementation across the organization in an integrated manner. The Executive Leadership draw them from the upper management. Champions also act as mentor to Black Belts.

Master Black Belts, identified by champions, act as in-house expert coach for the organization on Six Sigma. They devote 100% of their time to Six Sigma. They assist champions and guide Black Belts and Green Belts. Apart from the usual rigor of statistics, their time is spent on ensuring integrated deployment of Six Sigma across various functions and departments.

Black Belts operate under Master Black Belts to apply Six Sigma methodology to specific projects. They devote 100% of their time to Six Sigma. They primarily focus on Six Sigma project execution, whereas Champions and Master Black Belts focus on identifying projects/functions for Six Sigma.

Green Belts are the employees who take up Six Sigma implementation along with their other job responsibilities. They operate under the guidance of Black Belts and support them in achieving the overall results.

Note: If you are going for project manager position then you will definitely need to prepare yourself in the area of estimation to a good extent. In the coming sections we will run through estimation related questions which are asked for project manager position. Estimation is a real weakness in software industry today. Different technologies, different company approaches and custom processes followed by software companies it still does not have a standard. So we will try to run through the most embraced estimation technologies by software industry.

(I)   What are function points?

Twist: Define Elementary process in FPA?

FPA is breaking huge systems in to smaller pieces and analyzing them. Software application is combination of set of elementary processes. EP is smallest unit of activity that is meaningful to the user. EP must be self contained and leave the application in a consistent state. Elementary process is not necessarily completely independent or can exist by itself. But it should leave the application in a consistent state.

(I)   What are the different types of elementary process in FPA?

There are two types of elementary process

√   Dynamic Elementary process

√   Static Elementary process

Dynamic elementary process moves data from internal application boundary to external application boundary or vice-versa.

Examples of dynamic elementary process:

√   Input data screen where user inputs data in to application. Data moves from the input screen inside application.

√   Transaction exported in export files in XML or any other standard.

√   Display reports which can come from external application boundary and internal application boundary.

Static elementary process maintains data of application either inside application boundary or in external application boundary.

Examples of static elementary process:

√   In a customer maintenance screen maintaining customer data is static elementary process.

(I)   What are the different elements in Functions points?

The different elements in function points are as follows:

√   Internal Logical Files (ILF)

√   External Interface File (EIF)

√   Record Element Type (RET)

√   DET (Data element types)

√   File Type Reference (FTR)

√   External Input (EI)

√   External Inquiry (EQ)

√   External Output (EO)

Let's run in detail through each of them.

Internal Logical Files (ILF)

Following are points to be noted for ILF:

√   ILF are logically related data from user point of view.

√   They reside in Internal Application boundary and are maintained through elementary process of application.

√   ILF may have maintenance screen or probably not.

Supplier	Product	Location
SK Enterprise	Bottles	Delhi
Bell Corporate	Computers	Mumbai
Bell Corporate	Computer	Kerala
MD Motors	Car	Madras

Figure 12.11: Supplier ER database diagram

Note: *Do not make a mistake of mapping one to one relationship between ILF and technical database design in that case FPA can go very misleading. The main difference between ILF and technical database is ILF is logical view and database is physical structure (Technical Design). Example Supplier database design will have tables like Supplier, Supplier Address, and Supplier Phone numbers but from ILF point of view it's only Supplier. As logically they are all Supplier details.*

External Interface file (EIF)

They are logically related data from user point of view.

√   EIF reside in external application boundary.

√   EIF is used only for reference purpose and are not maintained by internal application.

√   EIF is maintained by external application.

Record Element Type (RET)

Following are points to be noted for RET

√   RET are sub-group element data of ILF or EIF.

√   If there is no sub-group of ILF then count the ILF itself as one RET.

√   A group of RET within ILF are logically related, most probably with a parent Child relationship.

Example: Supplier had multiple addresses and every address can have multiple phone numbers (see the image below which shows database diagrams). So Supplier, SupplierAddress and Supplier phone numbers are RET.

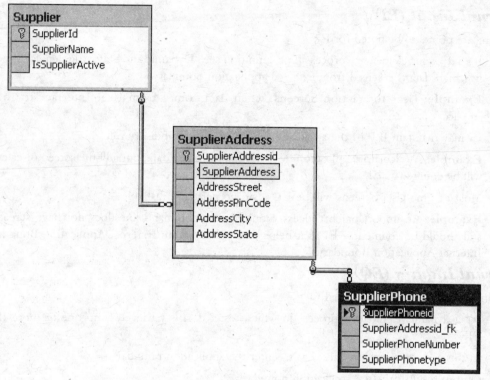

Figure 12.12: Whole supplier is one ILF.

> *Note: The whole database is one supplier ILF as all belong to one logical section.*

√   RET quantifies the relationship complexity of ILF and EIF.

DET (Data element types)

Following are the points to be noted for DET counting:

√   Each DET should be User recognizable. Example in the above given figure we have kept auto increment field (Supplierid) for primary key. Supplierid field from user point of view never exists at all, it's only from software designing aspect, so does not qualifies for DET.

√   DET should be non-recursive field in ILF. DET should not repeat in the same ILF again, it should be counted only once.

√   Count foreign keys as one DET. "Supplierid" does not qualifies as DET but its relationship in "supplieraddress" table is counted as DET. So "Supplierid_fk" in supplieraddress table is counted as DET. Same holds true for "Supplieraddressid_fk".

File Type Reference (FTR)

Following are points to be noted for FTR:

√   FTR is files or data referenced by a transaction.

√   FTR should be ILF or EIF. So count each ILF or EIF read during process.

√   If the EP is maintaining an ILF then count that as FTR. So by default you will always have one FTR in any EP.

External Input (EI)

Following are points to be noted for EI:

√   It's a dynamic elementary process [For definition see "Dynamic and Static Elementary Process"] in which data is received from external application boundary.

Example: User Interaction Screens, when data comes from User Interface to Internal Application.

√   EI may maintain ILF of the application, but it is not compulsory rule.

Example: A calculator application does not maintain any data, but still the screen of calculator will be counted as EI.

√   Most of time User Screens will be EI, again no hard and fast rule.

Example: An import batch process running from command line does not have screen, but still should be counted as EI as it helps passing data from External Application Boundary to Internal Application Boundary.

External Inquiry (EQ)

Following are points to be noted for EQ

√   It's a dynamic elementary process in which result data is retrieved from one or more ILF or EIF.

√   In this EP some input request has to enter the application boundary.

√   Output results exits the application boundary.

√   EQ does not contain any derived data. Derived data means any complex calculated data. Derived data is not just mere retrieval but are combined with additional formulae to generate results. Derived data is not part of ILF or EIF, they are generated on fly.

√   EQ does not update any ILF or EIF.

√   EQ activity should be meaningful from user perspective.

√   EP is self contained and leaves the business in consistent state.

√   DET and processing logic is different from other EQ's.

√   Simple reports form good base as EQ.

> *Note: No hard and fast rules that only simple reports are EQ. Simple view functionality can also be counted as EQ.*

External Output (EO)

Following are points to be noted for EO:

√   It's a dynamic elementary process in which derived data crosses from Internal Application Boundary to External Application Boundary.

√   EO can update an ILF or EIF.

√   Process should be the smallest unit of activity that is meaningful to end user in business.

√   EP is self contained and leaves the business in a consistent state.

√   DET is different from other EO's. So this ensures to us that we do not count EO's twice.

√   They have derived data or formulae calculated data.

√   Major difference between EO and EQ is that data passes across application boundary.

Example: Exporting Accounts transaction to some external file format like XML or some other format. This can be later imported by the external accounting software. Second important difference is in EQ has non-derived data and EO has derived data.

(A)   Can you explain in GSC and VAF in function points?

In GSC (General System Characteristic) there are 14 factors which are rated on 1 to 5 depending on the complexity of the factor. Below are the 14 factors:

√   **Data communications:** How many communication facilities are there to aid in the transfer or exchange of information with the application or system?

√   **Distributed data processing:** How are distributed data and processing functions handled?

√   **Performance:** Did the user require response at times or throughout?

√   **Heavily used configuration:** How heavily used is the current hardware platform where the application will be executed?

√   **Transaction rate:** How frequently are transactions executed; daily, weekly, monthly, etc.?

√   **On-Line data entry:** What percentage of the information is entered On-Line?

√   **End-user efficiency:** Was the application designed for end-user efficiency?

√   **On-Line update:** How many ILF's are updated by On-Line transaction?

√   **Complex processing:** Does the application have extensive logical or mathematical processing?.

√   **Reusability:** Was the application developed to meet one or many users needs?

√   **Installation ease:** How difficult is conversion and installation?

√   **Operational ease:** How effective and/or automated are start-up, back up, and recovery procedures?

√   **Multiple sites:** Was the application specifically designed, developed, and supported to be installed at multiple sites for multiple organizations?

√   **Facilitate change:** Was the application specifically designed, developed, and supported to facilitate change?

Performance	throughput?	5
Heavily used configuration	How heavily used is the current hardware platform where the application will be executed?	1
Transaction rate	How frequently are transactions executed; daily, weekly, monthly, etc.?	5
On-Line data entry	What percentage of the information is entered On-Line?	5
End-user efficiency	Was the application designed for end-user efficiency?	1
On-Line update	How many ILF's are updated by On-Line transaction?	5
Complex processing	Does the application have extensive logical or mathematical processing?	5
Reusability	Was the application developed to meet one or many user's needs?	5
Installation ease	How difficult is conversion and installation?	5
Operational ease	How effective and/or automated are start-up, back up, and recovery procedures?	5
Multiple sites	Was the application specifically designed, developed, and supported to be installed at multiple sites for multiple organizations?	5
Facilitate change	Was the application specifically designed, developed, and supported to facilitate change?	5
GSC		**1.23**

Figure 12.13: GSC rated in estimation sheet

F   SC we g   VAF i.e. Value added function points by the below formulae.

0.65   sum of all GSC factor)/100).

unadjusted function points and how is it

Un   nctio.   = ILF + EIF + EI + EQ + EO.

Below is the table ref   for getting ILF, EIF, EI, EQ and EO.

EI Rating Table

FTR	Data Elements		
	1 to 4	5 to 15	> 15
Less than 2	3	3	4
Equal to 2	3	4	6
Greater than 2	4	6	6

EO Rating Table

FTR	Data Elements		
	1 to 5	6 to 19	> 19
Less than 2	4	4	5
2 or 3	4	5	7
Greater than 2	5	7	7

EQ Rating Table

FTR	Data Elements		
	1 to 5	6 to 19	> 19
Less than 2	3	3	4
2 or 3	3	4	6
Greater than 2	4	6	6

ILF Rating Table

RET	Data Elements		
	1 to 19	20 to 50	>= 51
1	7	7	10
2 to 5	7	10	15
Greater than 6	10	15	15

EIF Rating Table

RET	Data Elements		
	1 to 19	20 to 50	>= 51
1	5	5	7
2 to 5	5	7	10
Greater than 6	7	10	10

Figure 12.14: Rating tables

(I)   Can you explain steps in function points?

Below are the steps in function points:

√   First Count ILF, EIF, EI, EQ, RET, DET, FTR and use the rating tables. After you have counted all the elements you will get the unadjusted function points.

√   Put rating values 0 to 5 to all 14 GSC. Adding total of all 14 GSC to come out with total VAF. Formula for VAF = 0.65 + (sum of all GSC factor/100).

√   Finally, make the calculation of adjusted function point. Formula: Total function point = VAF * Unadjusted function point.

√   Make estimation how many function points you will do per day. This is also called as "Performance factor".

√   On basis of performance factor, you can calculate Man/Days.

(I) What is the FP per day in your current company?

Twist: What is your company's productivity factor ?

Left to the readers as every company has his own FP per Day.

> *Note:* *There is a free PDF provided "How to prepare Software Quotations?" Please do refer Function point chapter.*

(A)   Do you know Use Case points?

In CD we have a complete free PDF tutorial of how to prepare software quotation. It has all the estimation technology that today's software industry uses.

(A)   What is COCOMO I, COCOMOII and COCOMOIII?

In CD we have a complete free PDF tutorial of how to prepare software quotation. It has all the estimation technology that today's software industry uses.

(A)   What is SMC approach of estimation?

Look for the PDF in the CD.

(A)   How do you estimate maintenance project and change requests?

Left for the readers to answer.

13

Database

(B) What is database or database management systems (DBMS)?

Twist: What's the difference between file and database? Can files qualify as a database?

> *Note: Probably these questions are too basic for experienced guys. But from freshers point of view it can be a difference between getting a job and to be jobless.*

Database provides a systematic and organized way of storing, managing and retrieving from collection of logically related information.

Secondly the information has to be persistent, that means even after the application is closed the information should be persisted.

Finally it should provide an independent way of accessing data and should not be dependent on the application to access the information.

Ok let me spend a few sentence more on explaining the third aspect. Below is a simple figure of a text file which has personal detail information. The first column of the information is Name, Second address and finally the phone number. This is a simple text file which was designed by a programmer for a specific application.

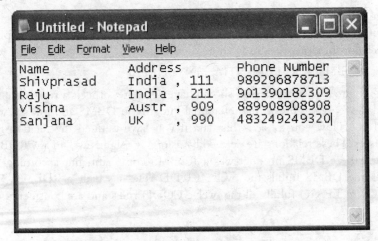

Figure 13.1: Non-Uniform Text File

It works fine in the boundary of the application. Now some years down the line a third party application has to be integrated with this file , so in order the third party application integrates properly it has the following options:

√   Use interface of the original application.

√   Understand the complete detail of how the text file is organized, example the first column is Name, then address and finally phone number. After analyzing write a code which can read the file, parse it etc ....Hmm lot of work right.

That's what the main difference between a simple file and database; database has independent way (SQL) of accessing information while simple files do not (That answers my twisted question defined above). File meets the storing, managing and retrieving part of a database but not the independent way of accessing data.

> *Note: Many experienced programmers think that the main difference is that file can not provide multi-user capabilities which a DBMS provides. But if you look at some old COBOL and C programs where file where the only means of storing data, you can see functionalities like locking, multi-user etc provided very efficiently. So it's a matter of debate if some interviewers think this as a main difference between files and database accept it... going in to debate is probably loosing a job.*

(Just a note for fresher's multi-user capabilities means that at one moment of time more than one user should be able to add, update, view and delete data. All DBMS provides this as in built functionalities but if you are storing information in files it's up to the application to write a logic to achieve these functionalities)

(B)   What is SQL ?

SQL stands for Structured Query Language.SQL is an ANSI (American National Standards Institute) standard computer language for accessing and manipulating database systems. SQL statements are used to retrieve and update data in a database.

(I)   What's difference between DBMS and RDBMS ?

Ok as said before DBMS provides a systematic and organized way of storing, managing and retrieving from collection of logically related information. RDBMS also provides what DBMS provides but above that it provides relationship integrity. So in short we can say

        RDBMS = DBMS + REFERENTIAL INTEGRITY

Example in above figure 13.1 every person should have an address this is a referential integrity between "Name" and "Address". If we break this referential integrity in DBMS and File's it will not complain, but RDBMS will not allow you to save this data if you have defined the relation integrity between person and addresses. These relations are defined by using "Foreign Keys" in any RDBMS.Many DBMS companies claimed there DBMS product was a RDBMS compliant, but according to industry rules and regulations if the DBMS fulfills the twelve CODD rules it's truly a RDBMS. Almost all DBMS (SQL SERVER, ORACLE etc) fulfills all the twelve CODD rules and are considered as truly RDBMS.

(A) What are CODD rules?

In 1969 Dr. E. F. Codd laid down some 12 rules which a DBMS should adhere in order to get the logo of a true RDBMS.

Rule 1: Information Rule.

"All information in a relational data base is represented explicitly at the logical level and in exactly one way - by values in tables."

Rule 2: Guaranteed access Rule.

"Each and every datum (atomic value) in a relational data base is guaranteed to be logically accessible by resorting to a combination of table name, primary key value and column name."

In flat files we have to parse and know exact location of field values. But if a DBMS is truly RDBMS you can access the value by specifying the table name, field name, for instance Customers.Fields ['Customer Name'].

Rule 3: Systematic treatment of null values.

"Null values (distinct from the empty character string or a string of blank characters and distinct from zero or any other number) are supported in fully relational DBMS for representing missing information and inapplicable information in a systematic way, independent of data type."

Rule 4: Dynamic on-line catalog based on the relational model.

"The data base description is represented at the logical level in the same way as ordinary data, so that authorized users can apply the same relational language to its interrogation as they apply to the regular data."The Data Dictionary is held within the RDBMS, thus there is no-need for off-line volumes to tell you the structure of the database.

Rule 5: Comprehensive data sub-language Rule.

"A relational system may support several languages and various modes of terminal use (for example, the fill-in-the-blanks mode). However, there must be at least one language whose statements are expressible, per some well-defined syntax, as character strings and that is comprehensive in supporting all the following items

√   Data Definition

√   View Definition

√   Data Manipulation (Interactive and by program).

√   Integrity Constraints

√   Authorization.

√   Transaction boundaries (Begin , commit and rollback)

> *Note: According to this rule CODD has only mentioned that some language should be present to support it, but not necessary that it should be SQL. Before 80's different database vendors where providing there own flavor of syntaxes until in 80 ANSI-SQL came into standardize this variation between vendors. As ANSI-SQL is quiet limited, every vendor including Microsoft introduced there additional SQL syntaxes in addition to the support of ANSI-SQL. You can see SQL syntaxes varying from vendor to vendor.*

Rule 6: .View updating Rule

"All views that are theoretically updatable are also updatable by the system."

Rule 7: High-level insert, update and delete.

"The capability of handling a base relation or a derived relation as a single operand applies not only to the retrieval of data but also to the insertion, update and deletion of data."

Rule 8: Physical data independence.

"Application programs and terminal activities remain logically unimpaired whenever any changes are made in either storage representations or access methods."

Rule 9: Logical data independence.

"Application programs and terminal activities remain logically unimpaired when information-preserving changes of any kind that theoretically permit un-impairment are made to the base tables."

Rule 10: Integrity independence.

"Integrity constraints specific to a particular relational data base must be definable in the relational data sub-language and storable in the catalog, not in the application programs."

Rule 11: Distribution independence.

"A relational DBMS has distribution independence."

Rule 12: Non-subversion Rule.

"If a relational system has a low-level (single-record-at-a-time) language, that low level cannot be used to subvert or bypass the integrity Rules and constraints expressed in the higher level relational language (multiple-records-at-a-time)."

(B)   What are E-R diagrams?

E-R diagram also termed as Entity-Relationship diagram shows relationship between various tables in the database.

Example: Table "Customer" and "CustomerAddresses" have a one to many relationships (i.e. one customer can have multiple addresses) this can be shown using the ER diagram. ER diagrams are drawn during the initial stages of project to forecast how the database structure will shape up. Below is a screen shot of a sample ER diagram of "Asset Management" which ships free with access.

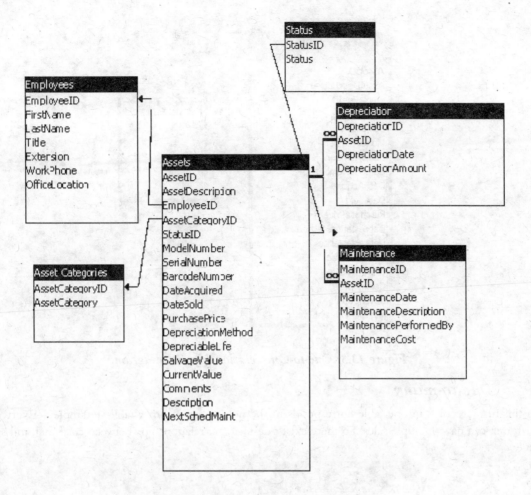

Figure 13.2: Asset management ER diagram.

(B) How many types of relationship exist in database designing?

There are three major relationship models:

√ One-to-one

As the name suggests you have one record in one table and corresponding to that you have one record in other table. We will take the same sample ER diagram defined for asset management. In the below diagram "Assets" can only have one "Status" at moment of time (Outdated / Need Maintenance and New Asset). At any moment of time "Asset" can only have one status of the above, so there is one-to-one relationship between them.

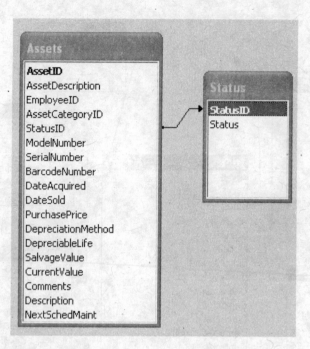

Figure 13.3: One-to-One relationship ER diagram

√ One-to-many

In this many records in one table corresponds to the one record in other table. Example: - Every one customer can have multiple sales. So there exist one-to-many relationships between customer and sales table.

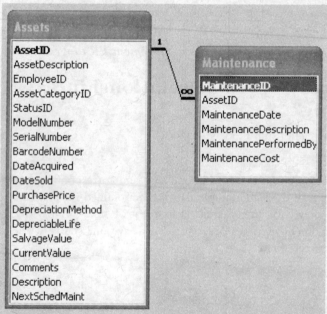

Figure 13.4: One-to-Many Relationship ER diagram

One "Asset" can have multiple "Maintenance". So "Asset" entity has one-to-many relationship between them as the ER model shows below.

√ *Many-to-many*

In this one record in one table corresponds to many rows in other table and also vice-versa. For instance: In a company one employee can have many skills like java , c# etc and also one skill can belong to many employees.

Given below is a sample of many-to-many relationship. One employee can have knowledge of multiple "Technology". So in order to implement this we have one more table "EmployeeTechnology" which is linked to the primary key of "Employee" and "Technology" table.

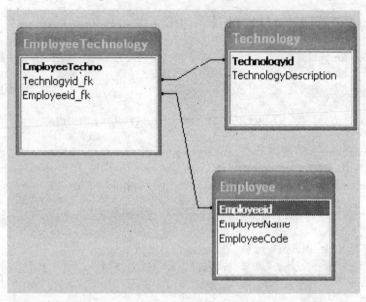

Figure 13.5: Many-to-Many Relationship ER diagram

(B) What is normalization? What are different type of normalization?

Note: *A regular JAVA rogrammer working on projects often stumbles in this question ,which is but obvious.Bad part is sometimes interviewer can take this as a very basic question to be answered and it can be a turning point for the interview.So let's cram it.*

It is set of rules that has been established to aid in the design of tables that are meant to be connected through relationships. This set of rules is known as Normalization.

Benefits of Normalizing your database include:

√ Avoiding repetitive entries

√ Reducing required storage space

√ Preventing the need to restructure existing tables to accommodate new data.

√ Increased speed and flexibility of queries, sorts, and summaries.

> Note: *During interview people expect to answer maximum of three normal forms and thats what is expected practically. Actually you can normalize database to fifth normal form. But believe this book answering three normal forms will put you in decent shape during interview.*

Following are the three normal forms:

First Normal Form

For a table to be in first normal form, data must be broken up into the smallest units possible. In addition to breaking data up into the smallest meaningful values, tables in first normal form should not contain repetitions groups of fields.

Customer id	Customer Name	City1	City2	Unit Price	Qty	Total
3243244	Shivprasad koirala	xyz	PQR	1	12	12$
3043244	Sanjana koirala	xcv	123	10	1	10$

Figure 13.6: Repeating groups example

For in the above example city1 and city2 are repeating. In order this table to be in First normal form you have to modify the table structure as follows. Also not that the Customer Name is now broken down to first name and last name (First normal form data should be broken down to smallest unit).

Customer id	First Name	Last Name	City	Unit Price	Qty	Total
3243244	Shivprasad	Koirala	xyz	1	12	12$
3243244	Shivprasad	koirala	PQR	1	12	12$
3043244	Sanjana	koirala	xcv	2	20	40$
3043244	sanjana	Koirala	123	2	20	40$

Figure 13.7: Customer table normalized to first normal form

Second Normal form

The second normal form states that each field in a multiple field primary keytable must be directly related to the entire primary key. Or in other words, each non-key field should be a fact about all the fields in the primary key.

In the above table of customer , city is not linked to any primary field.

Customer id	First Name	Last Name	City	Unit Price	Qty	Total
3243244	Shivprasad	Koirala	xyz	1	12	12$
3243244	Shivprasad	koirala	PQR	1	12	12$.
3043244	Sanjana	koirala	xcv	2	20	40$
3043244	sanjana	Koirala	123	2	20	40$

Figure 13.8: Normalized customer table.

City id	City
1	xyz
2	PQR
3	xcv
4	123

Figure 13.9: City is now shifted to a different master table.

That takes our database to a second normal form.

Third normal form

A non-key field should not depend on other Non-key field. The field "Total" is dependent on "Unit price" and "qty".

Customer id	First Name	Last Name	City	Unit Price	Qty
3243244	Shivprasad	Koirala	xyz	1	12
3243244	Shivprasad	koirala	PQR	1	12
3043244	Sanjana	koirala	xcv	2	20
3043244	sanjana	Koirala	123	2	20

Figure 13.10: Fill third normal form

So now the "Total" field is removed and is multiplication of Unit price * Qty.

(B)   What is denormalization ?

Denormalization is the process of putting one fact in numerous places (its vice-versa of normalization). Only one valid reason exists for denormalizing a relational design - to enhance performance. The sacrifice to performance is that you increase redundancy in database.

(DB) Can you explain Fourth Normal Form?

> *Note: Whenever interviewer is trying to go above third normal form it can have two reasons ego or to fail you. Three normal forms are really enough, practically anything more than that is an overdose.*

In fourth normal form it should not contain two or more independent multi-valued facts about an entity and it should satisfy "Third Normal form".

Supplier	Product	Location
SK Enterprise	Bottles	Delhi
Bell Corporate	Computers	Mumbai
Bell Corporate	Computer	Kerala
MD Motors	Car	Madras

Figure 13.11: Multi-valued facts

So let's try to see what multi-valued facts are. If there are two or more many-to-many relationship in one entity and they tend to come to one place is termed as "multi-valued facts".

In the above table you can see there are two many-to-many relationship between "Supplier" / "Product" and "Supplier" / "Location" (or in short multi-valued facts). In order the above example satisfies fourth normal form, both the many-to-many relationship should go in different tables.

Supplier	Product	Supplier	Location
SK Enterprise	Bottles	SK Enterprise	Delhi
Bell Corporate	Computers	Bell Corporate	Mumbai
MD Motors	Car	Bell Corporate	Kerala
		MD Motors	Madras

Figure 13.12: Normalized to Fourth Normal form.

(DB) Can you explain Fifth Normal Form?

Note: UUUHHH if you get his question after joining the company do ask him, did he himself really use it?

Fifth normal form deals with reconstructing information from smaller pieces of information. These smaller pieces of information can be maintained with less redundancy.

Example: "Dealers" sells "Product" which can be manufactured by various "Companies". "Dealers" in order to sell the "Product" should be registered with the "Company". So these three entities have very much mutual relationship within them.

Dealers	Product	Companies
JM Associate	Sweets	Cadbury
Shiv Networks	Shoes	Nike
Star Sellers	Magazine	Times
Hari Publishers	Books	KM Publications

Figure 13.13: Not in Fifth Normal Form.

The above table shows some sample data. If you observe closely a single record is created using lot of small information's. For instance: - "JM Associate" can sell sweets in the following two conditions:

√   "JM Associate" should be an authorized dealer of "Cadbury".

√   "Sweets" should be manufactured by "Cadbury" company.

Dealers	Product	Dealers	Companies
JM Associate	Sweets	JM Associate	Cadbury
Shiv Networks	Shoes	Shiv Networks	Nike
Star Sellers	Magazine	Star Sellers	Times
Hari Publishers	Books	Hari Publishers	KM Publications

Product	Companies
Sweets	Cadbury
Shoes	Nike
Magazine	Times
Books	KM Publications

Figure 13.14: Complete Fifth Normal Form

These two smaller information forms one record of the above given table. So in order that the above information to be "Fifth Normal Form" all the smaller information should be in three different places. Below is the complete fifth normal form of the database.

(DB) What's the difference between Fourth and Fifth normal form?

> *Note: There is huge similarity between Fourth and Fifth normal form i.e. they address the problem of "Multi-Valued facts".*

"Fifth normal form" multi-valued facts are interlinked and "Fourth normal form" values are independent. For instance in the above two questions "Supplier/Product" and "Supplier/Location" are not linked. While in fifth form the "Dealer/Product/Companies" are completely linked.

(DB) Have you heard about sixth normal form?

> *Note: Arrrrggghhh yes there exists a sixth normal form also. But note guys you can skip this statement or just in case if you want to impress the interviewer.*

If you want relational system in conjunction with time you use sixth normal form. At this moment very few databases support this.

(B) What are DML and DDL statements?

DML stands for Data Manipulation Statements. They update data values in table. Below are the most important DDL statements:

√   SELECT - gets data from a database table

√   UPDATE - updates data in a table

√   DELETE - deletes data from a database table

√   INSERT INTO - inserts new data into a database table

DDL stands for Data definition Language. They change structure of the database objects like table, index etc. Most important DDL statements are as shown below:

√   CREATE TABLE - creates a new table in the database.

√   ALTER TABLE – changes table structure in database.

√   DROP TABLE - deletes a table from database

√   CREATE INDEX - creates an index

√   DROP INDEX - deletes an index

(B) How do we select distinct values from a table?

DISTINCT keyword is used to return only distinct values. Below is syntax:

SELECT DISTINCT Mycolumn FROM MyTable

(B) What is Like operator for and what are wild cards?

LIKE operator is used to match patterns. A "%" sign is used to define the pattern.

Below SQL statement will return all words with letter "S"

> SELECT * FROM Employee WHERE EmpName LIKE 'S%'

Below SQL statement will return all words which end with letter "S"

> SELECT * FROM Employee WHERE EmpName LIKE '%S'

Below SQL statement will return all words having letter "S" in between

> SELECT * FROM Employee WHERE EmpName LIKE '%S%'

(B)   Can you explain Insert, Update and Delete query?

Insert statement is used to insert new rows in to table. Update to update existing data in the table. Delete statement to delete a record from the table. Below code snippet for Insert, Update and Delete:

```
INSERT INTO Employee VALUES ('Shiv', 'Vishna', 'Sanjana', 'Simran')
UPDATE Employee SET Address = 'Mulund Mumbai', City = 'Mumbai' WHERE
LastName = 'Koirala'
DELETE FROM Employee WHERE LastName = 'Koirala'
```

(B)   What is order by clause?

ORDER BY clause helps to sort the data in either ascending order to descending order.

Ascending order sort query

> SELECT LastName FROM Employee ORDER BY EmpSalary ASC

Descending order sort query

> SELECT LastName FROM Employee ORDER BY EmpSalary DESC

(B)   What is the SQL In clause?

SQL IN operator is used to see if the value exists in a group of values. For instance the below SQL checks if the LastName is either 'Shiv' or 'Koirala'

> SELECT * FROM EmployeeName WHERE LastName IN ('Shiv','Koirala')

Also you can specify a not clause with the same.

> SELECT * FROM EmployeeName WHERE LastName NOT IN ('Shiv','Koirala')

(B)   Can you explain the between clause?

Below SQL selects employees born between '01/01/1975' AND '01/01/1978'

> SELECT * FROM EmployeeName WHERE DateOfBirth BETWEEN '01/01/1975' AND '01/01/1978'

(A) I have an employee salary table how do we find the second highest from it?

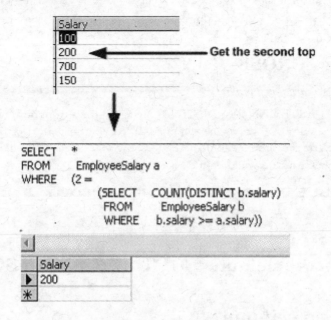

Figure 13.15: SQL for Second highest

(B) What are different types of joins in SQL?

INNER JOIN

Inner join shows matches only when they exist in both tables. Example in the below SQL there are two tables Customers and Orders and the inner join in made on Customers.Customerid and Orders.Customerid. So this SQL will only give you result with customers who have orders. If the customer does not have order it will not display that record.

    SELECT Customers.*, Orders.* FROM Customers INNER JOIN Orders ON
    Customers.CustomerID =Orders.CustomerID

LEFT OUTER JOIN

Left join will display all records in left table of the SQL statement. In SQL below customers with or without orders will be displayed. Order data for customers without orders appears as NULL values. For example, you want to determine the amount ordered by each customer and you need to see who has not ordered anything as well. You can also see the LEFT OUTER JOIN as a mirror image of the RIGHT OUTER JOIN (Is covered in the next section) if you switch the side of each table.

    SELECT Customers.*, Orders.* FROM Customers LEFT OUTER JOIN Orders ON
    Customers.CustomerID =Orders.CustomerID

RIGHT OUTER JOIN·

Right join will display all records in right table of the SQL statement. In SQL below all orders with or without matching customer records will be displayed. Customer. data for orders without customers appears as NULL values. For example, you want to determine if there are any orders in the data with undefined CustomerID values (say, after a conversion or something like it). You can also see the RIGHT OUTER JOIN as a mirror image of the LEFT OUTER JOIN if you switch the side of each table.

> SELECT Customers.*, Orders.* FROM Customers RIGHT OUTER JOIN Orders ON Customers.CustomerID =Orders.CustomerID

(B) What is "CROSS JOIN"?

> *Twist: What is Cartesian product?*

"CROSS JOIN" or "CARTESIAN PRODUCT" combines all rows from both tables. Number of rows will be product of the number of rows in each table. In real life scenario I can not imagine where we will want to use a Cartesian product. But there are scenarios where we would like permutation and combination probably Cartesian would be the easiest way to achieve it.

(B) You want to select the first record in a given set of rows?

Select top 1 * from sales.salesperson

(B) What is the default "SORT" order for a SQL?

ASCENDING

(B) What is a self-join?

If you want to join two instances of the same table you can use self-join.

(B) What's the difference between DELETE and TRUNCATE ?

Following are difference between them:

√   DELETE TABLE syntax logs the deletes thus making the delete operation slow. TRUNCATE table does not log any information but it logs information about deallocation of data page of the table. So TRUNCATE table is faster as compared to delete table.

√   DELETE table can have criteria while TRUNCATE can not.

√   TRUNCATE table can not have triggers.

(B) What are Wildcard operators ?

> *Twist: What is like clause in SQL?*

> *Note: For showing how the wildcards work I will be using the "person.address" table in adventureworks.*

There are basically two types of operator:

"%" operator (During Interview you can spell it as "Percentage Operator").

"%" operator searches for one or many occurrences. So when you fire a query using "%" database searches for one or many occurrences. In the below SQL I have applied "%" operator to "S" character.

> Select AddressLine1 from person.address where AddressLine1 like 'S%'

```
Select AddressLine1 from person.address where AddressLine1 like 'S%'
```

	AddressLine1
1	S Sound Ctr Suite 25300
2	Saltonstall Parkway
3	San Diego Factory
4	Sapp Road West
5	Savannah Festival Outlet
6	Science Park South, Birchwood
7	Silver Sands Factory Outlet
8	Simi @ The Plaza
9	Southgate Mall
10	Southwest Outlet
11	Sports Store At Park City
12	Sports Stores @ Tuscola
13	Spring Meadows Place
14	St. Louis Marketplace
15	Stateline Plaza
16	Station E
17	Stevens Creek Shopping Center
18	Stonewood Mall

Figure 13.16: "%" operator in action.

"_" operator (During Interview you spell it as "Underscore Operator").

"_" operator is the character defined at that point. In the below sample I have fired a query

Select AddressLine1 from person.address where AddressLine1 like '_h%'

So all data where second letter is "h" is returned.

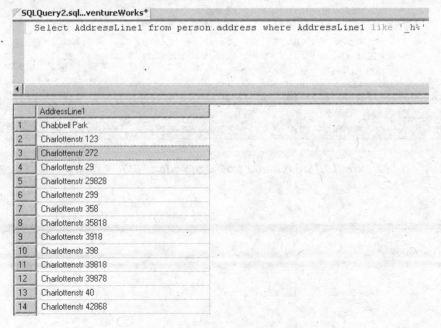

Figure 13.17: "_" operator in action

(B) What's the difference between "UNION" and "UNION ALL" ?

UNION SQL syntax is used to select information from two tables. But it selects only distinct records from both the table. , while UNION ALL selects all records from both the tables.

To explain it practically below are two images one fires "UNION" and one "UNION ALL" on the "person.address" table of the "AdventureWorks" database.

> Select * from person.address

Union

> Select * from person.address

This returns 19614 rows (that's mean it removes duplicates)

> Select * from person.address

union all

> Select * from person.address

This returns 39228 rows ("unionall" does not check for duplicates so returns double the record show up)

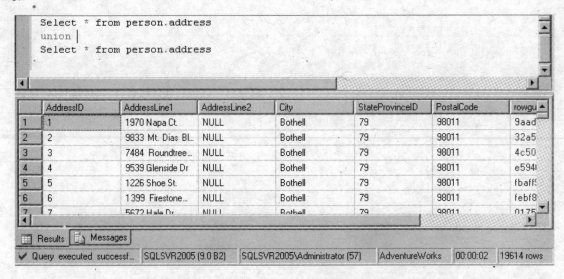

Figure 13.18: Union keyword in action (19614 rows)

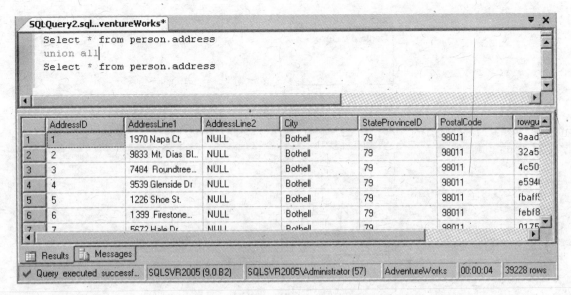

Figure 13.19: Union All in action (39228 rows)

> Note: Selected records should have same data type or else the syntax will not work.

> Note: In the coming questions you will see some 5 to 6 questions on cursors. Though not a much discussed topic but still from my survey 5% of interviews have asked questions on cursors. So let's leave no stone for the interviewer to reject us.

(I) What are cursors and what are the situations you will use them?

SQL statements are good for set at a time operation. So it is good at handling set of data. But there are scenarios where you want to update row depending on certain criteria. You will loop through all rows and update data accordingly. There's where cursors come in to picture.

(I) What are the steps to create a cursor?

Below are the basic steps to execute a cursor.

√ Declare

√ Open

√ Fetch

√ Operation

√ Close and Deallocate

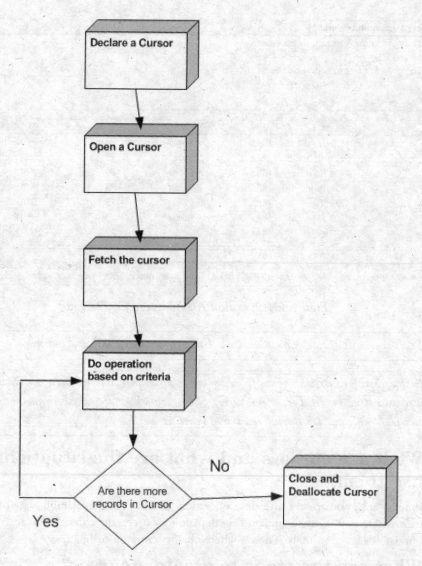

Figure 13.20: Steps to process a cursor

This is a small sample which uses the "person.address" class. This program will only display records which have "@Provinceid" equal to "7".

```
DECLARE @provinceid int
-- Declare Cursor
DECLARE provincecursor CURSOR FOR
SELECT stateprovinceid
FROM Person.Address
-- Open cursor
OPEN provincecursor
-- Fetch data from cursor in to variable
FETCH NEXT FROM provincecursor
```

```
INTO @provinceid
WHILE @@FETCH_STATUS = 0
BEGIN
-- Do operation according to row value
if @Provinceid=7
begin
PRINT @Provinceid
end
-- Fetch the next cursor
FETCH NEXT FROM provincecursor
INTO @provinceid
END
-- Finally do not forget to close and deallocate the cursor
CLOSE provincecursor
DEALLOCATE provincecursor
```

(B)   What is "Group by" clause?

"Group by" clause group similar data so that aggregate values can be derived. In "AdventureWorks" there are two tables "Salesperson" and "Salesterritory". In below figure "Actual data" is the complete view of "Salesperson". But now we want a report that per territory wise how many sales people are there. So in the second figure I made a group by on territory id and used the "count" aggregate function to see some meaningful data. "Northwest" has the highest number of sales personnel.

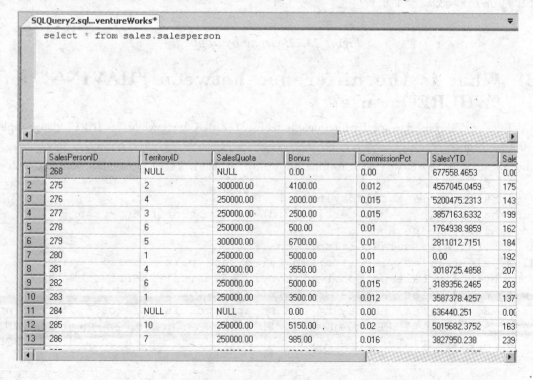

Figure 13.21: Actual Data

SQLQuery2.sql...ventureWorks*

```
select sales.salesterritory.name ,
count(sales.salesperson.territoryid) as numberofsalesperson
from sales.salesperson
inner join sales.salesterritory on
sales.salesterritory.territoryid=sales.salesperson.territoryid
group by sales.salesperson.territoryid,sales.salesterritory.name
```

	name	numberofsalesperson
1	Northwest	3
2	Northeast	1
3	Central	1
4	Southwest	2
5	Southeast	1
6	Canada	2
7	France	1
8	Germany	1
9	Australia	1
10	United Kingdom	1

Figure 13.22: Group by applied

(B) What is the difference between "HAVING" and "WHERE" clause?

"HAVING" clause is used to specify filtering criteria for "GROUP BY", while "WHERE" clause applies on normal SQL.

In the above example we if we want to filter on territory which has sales personnel count above 2.

```
select sales.salesterritory.name ,
count(sales.salesperson.territoryid) as numberofsalesperson
from sales.salesperson
inner join sales.salesterritory on
sales.salesterritory.territoryid=sales.salesperson.territoryid
group by sales.salesperson.territoryid,sales.salesterritory.name
having count(sales.salesperson.territoryid) >= 2
Note:- You can see the having clause applied. In this case you can not
specify it with "WHERE" clause it will throw an error. In short "HAVING"
clause applies filter on a group while "WHERE" clause on a simple SQL.
```

(B)   What is a Sub-Query?

A query nested inside a SELECT statement is known as a subquery and is an alternative to complex join statements. A subquery combines data from multiple tables and returns results that are inserted into the WHERE condition of the main query. A subquery is always enclosed within parentheses and returns a column. A subquery can also be referred to as an inner query and the main query as an outer query. JOIN gives better performance than a subquery when you have to check for the existence of records.

For example, to retrieve all EmployeeID and CustomerID records from the ORDERS table that have the EmployeeID greater than the average of the EmployeeID field, you can create a nested query, as shown:

```
SELECT DISTINCT EmployeeID, CustomerID
FROM ORDERS
WHERE EmployeeID > (SELECT AVG(EmployeeID)
FROM ORDERS)
```

(B)   What are Aggregate and Scalar Functions?

Aggregate and Scalar functions are in built function for counting and calculations.

Aggregate functions operate against a group of values but returns only one value.

AVG(column): Returns the average value of a column

COUNT(column): Returns the number of rows (without a NULL value) of a column

COUNT(*): Returns the number of selected rows

MAX(column): Returns the highest value of a column

MIN(column): Returns the lowest value of a column

Scalar functions operate against a single value and return value on basis of the single value.

UCASE(c): Converts a field to upper case

LCASE(c): Converts a field to lower case

MID(c,start[,end]): Extract characters from a text field

LEN(c): Returns the length of a text

(B)   Can you explain the SELECT INTO Statement?

SELECT INTO statement is used mostly to create backups. The below SQL backsup the Employee table in to the EmployeeBackUp table. One point to be noted is that the structure of EmployeeBackup and Employee table should be same.

      SELECT * INTO EmployeeBackup FROM Employee

(B)   What is a View?

View is a virtual table which is created on the basis of the result set returned by the select statement.

CREATE VIEW [MyView] AS SELECT * from EmployeeName where LastName = 'Shivprasad Koirala'

In order to query the view

        SELECT * FROM [MyView]

(B)   What is "Correlated Subqueries"?

A simple subquery retrieves rows that are then passed to the outer query to produce the desired result set. Using Correlated Subqueries, the outer query retrieves rows that are then passed to the subquery. The subquery runs for each row that is processed by the outer query. Below is an example of a simple co-related subquery. You execute it in "AdventureWorks" to see the results.

```
Select salespersonid , (Select name from sales.salesterritory where
sales.salesterritory.territoryid= sales.Salesperson.Territoryid)
from sales.Salesperson
```

(A)   What is SQl injection ?

It is a Form of attack on a database-driven Web site in which the attacker executes unauthorized SQL commands by taking advantage of insecure code on a system connected to the Internet, bypassing the firewall. SQL injection attacks are used to steal information from a database from which the data would normally not be available and/or to gain access to an organization's host computers through the computer that is hosting the database.

SQL injection attacks typically are easy to avoid by ensuring that a system has strong input validation.

As name suggest we inject SQL which can be relatively dangerous for the database. Example this is a simple SQL

```
SELECT email, passwd, login_id, full_name
    FROM members
    WHERE email = 'x'
Now somebody does not put "x" as the input but puts  "x ; DROP TABLE
members;". So the actual SQL which will execute is :-
SELECT email, passwd, login_id, full_name
    FROM members
    WHERE email = 'x'  ; DROP TABLE members;
```

Think what will happen to your database.

(A)   What is "Data Warehousing"?

"Data Warehousing "is a process in which the data is stored and accessed from central location and is meant to support some strategic decisions. "Data Warehousing" is not a requirement for "Data mining". But just makes your Data mining process more efficient.

Data warehouse is a collection of integrated, subject-oriented databases designed to support the decision-support functions (DSF), where each unit of data is relevant to some moment in time.

(A)   What are Data Marts?

Data Marts are smaller section of Data Warehouses. They help data warehouses collect data. For example your company has lot of branches which are spanned across the globe. Head-office of the company decides to collect data from all these branches for anticipating market. So to achieve this IT department can setup data mart in all branch offices and a central data warehouse where all data will finally reside.

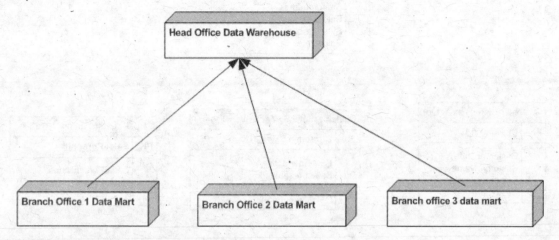

Figure 13.23: Data Mart in action

(A) What are Fact tables and Dimension Tables?

Twist: What is Dimensional Modeling?

Twist: What is Star Schema Design?

When we design transactional database we always think in terms of normalizing design to its least form. But when it comes to designing for Data warehouse we think more in terms of "denormalizing" the database. Data warehousing databases are designed using "Dimensional Modeling". Dimensional Modeling uses the existing relational database structure and builds on that.

There are two basic tables in dimensional modeling:-

√   Fact Tables.

√   Dimension Tables.

Fact tables are central tables in data warehousing. Fact tables have the actual aggregate values which will be needed in a business process. While dimension tables revolve around fact tables. They describe the attributes of the fact tables. Let's try to understand these two conceptually.

In the above example we have three tables which are transactional tables:-

√   **Customer:** It has the customer information details.

√   **Salesperson:** Sales person who are actually selling products to customer.

√   **CustomerSales:** This table has data of which sales person sold to which customer and what was the sales amount.

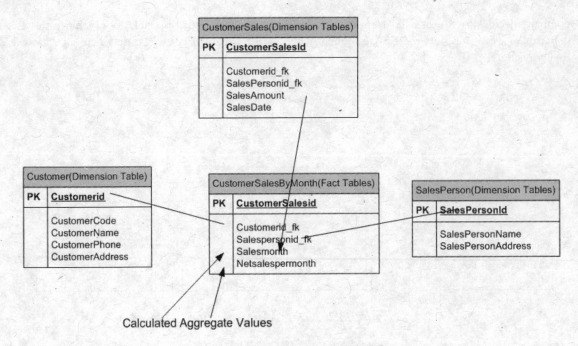

Figure 13.24: Dimensional Modeling

Below is the expected report Sales / Customer / Month. You will be wondering if we make a simple join query from all three tables we can easily get this output. But imagine if you have huge records in these three tables it can really slow down your reporting process. So we introduced a third dimension table "CustomerSalesByMonth" which will have foreign key of all tables and the aggregate amount by month. So this table becomes the dimension table and all other tables become fact tables. All major data warehousing design use Fact and Dimension model.

Customer Name	Sales Person Name	Month	Sales Amount Per Month
Man Brothers	Rajesh	Jan	1000
Suman Motela	Shiv	Jan	2000
KL enterprises	Rajesh	feb	500
KL enterprises	Shiv	Jan	1000

Figure 13.25: Expected Report.

The above design is also called as Star Schema design.

> *Note: For a pure data warehousing job this question is important. So try to understand why we modeled out design in this way rather than using the traditional approach - normalization.*

(A)What is Snow Flake Schema design in database?

Twist: What's the difference between Star and Snow flake schema?

Star schema is good when you do not have big tables in data warehousing. But when tables start becoming really huge it is better to denormalize. When you denormalize star schema it is nothing but snow flake design. For instance below "customeraddress" table is been normalized and is a child table of "Customer" table. Same holds true for "Salesperson" table.

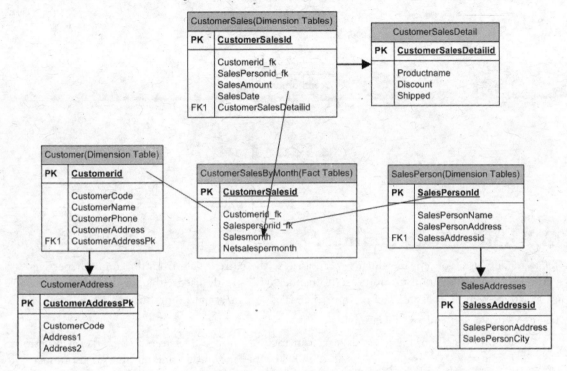

Figure 13.26: Snow Flake Schema

(A)   What is ETL process in Data warehousing?

Twist: What are the different stages in "Data warehousing"?

ETL (Extraction, Transformation and Loading) are different stages in Data warehousing. Like when we do software development we follow different stages like requirement gathering, designing, coding and testing. In the similar fashion we have for data warehousing.

Extraction

In this process we extract data from the source. In actual scenarios data source can be in many forms EXCEL, ACCESS, Delimited text, CSV (Comma Separated Files) etc. So extraction process handle's the complexity of understanding the data source and loading it in a structure of data warehouse.

Transformation

This process can also be called as cleaning up process. It's not necessary that after the extraction process data is clean and valid. For instance all the financial figures have NULL values but you want it to be ZERO for better analysis. So you can have some kind of stored procedure which runs through all extracted records and sets the value to zero.

Loading

After transformation you are ready to load the information in to your final data warehouse database.

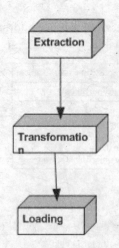

Figure 13.27: ETL stages

(A) What is "Data mining"?

"Data mining" is a concept by which we can analyze the current data from different perspectives and summarize the information in more useful manner. It's mostly used either to derive some valuable information from the existing data or to predict sales to increase customer market.

There are two basic aims of "Data mining":

√   **Prediction:** From the given data we can focus on how the customer or market will perform. For instance we are having a sale of 40000 $ per month in India, if the same product is to be sold with a discount how much sales can the company expect.

√   **Summarization:** To derive important information to analyze the current business scenario. For example a weekly sales report will give a picture to the top management how we are performing on a weekly basis?

(A)   Compare "Data mining" and "Data Warehousing"?

"Data Warehousing" is technical process where we are making our data centralized while "Data mining" is more of business activity which will analyze how good your business is doing or predict how it will do in the future coming times using the current data.

As said before "Data Warehousing" is not a need for "Data mining". It's good if you are doing "Data mining" on a "Data Warehouse" rather than on an actual production database. "Data Warehousing" is essential when we want to consolidate data from different sources, so it's like a cleaner and matured data which sits in between the various data sources and brings then in to one format.

"Data Warehouses" are normally physical entities which are meant to improve accuracy of "Data mining" process. For example you have 10 companies sending data in different format, so you create one physical database for consolidating all the data from different company sources, while "Data mining" can be a physical model or logical model. You can create a database in "Data mining" which gives you reports of net sales for this year for all companies. This need not be a physical database as such but a simple query.

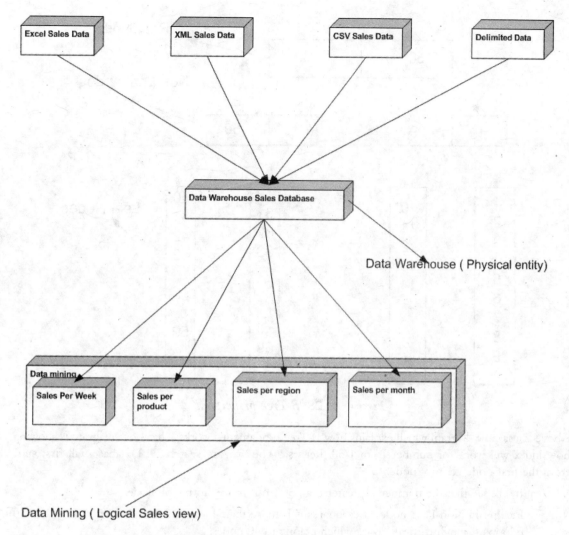

Figure 13.28 : Data Warehouse and Data mining

The above figure gives a picture how these concepts are quiet different. "Data Warehouse" collects cleans and filters data through different sources like "Excel", "XML" etc. But "Data Mining" sits on the top of "Data Warehouse" database and generates intelligent reports. Now either it can export to a different database or just generate report using some reporting tool like "Reporting Services".

(B) What are indexes?

Index makes your search faster. So defining indexes to your database will make your search faster.

(A) What are B-Trees?

Most of the indexing fundamentals use "B-Tree" or "Balanced-Tree" principle. It's not a principle that is something is created by SQL Server or ORACLE but is a mathematical derived fundamental.

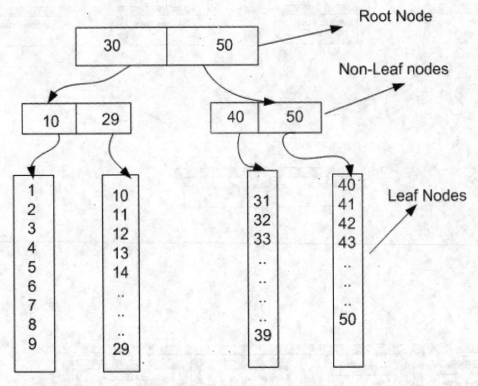

Figure 13.29: B-Tree principle.

Above is a sample diagram which explains how B-Tree fundamental works. The above diagram is showing how index will work for number from 1-50. Let's say you want to search 39. Database will first start from the first node i.e. root node.

√   It will see that the number is greater than 30, so it moves to the 50 node.

√   Further in Non-Leaf nodes it compares is it more than 40 or less than 40. As it's less than 40 it loops through the leaf nodes which belong to 40 nodes.

You can see that this is all attained in only two steps...faster aaah. That is how exactly indexes work in Database.

(I)   I have a table which has lot of inserts, is it a good database design to create indexes on that table?

> *Twist: Insert's are slower on tables which have indexes, justify it?*
>
> *Twist: Why do page splitting happen?*

"B-Tree" stands for balanced tree. In order that "B-tree" fundamental work properly both of the sides should be balanced. All indexing fundamentals in database use "B-tree" fundamental. Now whenever there is new data inserted or deleted the tree tries to become unbalance. In order that we can understand the fundamental properly let's try to refer the figure down.

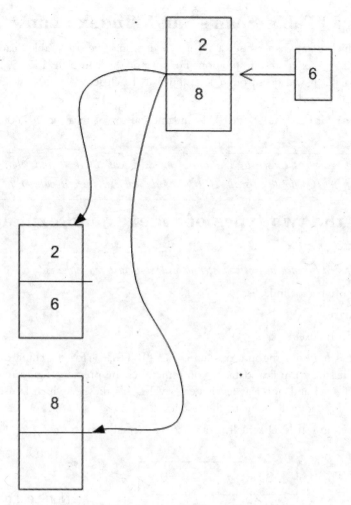

Figure 13.30: Page split for Indexed tables

If you see the first level index there is "2" and "8", now let say we want to insert "6". In order to balance the "B-TREE" structure rows it will try to split in two pages, as shown. Even though the second page split has some empty area it will go ahead because the primary thing for him is balancing the "B-TREE" for fast retrieval.

Now if you see during the split it is doing some heavy duty here:

√   Creates a new page to balance the tree.

√   Shuffle and move the data to pages.

So if your table is having heavy inserts that means it's transactional, then you can visualize the amount of splits it will be doing. This will not only increase insert time but will also upset the end-user who is sitting on the screen.

So when you forecast that a table has lot of inserts it's not a good idea to create indexes.

(I)   What are "Table Scan's" and "Index Scan's"?

These are ways by which database searches a record or data in table. In "Table Scan" database loops through all the records to get to the destination. For instance if you have 1, 2, 5, 23, 63 and 95. If you want to search for 23 it will go through 1, 2 and 5 to reach it. Worst if it wants to search 95 it will loop through all the records.

While for "Index Scan's" it uses the "B-TREE" fundamental to get to a record. For "B-TREE" refer previous questions.

> *Note: Which way to search is chosen by Database engine. Example if it finds that the table records are very less it will go for table scan. If it finds the table is huge it will go for index scan.*

(B) What are the two types of indexes and explain them in detail?

Twist: What's the difference between clustered and non-clustered indexes?

There are basically two types of indexes:

√   Clustered Indexes.

√   Non-Clustered Indexes.

Ok every thing is same for both the indexes i.e. it uses "B-TREE" for searching data. But the main difference is the way it stores physical data. If you remember the previous figure (give figure number here) there where leaf level and non-leaf level. Leaf level holds the key which is used to identify the record. And non-leaf level actually point to the leaf level.

In clustered index the non-leaf level actually points to the actual data.

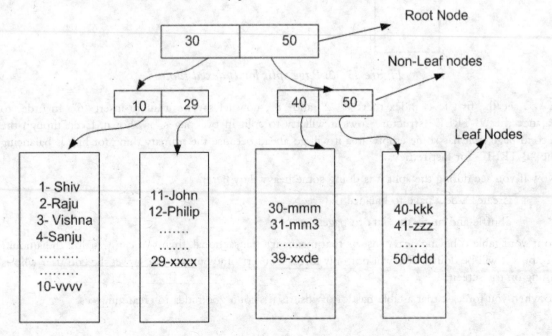

Figure 13.31: Clustered Index Architecture

In Non-Clustered index the leaf nodes point to pointers (they are rowid's) which then point to actual data.

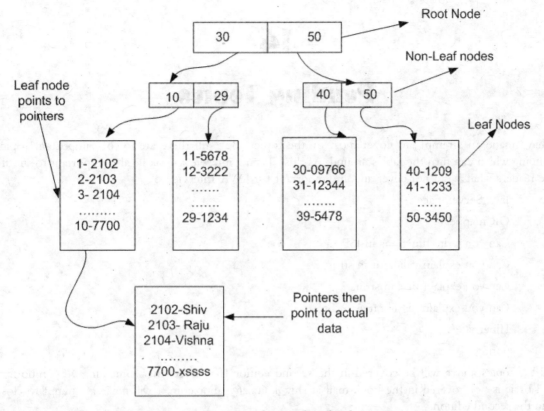

Figure 13.32: Non-Clustered Index has pointers.

So here's what the main difference is in clustered and non-clustered , in clustered when we reach the leaf nodes we are on the actual data. In non-clustered indexes we get a pointer, which then points to the actual data.

So after the above fundamentals following are the basic differences between them:

√ Also note in clustered index actual data as to be sorted in same way as the clustered indexes are. While in non-clustered indexes as we have pointers which is logical arrangement we do need this compulsion.

√ So we can have only one clustered index on a table as we can have only one physical order while we can have more than one non-clustered indexes.

If we make non-clustered index on a table which has clustered indexes, how does the architecture change?

The only change is that the leaf node point to clustered index key. Using this clustered index key can then be used to finally locate the actual data. So the difference is that leaf node has pointers while in the next half it has clustered keys. So if we create non-clustered index on a table which has clustered index it tries to use the clustered index.

14

Pending Topics

I have made an attempt to cover most of the topics. But still there are lot of important topics pending which can turn the tables around. As this been a interview book its also important to notify the readers what it did not cover and are important for JAVA Interviews.

√   Java Server Faces.

√   OR mappers

√   Can you write functions in JSP ?.

√   Can you explain validator in struts ?

√   Can you explain tiles in struts ?

√   Can you explain tag libraries of Struts ?

√   Hibernate

√   Spring

All the topics above will be covered in the second edition.If you feel that something very important and basic is not covered in the book mail at shiv_koirala@yahoo.com. I will make a attempt to close it in the second edition.

15

.Net Interview Questions

Basic .NET Framework

What is a IL?

> *Twist: What is MSIL or CIL , What is JIT?*

What is a CLR?

What is a CTS?

What is a CLS(Common Language Specification)?

What is a Managed Code?

What is a Assembly ?

What are different types of Assembly?

What is NameSpace?

What is Difference between NameSpace and Assembly?

If you want to view a Assembly how to you go about it ?

> *Twist: What is ILDASM ?*

What is Manifest?

Where is version information stored of a assembly ?

Is versioning applicable to private assemblies?

What is GAC ?

> *Twist: What are situations when you register .NET assembly in GAC ?*

What is concept of strong names ?

> *Twist: How do we generate strong names or what is the process of generating strong names , What is use of SN.EXE , How do we apply strong names to assembly ? , How do you sign an assembly ?*

How to add and remove a assembly from GAC?

What is Delay signing ?

What is garbage collection?

Can we force garbage collector to run ?

What is reflection?

What are different type of JIT ?

What are Value types and Reference types ?

What is concept of Boxing and Unboxing ?

What's difference between VB.NET and C# ?

What's difference between System exceptions and Application exceptions?

What is CODE Access security?

What is a satellite assembly?

How to prevent my .NET DLL to be decompiled?

What's the difference between Convert.toString and .toString() method ?

What is Native Image Generator (Ngen.exe)?

We have two version of the same assembly in GAC? I want my client to make choice of which assembly to choose?

What is CodeDom?

.NET Interoperability

How can we use COM Components in .NET?

> *Twist: What is RCW ?*

Once i have developed the COM wrapper do i have to still register the COM in registry?

How can we use .NET components in COM?

> *Twist: What is CCW (COM callable wrapper) ?, What caution needs to be taken in order that .NET components is compatible with COM ?*

How can we make Windows API calls in .NET?

When we use windows API in .NET is it managed or unmanaged code ?

What is COM ?

What is Reference counting in COM ?

Can you describe IUKNOWN interface in short ?

Can you explain what is DCOM ?

How do we create DCOM object in VB6?

How to implement DTC in .NET ?

How many types of Transactions are there in COM + .NET ?

How do you do object pooling in .NET ?

What are types of compatibility in VB6?

What is equivalent for regsvr32 exe in .NET ?

Threading

What is Multi-tasking ?

What is Multi-threading ?

What is a Thread ?

Did VB6 support multi-threading ?

Can we have multiple threads in one App domain ?

Which namespace has threading ?

Can you explain in brief how can we implement threading ?

How can we change priority and what the levels of priority are provided by .NET ?

What does Addressof operator do in background ?

How can you reference current thread of the method ?

What's Thread.Sleep() in threading ?

How can we make a thread sleep for infinite period ?

What is Suspend and Resume in Threading ?

What the way to stop a long running thread ?

How do i debug thread ?

What's Thread.Join() in threading ?

What are Daemon thread's and how can a thread be created as Daemon?

When working with shared data in threading how do you implement synchronization ?

Can we use events with threading ?

How can we know a state of a thread?

What is a monitor object?

What are wait handles ?

> *Twist: What is a mutex object ?*

what is ManualResetEvent and AutoResetEvent ?

What is ReaderWriter Locks ?

How can you avoid deadlock in threading ?

What's difference between thread and process?

Remoting and Webservices

What is a application domain?

What is .NET Remoting ?

Which class does the remote object has to inherit ?

What are two different types of remote object creation mode in .NET ?

Describe in detail Basic of SAO architecture of Remoting?

What are the situations you will use singleton architecture in remoting ?

What is fundamental of published or precreated objects in Remoting ?

What are the ways client can create object on server in CAO model ?

Are CAO stateful in nature ?

In CAO model when we want client objects to be created by "NEW" keyword is there any precautions to be taken ?

Is it a good design practice to distribute the implementation to Remoting Client ?

What is LeaseTime,SponsorshipTime ,RenewonCallTime and LeaseManagerPollTime?

Which config file has all the supported channels/protocol ?

How can you specify remoting parameters using Config files ?

Can Non-Default constructors be used with Single Call SAO?

      Twist: What are the limitation of constructors for Single call SAO ?

How can we call methods in remoting Asynchronously ?

What is Asynchronous One-Way Calls ?

What is marshalling and what are different kinds of marshalling ?

What is ObjRef object in remoting ?

What is a WebService ?

What is UDDI ?

What is DISCO ?

What is WSDL?

What the different phase/steps of acquiring a proxy object in Webservice ?

What is file extension of Webservices ?

Which attribute is used in order that the method can be used as WebService ?

What are the steps to create a webservice and consume it ?

Do webservice have state ?

Caching Concepts

What is application object ?

What's the difference between Cache object and application object ?

How can get access to cache object ?

What are dependencies in cache and types of dependencies ?

Can you show a simple code showing file dependency in cache ?

What is Cache Callback in Cache ?

What is scavenging ?

What are different types of caching using cache object of ASP.NET?

How can you cache different version of same page using ASP.NET cache object ?

How will implement Page Fragment Caching ?

What are   ASP.NET session and compare ASP.NET session with classic ASP session variables?

Which various modes of storing ASP.NET session ?

Is Session_End event supported in all session modes ?

What are the precautions you will take in order that StateServer Mode work properly ?

What are the precautions you will take in order that SQLSERVER Mode work properly ?

Where do you specify session state mode in ASP.NET ?

What are the other ways you can maintain state ?

What are benefits and Limitation of using Hidden fields ?

What is ViewState ?

Do performance vary for viewstate according to User controls ?

What are benefits and Limitation of using Viewstate for state management?

How an you use Hidden frames to cache client data ?

What are benefits and Limitation of using Hidden frames?

What are benefits and Limitation of using Cookies?

What is Query String and What are benefits and Limitation of using Query Strings?

OOPS

What is Object Oriented Programming ?

What's a Class ?

What's a Object ?

What's the relation between Classes and Objects ?

What are different properties provided by Object-oriented systems ?

> *Twist: Can you explain different properties of Object Oriented Systems?*

> *Twist: What's difference between Association, Aggregation and Inheritance relationships?*

How can we acheive inheritance in VB.NET ?

What are abstract classes ?

What's a Interface ?

What is difference between abstract classes and interfaces?

What is a delegate ?

What are event's ?

Do events have return type ?

Can event's have access modifiers ?

Can we have shared events ?

What is shadowing ?

What's difference between Shadowing and Overriding ?

What's difference between delegate and events?

If we inherit a class do the private variables also get inherited ?

What are different accessibility levels defined in .NET ?

Can you prevent a class from overriding ?

What's the use of "MustInherit" keyword in VB.NET ?

Why can not you specify accessibility modifier in Interface ?

What are similarities between Class and structure ?

What's the difference between Class and structure's ?

What does virtual keyword mean ?

What are shared (VB.NET)/Static(C#) variables?

What is Dispose method in .NET ?

Whats the use of "OverRides" and "Overridable" keywords ?

Where are all .NET Collection classes located ?

What is ArrayList ?

What's a HashTable ?

>   *Twist: What's difference between HashTable and ArrayList ?*

What are queues and stacks ?

What is ENUM ?

What is nested Classes ?

What's Operator Overloading in .NET?

In below sample code if we create a object of class2 which constructor will fire first ?

What's the significance of Finalize method in .NET?

Why is it preferred to not use finalize for clean up?

How can we suppress a finalize method?

What's the use of DISPOSE method?

How do I force the Dispose method to be called automatically, as clients can forget to call Dispose method?

In what instances you will declare a constructor to be private?

Can we have different access modifiers on get/set methods of a property ?

If we write a goto or a return statement in try and catch block will the finally block execute ?

What is Indexer ?

Can we have static indexer in C# ?

In a program there are multiple catch blocks so can it happen that two catch blocks are executed ?

What is the difference between System.String and System.StringBuilder classes?

ASP.NET

What's the sequence in which ASP.NET events are processed ?

In which event are the controls fully loaded ?

How can we identify that the Page is PostBack ?

How does ASP.NET maintain state in between subsequent request ?

What is event bubbling ?

How do we assign page specific attributes ?

Administrator wants to make a security check that no one has tampered with ViewState , how can he ensure this ?

What's the use of @ Register directives ?

What's the use of SmartNavigation property ?

What is AppSetting Section in "Web.Config" file ?

Where is ViewState information stored ?

What's the use of @ OutputCache directive in ASP.NET?

How can we create custom controls in ASP.NET ?

How many types of validation controls are provided by ASP.NET ?

Can you explain what is "AutoPostBack" feature in ASP.NET ?

How can you enable automatic paging in DataGrid ?

What's the use of "GLOBAL.ASAX" file ?

What's the difference between "Web.config" and "Machine.Config" ?

What's a SESSION and APPLICATION object ?

What's difference between Server.Transfer and response.Redirect ?

What's difference between Authentication and authorization?

What is impersonation in ASP.NET ?

Can you explain in brief how the ASP.NET authentication process works?

What are the various ways of authentication techniques in ASP.NET?

How does authorization work in ASP.NET?

What's difference between Datagrid , Datalist and repeater ?

From performance point of view how do they rate ?

What's the method to customize columns in DataGrid?

How can we format data inside DataGrid?

How will decide the design consideration to take a Datagrid , datalist or repeater ?

Difference between ASP and ASP.NET?

What are major events in GLOBAL.ASAX file ?

What order they are triggered ?

Do session use cookies ?

How can we force all the validation control to run ?

How can we check if all the validation control are valid and proper ?

If you have client side validation is enabled in your Web page , Does that mean server side code is not run?

Which JavaScript file is referenced for validating the validators at the client side ?

How to disable client side script in validators?

I want to show the entire validation error message in a message box on the client side?

You find that one of your validation is very complicated and does not fit in any of the validators, so what will you do ?

What is Tracing in ASP.NET ?

How do we enable tracing ?

What exactly happens when ASPX page is requested from Browser?

How can we kill a user session ?

How do you upload a file in ASP.NET ?

How do I send email message from ASP.NET ?

What are different IIS isolation levels?

ASP used STA threading model , whats the threading model used for ASP.NET ?

Whats the use of <%@ page aspcompat=true %> attribute ?

Explain the differences between Server-side and Client-side code?

Can you explain Forms authentication in detail ?

How do I sign out in forms authentication ?

If cookies are not enabled at browser end does form Authentication work?

How to use a checkbox in a datagrid?

What are the steps to create a windows service in VB.NET ?

What's the difference between "Web farms" and "Web garden"?

How do we configure "WebGarden"?

What is the main difference between Gridlayout and FlowLayout ?

.NET Architecture

What are design patterns ?

What's difference between Factory and Abstract Factory Pattern's?

What's MVC pattern?

> *Twist: How can you implement MVC pattern in ASP.NET?*

How can we implement singleton pattern in .NET?

How do you implement prototype pattern in .NET?

> *Twist: How to implement cloning in .NET ? , What is shallow copy and deep copy ?*

What are the situations you will use a Web Service and Remoting in projects?

Can you give a practical implementation of FAÇADE patterns?

How can we implement observer pattern in .NET?

What is three tier architecture?

Have you ever worked with Microsoft Application Blocks, if yes then which?

What is Service Oriented architecture?

What are different ways you can pass data between tiers?

What is Windows DNA architecture?

What is aspect oriented programming?

ADO.NET

What is the namespace in which .NET has the data functionality classes ?

Can you give a overview of ADO.NET architecture ?

What are the two fundamental objects in ADO.NET ?

What is difference between dataset and datareader ?

What are major difference between classic ADO and ADO.NET ?

What is the use of connection object ?

What is the use of command objects and what are the methods provided by the command object ?

What is the use of dataadapter ?

What are basic methods of Dataadapter ?

What is Dataset object?

What are the various objects in Dataset ?

How can we connect to Microsoft Access, Foxpro, Oracle etc ?

How do we connect to SQL SERVER , which namespace do we use ?

How do we use stored procedure in ADO.NET and how do we provide parameters to the stored procedures?

How can we force the connection object to close after my datareader is closed ?

I want to force the datareader to return only schema of the datastore rather than data ?

How can we fine tune the command object when we are expecting a single row or a single value ?

Which is the best place to store connectionstring in .NET projects ?

What are steps involved to fill a dataset ?

Twist: How can we use dataadapter to fill a dataset ?

What are the various methods provided by the dataset object to generate XML?

How can we save all data from dataset ?

How can we check that some changes have been made to dataset since it was loaded ?

Twist: How can we cancel all changes done in dataset ? How do we get values which are changed in a dataset ?

How can we add/remove row's in "DataTable" object of "DataSet" ?

What's basic use of "DataView" ?

What's difference between "DataSet" and "DataReader" ?

Twist: Why is DataSet slower than DataReader ?

How can we load multiple tables in a DataSet ?

How can we add relation's between table in a DataSet ?

What's the use of CommandBuilder ?

What's difference between "Optimistic" and "Pessimistic" locking ?

How many way's are there to implement locking in ADO.NET ?

How can we perform transactions in .NET?

What's difference between Dataset. clone and Dataset. copy ?

Can you explain the difference between an ADO.NET Dataset and an ADO Recordset?

Explain in detail the fundamental of connection pooling?

What is Maximum Pool Size in ADO.NET Connection String?

How to enable and disable connection pooling?

SQL SERVER

What is normalization? What are different type of normalization?

What is denormalization ?

What is a candidate key ?

What are different types of joins and whats the difference between them ?

What are indexes and What is the difference between clustered and nonclustered indexes?

How can you increase SQL performance ?

What is the use of OLAP ?

What's a measure in OLAP ?

What are dimensions in OLAP ?

What are levels in dimensions ?

What are fact tables and dimension tables in OLAP ?

      Twist: can you explain the star schema for OLAP ?

What is DTS?

What is fillfactor ?

      Twist: When does plage split occurs ?

What is RAID and how does it work ?

What's the difference between DELETE TABLE and TRUNCATE TABLE commands?

What are the problems that can occur if you do not implement locking properly in SQL SERVER ?

What are different transaction levels in SQL SERVER ?

      Twist: what are different types of locks in SQL SERVER ?

What are different locks in SQL SERVER ?

Can we suggest locking hints to SQL SERVER ?

What is LOCK escalation?

What are the different ways of moving data/databases between servers and databases in SQL Server?

What are advantages of SQL 2000 over SQl 7.0 ?

What is the difference between a HAVING CLAUSE and a WHERE CLAUSE?

What is difference between UNION and UNION ALL SQL syntax ?

How can you raise custom errors from stored procedure ?

What is ACID fundamental and what are transactions in SQL SERVER ?

What is DBCC?

What is purpose of Replication ?

What are different type of replication supported by SQL SERVER ?

What is BCP utility in SQL SERVER ?

What are different types of triggers in SQl SERVER 2000 ?

If we have multiple AFTER Triggers on table how can we define the sequence of the triggers ?

What is SQl injection ?

What's the difference between Stored Procedure (SP) and User Defined Function (UDF)?

UML

What is UML?

How many types of diagrams are there in UML ?

> *Twist: Explain in short all types of diagrams in UML ?*

What are advantages of using UML?

> *Twist: What is Modeling and why UML ?*

What's the sequence of UML diagrams in project?

> *Twist: How did you implement UML in your project?*

> *Just a small Twist: Do I need all UML diagrams in a project?*

Give a small brief explanation of all Elements in activity diagrams?

Explain Different elements of a collaboration diagram ?

Explain Component diagrams ?

Explain all parts of a deployment diagram?

Describe various components in sequence diagrams?

What are the element in State Chart diagrams ?

Describe different elements in Static Chart diagrams ?

Explain different elements of a Use Case ?

> *Twist: What's difference between Activity and sequence diagrams?(I leave this to the readers)*

Project Management

What is project management?

Is spending in IT project's constant through out the project?

Who is a stakeholder ?

Can you explain project life cycle ?

> *Twist: How many phases are there in software project ?*

Are risk constant through out the project ?

Can you explain different software development life cycles ?

What is triple constraint triangle in project management ?

What is a project baselines ?

What is effort variance?

How is normally a project management plan document organized ?

How do you estimate a project?

What is CAR (Causal Analysis and Resolution)?

What is DAR (Decision Analysis and Resolution)?

What is a fish bone diagram ?

> *Twist: What is Ishikawa diagram ?*

What is pareto principle ?

> *Twist: What is 80/20 principle ?*

How do you handle change request?

What is internal change request?

What is difference between SITP and UTP in testing ?

What are the software you have used for project management?

What are the metrics followed in project management?

> *Twist: What metrics will you look at in order to see the project is moving successfully?*

You have people in your team who do not meet there deadlines or do not perform what are the actions you will take ?

> *Twist: Two of your resources have conflict's between them how would you sort it out ?*

What is black box testing and White box testing?

What's the difference between Unit Testing, Assembly Testing and Regression testing?

What is V model in testing?

How do you start a project?

How did you do resource allocations?

How do you do code reviews ?

What is CMMI?

What are the five levels in CMMI?

What is continuous and staged representation?

Can you explain the process areas?

What is SIX sigma?

What is DMAIC and DMADV ?

What are the various roles in Six Sigma implementation?

What are function points?

Twist: Define Elementary process in FPA?

What are different types of elementary process in FPA?

What are the different elements in Functions points?

Can you explain in GSC and VAF in function points?

What are unadjusted function points and how is it calculated?

Can you explain steps in function points?

What is the FP per day in your current company?

Twist: What is your company's productivity factor ?

Do you know Use Case points?

What is COCOMO I, COCOMOII and COCOMOIII?

What is SMC approach of estimation?

How do you estimate maintenance project and change requests?

XML

What is XML?

What is the version information in XML?

What is ROOT element in XML?

If XML does not have closing tag will it work?

Is XML case sensitive?

What's the difference between XML and HTML?

Is XML meant to replace HTML?

Can you explain why your project needed XML?

What is DTD (Document Type definition)?

What is well formed XML?

What is a valid XML?

What is CDATA section in XML?

What is CSS?

What is XSL?

What is Element and attributes in XML?

Which are the namespaces in .NET used for XML?

What are the standard ways of parsing XML document?

In What scenarios will you use a DOM parser and SAX parser?

How was XML handled during COM times?

What's the main difference between MSML and .NET Framework XML classes?

What are the core functionalities in XML .NET framework? Can you explain in detail those functionalities?

What is XSLT?

Define XPATH?

What's the concept of XPOINTER?

What is an XMLReader Class?

What is XMLTextReader?

How do we access attributes using "XmlReader"?

Explain simple Walk through of XmlReader ?

What does XmlValidatingReader class do?

16
.SQL Server Interview Questions

Database Concepts

What is database or database management systems (DBMS)?

What's difference between DBMS and RDBMS ?

What are CODD rules?

Is access database a RDBMS?

What's the main difference between ACCESS and SQL SERVER?

What's the difference between MSDE and SQL SERVER 2000?

What is SQL SERVER Express 2005 Edition?

What is SQL Server 2000 Workload Governor?

What's the difference between SQL SERVER 2000 and 2005?

What are E-R diagrams?

How many types of relationship exist in database designing?

What is normalization? What are different type of normalization?

What is denormalization ?

Can you explain Fourth Normal Form?

Can you explain Fifth Normal Form?

What's the difference between Fourth and Fifth normal form?

Have you heard about sixth normal form?

What is Extent and Page?

What are the different sections in Page?

What are page splits?

In which files does actually SQL Server store data?

What is Collation in SQL Server?

Can we have a different collation for database and table?

SQL

Revisiting basic syntax of SQL?

What are "GRANT" and "REVOKE' statements?

What is Cascade and Restrict in DROP table SQL?

How to import table using "INSERT" statement?

What is a DDL, DML and DCL concept in RDBMS world?

What are different types of joins in SQL?

What is "CROSS JOIN"?

You want to select the first record in a given set of rows?

How do you sort in SQL?

How do you select unique rows using SQL?

Can you name some aggregate function is SQL Server?

What is the default "SORT" order for a SQL?

What is a self-join?

What's the difference between DELETE and TRUNCATE ?

Select addresses which are between '1/1/2004' and '1/4/2004'?

What are Wildcard operators in SQL Server?

What's the difference between "UNION" and "UNION ALL" ?

What are cursors and what are the situations you will use them?

What are the steps to create a cursor?

What are the different Cursor Types?

What are "Global" and "Local" cursors?

What is "Group by" clause?

What is ROLLUP?

What is CUBE?

What is the difference between "HAVING" and "WHERE" clause?

What is "COMPUTE" clause in SQL?

What is "WITH TIES" clause in SQL?

What does "SET ROWCOUNT" syntax achieves?

What is a Sub-Query?

What is "Correlated Subqueries"?

What is "ALL" and "ANY" operator?

What is a "CASE" statement in SQL?

What does COLLATE Keyword in SQL signify?

What is CTE (Common Table Expression)?

Why should you use CTE rather than simple views?

What is TRY/CATCH block in T-SQL?

What is PIVOT feature in SQL Server?

What is UNPIVOT?

What are RANKING functions?

What is ROW_NUMBER()?

What is RANK() ?

What is DENSE_RANK()?

What is NTILE()?

What is SQl injection ?

.NET Integration

What are steps to load a .NET code in SQL SERVER 2005?

How can we drop an assembly from SQL SERVER?

Are changes made to assembly updated automatically in database?

Why do we need to drop assembly for updating changes?

How to see assemblies loaded in SQL Server?

I want to see which files are linked with which assemblies?

Does .NET CLR and SQL SERVER run in different process?

Does .NET controls SQL SERVER or is it vice-versa?

Is SQLCLR configured by default?

How to configure CLR for SQL SERVER?

Is .NET feature loaded by default in SQL Server?

How does SQL Server control .NET run-time?

What's a "SAND BOX" in SQL Server 2005?

What is an application domain?

How are .NET Appdomain allocated in SQL SERVER 2005?

What is Syntax for creating a new assembly in SQL Server 2005?

Do Assemblies loaded in database need actual .NET DLL?

You have a assembly which is dependent on other assemblies, will SQL Server load the dependent assemblies?

Does SQL Server handle unmanaged resources?

What is Multi-tasking?

What is Multi-threading?

What is a Thread ?

Can we have multiple threads in one App domain?

What is Non-preemptive threading?

What is pre-emptive threading?

Can you explain threading model in SQL Server?

How does .NET and SQL Server thread work?

How is exception in SQLCLR code handled?

Are all .NET libraries allowed in SQL Server?

What is "Hostprotectionattribute" in SQL Server 2005?

How many types of permission level are there for an assembly?

In order that an assembly gets loaded in SQL Server what type of checks are done?

Can you name system tables for .NET assemblies?

Are two version of same assembly allowed in SQL Server?

How are changes made in assembly replicated?

Is it a good practice to drop a assembly for changes?

In one of the projects following steps where done, will it work?

What does Alter assembly with unchecked data signify?

How do I drop an assembly?

Can we create SQLCLR using .NET framework 1.0?

While creating .NET UDF what checks should be done?

How do you define a function from the .NET assembly?

Can you compare between T-SQL and SQLCLR?

With respect to .NET is SQL SERVER case sensitive?

Does case sensitive rule apply for VB.NET?

Can nested classes be accessed in T-SQL?

Can we have SQLCLR procedure input as array?

Can object datatype be used in SQLCLR?

How's precision handled for decimal datatypes in .NET?

How do we define INPUT and OUTPUT parameters in SQLCLR?

Is it good to use .NET datatypes in SQLCLR?

How to move values from SQL to .NET datatypes?

What is System.Data.SqlServer?

What is SQLContext?

Can you explain essential steps to deploy SQLCLR?

How do create function in SQL Server using .NET?

How do we create trigger using .NET?

How to create User Define Functions using .NET?

How to create aggregates using .NET?

What is Asynchronous support in ADO.NET?

What is MARS support in ADO.NET?

What is SQLbulkcopy object in ADO.NET?

How to select range of rows using ADO.NET?

What are different types of triggers in SQl SERVER 2000 ?

If we have multiple AFTER Triggers on table how can we define the sequence of the triggers ?

How can you raise custom errors from stored procedure ?

ADO.NET

Which are namespaces for ADO.NET?

Can you give a overview of ADO.NET architecture?

What are the two fundamental objects in ADO.NET?

What is difference between dataset and datareader?

What are major difference between classic ADO and ADO.NET?

What is the use of connection object?

What are the methods provided by the command object?

What is the use of "Dataadapter"?

What are basic methods of "Dataadapter"?

What is Dataset object?

What are the various objects in Dataset?

How can we connect to Microsoft Access, FoxPro, Oracle etc?

What's the namespace to connect to SQL Server?

How do we use stored procedure in ADO.NET?

How can we force the connection object to close?

I want to force the datareader to return only schema?

Can we optimize command object when there is only one row?

Which is the best place to store connectionstring?

What are steps involved to fill a dataset?

What are the methods provided by the dataset for XML?

How can we save all data from dataset?

How can we check for changes made to dataset?

How can we add/remove row's in "DataTable" object of "DataSet"?

What's basic use of "DataView"?

What's difference between "DataSet" and "DataReader"?

How can we load multiple tables in a DataSet?

How can we add relation's between table in a DataSet?

What's the use of CommandBuilder?

What's difference between "Optimistic" and "Pessimistic" locking?

How many way's are there to implement locking in ADO.NET?

How can we perform transactions in .NET?

What's difference between Dataset. clone and Dataset. copy?

Whats the difference between Dataset and ADO Recordset?

Notification Services

What are notification services?

What are basic components of Notification services?

Can you explain architecture of Notification Services?

Which are the two XML files needed for notification services?

What is Nscontrols command?

What are the situations you will use "Notification" Services?

Service Broker

What do we need Queues?

What is "Asynchronous" communication?

What is SQL Server Service broker?

What are the essential components of SQL Server Service broker?

What is the main purpose of having Conversation Group?

How to implement Service Broker?

How do we encrypt data between Dialogs?

XML Integration

What is XML?

What is the version information in XML?

What is ROOT element in XML?

If XML does not have closing tag will it work?

Is XML case sensitive?

What's the difference between XML and HTML?

Is XML meant to replace HTML?

Can you explain why your project needed XML?

What is DTD (Document Type definition)?

What is well formed XML?

What is a valid XML?

What is CDATA section in XML?

What is CSS?

What is XSL?

What is Element and attributes in XML?

Can we define a column as XML?

How do we specify the XML data type as typed or untyped?

How can we create the XSD schema?

How do I insert in to a table which has XSD schema attached to it?

What is maximum size for XML datatype?

What is Xquery?

What are XML indexes?

What are secondary XML indexes?

What is FOR XML in SQL Server?

Can I use FOR XML to generate SCHEMA of a table and how?

What is the OPENXML statement in SQL Server?

I have huge XML file which we want to load in database?

How to call stored procedure using HTTP SOAP?

What is XMLA?

Data Warehousing/Data Mining

What is "Data Warehousing"?

What are Data Marts?

What are Fact tables and Dimension Tables?

What is Snow Flake Schema design in database?

What is ETL process in Data warehousing?

How can we do ETL process in SQL Server?

What is "Data mining"?

Compare "Data mining" and "Data Warehousing"?

What is BCP?

How can we import and export using BCP utility?

During BCP we need to change the field position or eliminate some fields how can we achieve this?

What is Bulk Insert?

What is DTS?

Can you brief about the Data warehouse project you worked on?

What is an OLTP (Online Transaction Processing) System?

What is an OLAP (On-line Analytical processing) system?

What is Conceptual, Logical and Physical model?

What is Data purging?

What is Analysis Services?

What are CUBES?

What are the primary ways to store data in OLAP?

What is META DATA information in Data warehousing projects?

What is multi-dimensional analysis?

What is MDX?

How did you plan your Data ware house project?

What are different deliverables according to phases?

Can you explain how analysis service works?

What are the different problems that "Data mining" can solve?

What are different stages of "Data mining"?

What is Discrete and Continuous data in Data mining world?

What is MODEL is Data mining world?

DB)How are models actually derived?

What is a Decision Tree Algorithm?

Can decision tree be implemented using SQL?

What is Naïve Bayes Algorithm?

Explain clustering algorithm?

Explain in detail Neural Networks?

What is Back propagation in Neural Networks?

What is Time Series algorithm in data mining?

Explain Association algorithm in Data mining?

What is Sequence clustering algorithm?

What are algorithms provided by Microsoft in SQL Server?

How does data mining and data warehousing work together?

What is XMLA?

What is Discover and Execute in XMLA?

Integration Services/DTS

What is Integration Services import / export wizard?

What are prime components in Integration Services?

How can we develop a DTS project in Integration Services?

Replication

Whats the best way to update data between SQL Servers?

What are the scenarios you will need multiple databases with schema?

How will you plan your replication?

What are publisher, distributor and subscriber in "Replication"?

What is "Push" and "Pull" subscription?

Can a publication support push and pull at one time?

What are different models / types of replication?

What is Snapshot replication?

What are the advantages and disadvantages of using Snapshot replication?

What type of data will qualify for "Snapshot replication"?

What's the actual location where the distributor runs?

Can you explain in detail how exactly "Snapshot Replication" works?

What is merge replication?

How does merge replication works?

What are advantages and disadvantages of Merge replication?

What is conflict resolution in Merge replication?

What is a transactional replication?

Can you explain in detail how transactional replication works?

What are data type concerns during replications?

Reporting Services

Can you explain how can we make a simple report in reporting services?

How do I specify stored procedures in Reporting Services?

What is the architecture for "Reporting Services"?

Database Optimization

What are indexes?

What are B-Trees?

I have a table which has lot of inserts, is it a good database design to create indexes on that table?

What are "Table Scan's" and "Index Scan's"?

What are the two types of indexes and explain them in detail?

What is "FillFactor" concept in indexes?

What is the best value for "FillFactor"?

What are "Index statistics"?

How can we see statistics of an index?

How do you reorganize your index, once you find the problem?

What is Fragmentation?

How can we measure Fragmentation?

How can we remove the Fragmented spaces?

What are the criteria you will look in to while selecting an index?

What is "Index Tuning Wizard"?

What is an Execution plan?

How do you see the SQL plan in textual format?

What is nested join, hash join and merge join in SQL Query plan?

What joins are good in what situations?

What is RAID and how does it work ?

ction and Locks

... Database Transactions "?

...D?

What is "Begin Trans", "Commit Tran", "Rollback Tran" and "Save Tran"?

What are "Checkpoint's" in SQL Server?

What are "Implicit Transactions"?

Is it good to use "Implicit Transactions"?

What is Concurrency?

How can we solve concurrency problems?

What kind of problems occurs if we do not implement proper locking strategy?

What are "Dirty reads"?

What are "Unrepeatable reads"?

What are "Phantom rows"?

What are "Lost Updates"?

What are different levels of granularity of locking resources?

What are different types of Locks in SQL Server?

What are different Isolation levels in SQL Server?

What are different types of Isolation levels in SQL Server?

If you are using COM+ what "Isolation" level is set by default?

What are "Lock" hints?

What is a "Deadlock" ?

What are the steps you can take to avoid "Deadlocks" ?

How can I know what locks are running on which resource?